Praise for *Places Left Unfinished at the Time of Creation*

"This audaciously poetic and muscularly philosophical memoir is, alternately, a magical travelogue, a feverish reconstruction of family history, a perplexing detective novel, and finally, a personal spiritual odyssey back in time to Aztec mythology."
   —*San Jose Mercury News* (front page review)

"Santos is a vaquero poet at heart, but the laughter has turned to introspection and—may we still use this word?—wisdom."
   —*Chicago Tribune* (front page review)

"Santos counts the cost of immigration, assimilation and upward mobility in this graceful memoir, where intimate family chronicle alternates with introspective meditation on the Mexican past . . . he writes splendidly."
   —*The New York Times*

"In his impressive memoir, John Phillip Santos attempts to locate the origin of that lingering loss among the descendants of the conquered Indians, and he does so with grand success. . . . What a wonderful story he has told here, in a memoir that is a brave and beautiful attempt to redeem a people out of a limbo of forgetting."
   —*Los Angeles Times*

"Significant and unique . . . a beautiful, universal portrait of migration."
   —*The Washington Post*

"There is a remembering here that strikes a deep chord. Mr. Santos tells his stories with clarity and serenity, as one looking back on a long, wide, winding road."
   —*Dallas Morning News*

"[Santos] uses his talents to paint an incredibly rich portrait of his extended family . . . connecting the story to the birth of Mexico, the New World, the larger phenomenon of migration, and his brush with the apocalypse."
   —*The Village Voice*

"Too big to fit in a review, and almost too big to fit in one heart. *Places* is a book that only a journalist could dream, and only a poet could write."
   —*Austin Chronicle*

"[Santos] masterfully weaves the stories of various unforgettable characters with the landscape and fragrance of their memories."
   —*The Miami Herald*

"An unforgettable chronicle."
   —*Albuquerque Weekly Alibi*

W9-BEM-333

"An unrelentingly gorgeous memoir . . . [Santos] draws from centuries of history and great wells of emotion to construct a remembrance that flies in the face of his very words." —*Texas Monthly*

"A moving, intellectually powerful memoir of Mexican-American life . . . His fine memoir is certain to find a wide readership."
—*Kirkus Reviews* (starred)

"[An] elegantly crafted chronicle of one of the thousands of Mexican families who fled to El Norte during the Mexican Revolution. [Santo's] book is one of the most insightful investigations into Mexican-American border culture available."
—*Publishers Weekly* (starred)

"Many Americans will find themselves in the narrative of upheaval and migration; they will recognize the difference between labored nostalgia and heartfelt loss."
—*Booklist* (starred)

"It pains me when the incredible histories of our people are trivialized as magic realism; surviving is no magic act. In a time of global migrations and forgetting, these stories remember beyond the Alamo, beyond 1776, 1492, and 1519. I would recommend that the governors of Texas, California, and Arizona, the presidents of Mexico and the United States, and the director of the Immigration and Naturalization Service read this book. This is the map of one family, and perhaps all families who live on several borders. Here, then, are our documents, our papers. This story is our green card."
—Sandra Cisneros, bestselling author of *The House on Mango Street*

"This book is a tender treasure, a rare gift, a journey into the rich tapestry of a family's life and migrations. Exquisitely woven, intrinsically poetic, *Places Left Unfinished at the Time of Creation* moves fluidly among relatives and realities, cities and mysteries, unearthing, liking, shining deep light into the memory-caverns of our worlds. The best memoir I've ever read."
—Naomi Shihab Nye, author of *Never in a Hurry*

"John Phillip Santos invokes the muses of homelessness. He draws his silhouette in the twilight and inserts it in an ancient mural whose meaning is beyond him. His ultimate realization is that his is a wandering soul but he is not—has never been— alone. His memoir is a lesson in humility."
—Ilan Stavans

"John Santos's powerful memoir is not a simple walk down memory lane, but rather a poetic exploration of the ways in which remembering and forgetting inform our fragile modes of surviving and thriving. From Texas to Oxford, from grandparents to Borges, Santos takes us on a poignant pilgrimage that ends deep within our souls." —Cornel West, bestselling author of *Race Matters*

PENGUIN BOOKS

PLACES LEFT UNFINISHED
AT THE TIME OF CREATION

John Phillip Santos, born and raised in San Antonio, Texas, is the first Mexican American Rhodes scholar and the recipient of numerous literary awards. His articles on Latino culture, art, and politics have appeared in the *Los Angeles Times*, and the *San Antonio Express News*. He is writer and producer of more than forty television documentaries for CBS and PBS, three of them Emmy nominees. He lives in New York City, where he works in the Media Program of the Ford Foundation.

Places Left Unfinished at the Time of Creation

JOHN PHILLIP SANTOS

PENGUIN BOOKS

PENGUIN BOOKS
Published by the Penguin Group
Penguin Putnam Inc., 375 Hudson Street,
New York, New York 10014, U.S.A.
Penguin Books Ltd, 27 Wrights Lane,
London W8 5TZ, England
Penguin Books Australia Ltd, Ringwood,
Victoria, Australia
Penguin Books Canada Ltd, 10 Alcorn Avenue,
Toronto, Ontario, Canada M4V 3B2
Penguin Books (N.Z.) Ltd, 182–190 Wairau Road,
Auckland 10, New Zealand

Penguin Books Ltd, Registered Offices:
Harmondsworth, Middlesex, England

First published in the United States of America by Viking Penguin,
a member of Penguin Putnam Inc. 1999
Published in Penguin Books 2000

1   3   5   7   9   10   8   6   4   2

ILLUSTRATION CREDITS
Frontispiece: Front page of *La Prensa*, January 10, 1939
Testimonio: The Garcia sisters (top to bottom): Madrina, Uela, Tía Pepa
Mexico Viejo: *The Burning of the Idols*, detail from *La Descripción de
Tlaxcala*, used by permission of Glasgow University Library
Peregrinaje: Wedding portrait, Juan José and Margarita Santos, 1915
Volador: Detail from *Códice Fernandez Leal*, used by permission of
The Bancroft Library, University of California, Berkeley

CIP data available
ISBN 0-670-86808-6
ISBN 0 14 02.9202 0

Printed in the United States of America
Set in Bulmer
Designed by Deborah Kerner

Para mis padres,
who gave me the story

es de Espa[...]

SE TRATA DE JUAN SANTOS, DE 49 AÑOS

Su cuerpo fue encontrado flotando muy cerca de la calle Simpson

Es el cuarto suicidio que ocurre en los pocos días del año actual

El cuerpo inanimado de un mexicano fue encontrado el lunes en la mañana flotando en el río San Antonio, cerca de la calle Simpson, en el Parque Roosevelt.

El muerto, que era Juan Santos, de 49 años de edad, fue identificado por su hijo Juan Santos Jr. y por su cuñado Carlos García, quienes lo buscaban en esos momentos.

Los detectives Fred Littlepage y Ed Amacker, de la escuadra de homicidios, acudieron a investigar el caso, acompañados del juez Raymond Gerhart, y el departamento de bomberos envió el pulmotor para ver si por medio de la respiración artificial se lograba volverle la vida a Santos.

Por más de media hora se trabajó incesantemente, pero todo fue inútil, pues la muerte se había apoderado del mexicano, que se había arrojado al río, según pudo investigar el Juez Gerhart.

Según informes obtenidos por los detectives, Juan Santos salió de su residencia del 116 de la calle Par-[...] a las seis de la mañana, y a las siete sus familiares dieron parte a la policía de su desaparición, siendo encontrado aproximadamente una hora después por sus familiares.

Santos se encontraba empleado por la Petroleum Machino and Foundry Co., desde hace tiempo, y últimamente era víctima de una penosa y grave enfermedad.

Al principio, la policía supuso que se trataba de un caso de accidente, pero cuando el Juez Gerhart investigó, el caso a fondo, [...]ó en fallo de suicidio, el cuarto del año en [...]

DE VIOLAR LAS LEYES DE LA NEUTRALIDAD

Por haber hecho remesas de aeroplanos, destinados a su Gobierno

Los adquirieron en este país, enviándolos a través de México

ASSOCIATED PRESS

Washington, D. C., 9 de enero.— La Oficina de Control de Municiones informó hoy al Congreso, que el Departamento de Justicia, está fiscalizando "aparentes violaciones a la ley, por agentes del Embajador de España en México", en las cuales están comprendidas "compras de aeroplanos, que se creen fueron destinados al Gobierno de España".

La oficina de control de municiones agregó que se formularán acusaciones.

Declaró que un número de aeroplanos estuvieron embarcándose para México, siendo exportados sin contar con las licencias respectivas en cuyas remisiones, el país de destino de esos embarques fue falseado y que algunas violaciones caen dentro de las prevenciones que contiene la ley respectiva de 4 de mayo de 1937, prohibiendo la exportación directa o indirecta de armas, municiones o implementos de guerra para la lucha en España.

"Investigaciones del Departamento de Justicia", dicen además, dos aeroplanos fueron exportados de los Estados Unidos, que fueron desarmados y ensamblados en tos, se transportarlos para [...] a España, que de más fueron embarcados [...] paña en el "Eba[...]", que puerto de Veracruz, [...] nes.

(Véase: SE ACUS[...]

[...]e Lambert [...]os Nueceros

[...]esto al hablar con ciertos elementos para [...]os trabajadores mexicanos el derecho de [...]alarios que fija la ley respectiva

[...] American Federation of Labor, [...] de Nueceros no se fija

GRAN H[...] DE UN[...]

Contents

Peregrinaje

Volador

Family Trees

Los Garcias

Teofilo Garcia	Tomás Castillo
m.	*m.*
Petra Ortega	Fabiana Salazar

Jacobo Garcia *m.* Juanita Castillo

(Children in order of birth)

Francisco, Uncle Frank

Margarita, *Uela*, my grandmother

José

Santos

Juan

Tomasita *(died at birth)*

Tomasa, *Madrina*

Josefa, *Tía Pepa*

Jesús, Uncle Jesse

Gilberto, Uncle Gilbert

Manuel

Valentín *(Manuel's twin, died at birth)*

Carlos, Uncle Chale

Los Santos

Juan Nepumencio Santos *m.* Paula Sandoval

(Children in order of birth)

Mariano

Uvaldino

Juan José, my grandfather

Andrea

Francisca, *Tía Panchita*

Jesusa, *Tía Chita*

Manuela, *Tía Nela*

(Children by Juan Nepumencio's first marriage)

Pedro

José León

Guadalupe

Jesús María

Juan José Santos *m*. Margarita Garcia, *Uela*

(Children in order of birth)

Raul

Juan José, Jr., my father

Consuelo, AUNT CONNIE

Beatriz, AUNT BEA

Margarita, AUNT MARGIE

Rogelio, UNCLE ROGER

Juan José Santos, Jr., DADDY, *m*. Lucille Lopez, MOTHER

John Phillip

George David

Charles Daniel

Los Lopez

Leonides Lopez *m.* **Leandra Vela**, GRANDMOTHER

(Children in order of birth)

Leo William

Lauro Luis

Lydia Viola

Lily Amanda *(died at two)*

Ludovico Blas

Lucille Cecille, my mother

Places Left
Unfinished
at the Time
of Creation

I learned to breathe this way
when I left that body made of ashes,
river water, copal and huisache flowers.

When my breath was South
it was a feather as big as a palm frond.
The infinite miles were numbered in stars
and the earth was lit from inside.

My eyes were mirrors, my heart was wind.
The ground pulled my songs like a magnet.

The bananas were so ripe they spread like butter
when they first brought guns into the garden.

Our legacy is papaya, is *frijol*,
is sangria by the gallons.

Helix inside of helix, the color of blood.
Dead uncles. Lost friends. Forgotten *amantes*.

For five hundred years of impossible weather,
this lightning has smelled like night,
weaving its net of forgetting across these lands.

Testimonio

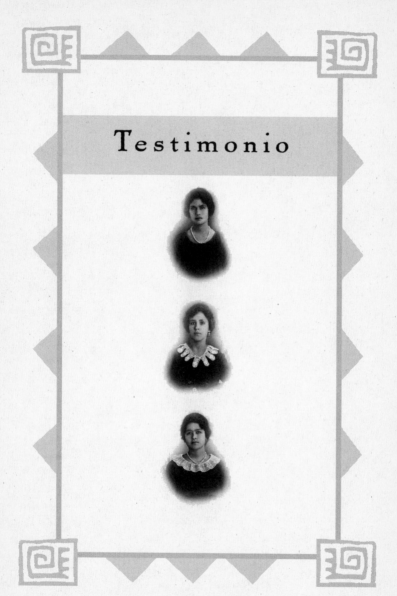

1

Tierra
de Viejitas

Land of Little Old Ladies

 *"Have all the Santos already died?"*

That's the question Madrina asks Aunt Connie several times a week, as she awakens from sleeping or daydreaming in front of the television.

"¿Ya se murieron todos los Santos?"

Madrina Tomasa is my grandmother's sister on my father's side of the family. She is the eldest living sibling of her brood of Garcias. She lives with my aunt and uncle in a bright, meticulously arranged room in a house in San Antonio, Texas, where she keeps time by TV novelas like Amor Salvaje, variety shows, and televised-live Sunday-morning masses from San Fernando Cathedral.

Like others of her generation, the present has lost its claim on her. Mostly she wanders, disembodied, through her ninety-five years, as if they were interlocking chambers of an enormous shell of memories. One

moment she is a child, bathing in morning light in the mercado of
Múzquiz, in the mountains of northern Mexico. Then it is 1921, and she
is overturning a Model A Ford on San Antonio's south side. She laughs
now, remembering the tumbling tin milk jugs from the dairy truck
she collided with, pouring out across the oily pavement on Nogalitos
Street.

Though she was married to my great-uncle Manuel for almost sixty
years, Madrina is still enamored with el tío Uvaldino Santos, my grand-
father's brother, whom she fell in love with as a teen. Aunt Connie says he
was the "love of her life," but they were not permitted to marry because in
Mexico it was considered improper for two sisters to marry two brothers.
Dead for more than ten years, Uvaldino comes to her in dreams, upright
and impeccable in his dark pin-striped suit, with mustache and eye-
brows perfectly combed, and presents her with large bunches of grapes.
And week to week, she asks my aunt that same question:

"¿Ya se murieron todos los Santos?"

My aunt replies, "Sí, Madrina, ya se murieron todos los Santos."
"All of the Santos have died."

Since Aunt Connie told me that story, I have wondered why she
told Madrina all the Santos are dead. Who are *we*?

Aren't we still unfolding the same great tapestry of a tale begun
long, long ago? Aren't my aunts and uncles, cousins, my parents and
brothers, all part of the same long dolorous poem that sings of the
epoch of ocean-plying caravelas and conquest, of Totonacas and Aztecas, of unimaginable treasures created from jade, silver, and gold? Of
gods worshipped and sacrificed to from on top of pyramids—of thousands upon thousands of Indios baptized for Christ in the saliva of
Franciscan monks? We may be latter-day Mexicanos, transplanted into
another millennium in *El Norte*, but we are still connected to the old
story, aren't we? The familia walked out of the mountain pueblos of

Mexico into the oldest precincts of San Antonio—then, finally, into the suburbs of the onetime colonial city, where the memory of our traditions has flickered like a votive flame, taken from the first fire.

It's a common name my family carries out of our Mexican past. It is a name that invokes the saints and embroiders daily prayers of Latinos in North and South America. The old ones in the family say the name was once *de Los Santos.* "From the saints." But no one remembers when or why it was shortened. There were Santos already in San Antonio two hundred years ago. In the records for the year 1793 at the Mission San Antonio de Valero, which later became the Alamo, you find the names of Manuel and Jorge de Los Santos, referred to as "Indios," but it's not clear whether they are our ancestors.

It sometimes seems as if Mexicans are to forgetting what the Jews are to remembering. We have made selective forgetting a sacramental obligation. Leave it all in the past, all that you were, and all that you could not be. There is pain enough in the present to go around. Some memories cannot be abandoned. Let the past reclaim all the rest, forever, and let stories come to their fitting end.

I never understood people's fascination with immortality. The idea of life without end gave me chills. Even as a kid, I wanted to be among my family and my ancestors, walking through our short time together, fully knowing it will end. I wanted to bind Texas and Mexico together like a raft strong enough to float out onto the ocean of time, with our past trailing in the wake behind us like a comet tail of memories.

But the past can be difficult to conjure again when so little has been left behind. A few photographs, a golden medal, a pair of eyeglasses as delicate as eggshells, an old Bible, a letter or two. Some families in Mexico have troves of their ancestors' belongings, from pottery of the ancients and exquisite paintings of Mexico City in the eighteenth century to helmets and shields of the Spaniards, and even hundred-year-old parrots and maguey plants that have been handed down, from the great-grandparents who first tended them.

By comparison, the Santos are traveling light through time. In my family, virtually nothing has been handed down, not because there was nothing to give, but after leaving Mexico to come to Texas—so many loved ones left behind, cherished places and things abandoned—the *antepasados* ceased to regard anything as a keepsake. Everything was given away. Or they may have secretly clung so closely to their treasured objects that they were never passed on.

Then they were lost.

My mother's mother, Leandra Lopez, whom we called simply "Grandmother," sat in her cluttered dark house on West Russell Street like an aged Tejana sphinx during the last ten years of her life. Through the year, she filed away embossed death notices and patron saint prayer cards of departed family and friends in the black leather address book I consulted to write out her Christmas cards every year. In early December, I would sit down with her and first cross out the entries for all those who had "passed onward," as she used to say. By each name in the book, she had already scratched a cross with thick black pencil lines.

Memo Montalvo from Hebbronville, Texas. According to Grandmother, a good man. He had married a not-very-pretty cousin from Laredo.

Efraín Vela from Mier, Tamaulipas. Son of a cousin on her father's side whom she never spoke to. Supposedly, he was the keeper of the family coat of arms, awarded to the family by the Viceroy of Nueva España himself. What would happen to it now?

Socorro Mendiola, from Alice, Texas. She and Grandmother had taught school together in a one-room schoolhouse in Cotulla in 1910. Then Socorro became a Franciscan nun, breaking the heart of Grandmother's cousin, Emeterio Vela, whom, she noted with a sigh, had died just last year.

And every year, by the degrees of each ended life, as the world grew older, our addressing marathons grew shorter—though Grandmother would change the subject if I pointed out this mortal ratio.

Inside her rolltop writing desk, she kept a mysterious wooden polygonal star that had a different swatch of old Mexican fabrics glued on each facet. The multicolored curiosity smelled like Mexico, all cumin, wild honey, and smoky rose, and when you shook it, a small solitary object rattled inside. A stone? A marble? A gem? To me, it seemed like some magician's puzzle, and locked inside were all of the secrets of old Mexico.

During one of our annual Christmas-card sessions, I asked her if I could have that star, instead of the customary reward of a box of animal crackers and five dollars in change, which she laboriously fished out of her zippered, yellowing plastic coin purse. Grandmother was almost completely blind by then, so I put her hand to the last of the Hallmark Christmas cards in the place for her to sign her name. She slowly scratched out LEANDRA VELA LOPEZ, and told me no, I could not have the star.

I never saw it again.

My uncle, Lico Lopez, her son, ferreted out the past as a passionate genealogist who used research, fantasy, and spells of breathless diabetic madness to craft his ancestral charts of the Lopez and Vela families. Some are elaborate discs, in which each outward concentric ring represents a new generation. In these, as you delve closer to the center, you also go deeper into the past. In others, quickly dashed off as notes to himself, ragged trees and jagged lines are drawn between names like Evaristo, Viviano, Blas, and Hermenegilda. In one, going back to 1763, the capstone slot contains the cryptic entry, from whom, presumably, he believed we were descended. Subtle faculties and proclivities were passed, speechlessly, through the flesh of successive generations. The ghosts of Spanish royalty mingled with Indios, Negros, and people from every part of the world—in Uncle Lico's secret genealogy of Mexico. Yet, despite the uninterest and ridicule of many, he managed to recover numerous family names and stories.

Lico knew I had some of the same magnetic attraction to the past that fueled his manic genealogies, as if the molecules of our bodies were polarized in a way that drew us both back in time, back, inexorably, toward the ancestors. Before he died, suddenly, in San Antonio, of a heart attack, he sent me all of the notes and charts accumulated in his forty years of digging in the family root cellars. He also gave me a receipt, dated May 25, 1928, laminated and mounted on wood, from my grandfather's grocery store, Leonides Lopez Groceries, in Cotulla, Texas. In my grandfather's filigreed wrought iron pencil script, it details a sale on that day of *harina* (flour), *azúcar* (sugar), *fideos* (vermicelli), *manteca* (lard), *papas* (potatoes), and other assorted dry goods, for a total of $5.05.

A relic like this is the exception, though. A trunkful of the Santos family photographs disappeared when Madrina moved out of the old house on Cincinnati Street. She swears she remembers seeing it fall off the truck near the corner of Zarzamora Street, where La Poblanita bakery was located. It was a pine box the size of a shipping trunk, stuffed with heirloom photographs. She can't remember why she said nothing at the time. It fell off a truck onto the dusty streets of old San Antonio de Bejar one day and was left behind, abandoned, lost.

In one photo that survived it is 1960, and the whole Santos tribe is standing on the porch of my grandmother's house, in early evening shadows. It must have been Easter because my many cousins and I are in church clothes, standing in the yard around the trunk of a great sycamore tree. My aunts and uncles are there, partly old Mexican, partly new American, looking handsome, hopeful, proud of the brood standing in front of them. In the very middle of the scene, *las Ancianas,* Grandmother Santos, whom we called "Uela," short for *abuela,* and Madrina, her sister, are standing regally in a perfect moment, radiating the indelible light of Mexico. On the porch, Mother and an aunt have my newborn twin brothers, George and Charles, wrapped in blankets in their arms. My father looks serious, with a distant gaze, in a dark suit and silky tie. To one side, standing apart from us, is one of my eldest cousins, René, who would be killed in Vietnam just seven years later.

These are the memento mori of the Santos. There are a few photographs, rosary chains of half-remembered stories, carried out of another time by the old Mexicans I grew up with. In dreams, the ancestors who have passed on visit with me, in this world, and in a world that lies perhaps within, amidst, and still beyond this world— a mystical limbo dimension that the descendants of the Aztecs call *el Inframundo.* In the *Inframundo,* all that has been forgotten still lives. Nothing is lost. All remembrance is redeemed from oblivion.

These ancestors, living and dead, have asked me the questions they were once asked: Where did our forebears come from and what have we amounted to in this world? Where have we come to in the span of all time, and where are we headed, like an arrow shot long ago into infinite empty space? What messages and markings of the ancient past do we carry in these handed-down bodies we live in today?

With these questions swirling inside me, I have rediscovered some stories of the family past in the landscapes of Texas and Mexico, in the timeless language of stone, river, wind, and trees. Tío Abrán, twin brother to my great-grandfather Jacobo, was a master of making charcoal. He lived in the hill country, where the cedars needed to make charcoal were planted a century ago to supply the industry. Today, long after he worked there, walking in that central Texas landscape crowded with deep green cedar, I feel old Abrán's presence, like the whisper of a tale still waiting to be told, wondering whether my intuition and the family's history are implicitly intertwined. Even if everything else had been lost—photographs, stories, rumors, and suspicions—if nothing at all from the past remained for us, the land remains, as the original book of the family.

It was always meant to be handed down.

I am one of the late twentieth-century Santos, born in *la Tierra de Viejitas,* "the Land of Little Old Ladies," a sun-drenched riverine empire in south Texas reigned over by a dynasty of Mexican *doñas* who held court in shady painted backyard arbors and parlors across the neighborhoods of San Antonio. To the uninitiated, *las Viejitas* might look fragile, with their bundled bluish hair, false teeth, and halting arthritic steps across the front porch. Their names were ciphers from the lost world: Pepa. Tomasa. Leandra. Margarita. Chita. Cuka. Fermina. They were grandmothers, great-aunts, sisters-in-law, and *comadres.*

Their houses smelled of cinnamon tea, marigolds, burning church candles, Maja brand Spanish talcum powder, and Pine-Sol. They tended garden plots of geraniums, squash, tomatoes, cilantro, and chile, decorated with stones that were painted to look like Popeye, Olive Oyl, and Cantinflas. The chickens in their backyards sometimes seemed to cluck to the sound of the polkas coming from the transistor radio left on in the bathroom. They healed children, and animals, with their *remedios,* potions and poultices made with herbs that had names like *el garrabato* and *la gobernadora.* Asking Tía Pepa how she learned the old remedies, cures, and healing arts, she once answered, "It's nothing special—just some little things I heard some people talking about when I was a little girl."

When she was fourteen, Pepa performed her first healing on a woman in her village of Palaú, Coahuila, in north Mexico. The woman was wasting away from a week of stomach cramps and nausea. She was *empachada,* afflicted by some alien spirit that had entered her body to block and torment her guts. Pepa explains how she laid the ailing señora on a large dining room table, rubbing her with freshly squeezed plant oils, tightly wrapping her in a blanket, "like an enchilada," and praying by her side for hours, petitioning the evil spirit to come out. The cramps subsided and the lady quickly got better.

Many years later, my brothers and I would be left with my grandmother and her old sisters when we were sick with colds. They wrapped hot, wet towels around our clasped hands and had us pray, "to preserve and concentrate the warmth of your body." The heat of the living rooms of *las Viejitas* was moist with the faint, burnt paraffin scent of the gas flames rising along the white-hot porcelain heating fixtures. While I lay dazed with the flu on a sofa, watching *The Andy Griffith Show, Let's Make a Deal,* or *The Mike Douglas Show,* they made *huevos rancheros* and *atole de arroz,* read the Bible, planted a new cactus in the backporch garden, and in the afternoon, took a long, tranquil siesta.

On their solo trips to Mexico, we heard how *las Viejitas* rode tough mares and swam in rushing rock-bed arroyos. After being dropped off across the border in Nuevo Laredo or Piedras Negras, they traveled by bus far into the old country to see *sobrinos y comadres* in Monterrey or Nueva Rosita, or deeper into Mexico to collect water from a spring in Querétaro said to have healing powers.

Some traded small parcels of real estate, purchased originally with insurance money from their long-departed husbands. Some loved parades—some wore fur coats in the middle of summer. Others prayed with eyes closed, their hands held to the breast and clasped so tightly the blood ran out. They wore powders and pomades, with small hand-kerchiefs always modestly folded into their cuffs or bodices.

Effortlessly, they seemed to know exactly what needed to be done. When a violent storm suddenly descended on the city, they pulled the windows closed and made crosses of lime on small cards, placing them under the beds, chairs, and tables.

They rolled tortillas while cooking beans and *carne guisada* on fiery stoves—and ended most days with a shot of tequila and a little juice glass filled with beer.

Then it was time for the rosary.

That there were no men among *las Viejitas* didn't seem strange at all. They seemed to have died so far in the past that no one ever spoke of them. The pictures of the grandfathers, and the great-grandfathers, were kept in loving regard in living room cabinets and bedroom bureaus—always with the claw mustaches, always unsmiling, stiff-spined in their heavy wool suits. In one old ivory frame, Uela and Abuelo Juan José, my father's parents, were caught in brisk midstride, staring ahead, snapped by a strolling photographer on the downtown sidewalk of Houston Street, under the marquis of the Texas Theater. I marveled at my grandfather's stance, with leg kicked out as if in a march. His expression was tender yet determined. But by the 1950s, most of the men were already distant memories. *Las Viejitas* had made it through without them, even if much of the century had been lonely.

They had raised their tribes—las familias—in *El Norte,* virtually alone. Most of their men fell early in the century, at an epic age's end when the memories and dreams of Old Mexico were receding quickly to the south like a tide falling back into an ancient inland sea, past Zarzamora Street in San Antonio, past the moonlit chalk bluffs of the Nueces River in south Texas, then farther south past the towns of Co-tulla, Hondo, Eagle Pass, and the Rio Grande.

After freely moving north and south for generations, the Santos were left on the north bank of this vanishing memory—*naufragios*—shipwrecked beyond the border. No one now remembered when Texas was Mexico, was Nueva España, was wilderness before the Europeans came.

There was revolution in the old country when the family set out for the north in this century. In 1914 they were Mestizo settlers, part Spanish, part Indian, on the edge of the ruins of ancient Mexico and New Spain. Even though these lands had been Mexican for nearly three centuries—Texas had been taken over by los Americanos in 1836—it was a new world they settled in, less than three hundred miles from home. Mexicanos could easily keep to themselves, but back then, there were some places you just didn't go. Mexicans knew to avoid completely the predominantly German Texas hill country towns of New Braunfels and Fredericksburg, where there had been trouble in the past with *"esa gente con las cabezas quadradas,"*—"those people with the square heads"—as Great-uncle Manuel Martinez, Madrina's husband, used to say.

There were outposts of the "pueblo Mexicano" in cities of the north like St. Louis and Chicago, in Detroit and Seattle, but the Mexican Americans mainly stayed in the lands we knew best, from California to Texas, not too far from *el otro lado,* "the other side," as Mexico was often referred to.

"The apple never falls too far from the tree," Uela used to say. By leaving Mexico, the family had become exiles in what was really our own homeland. But under the all-knowing gazes of these *Viejitas,* we never felt oppressed or downtrodden.

The world of the family in *la Tierra de Viejitas* was an echo of the worlds of families we knew in Mexico, where I spent a lot of time growing up. After the migration of the Santos and Garcias in 1914, during the time of the Mexican Revolution, only a few aunts and cousins had remained in Mexico, and many of them had died, or been lost by the time I was born. The Guerras of Sabinas, Coahuila, were such old family friends that they had become family, offering me a living root in the land the Santos had left behind fifty years before. I didn't know it then, but my visits to Sabinas, growing more frequent as I grew older, were also journeys to my family's former home in Mexico, there in that cluster of little-known northern towns in the coal-rich high desert country of Coahuila. These pilgrimages were almost involuntary, as if I had been pulled, inexplicably, in a strong Gulf undertow toward the ancestors. In towns such as Sabinas, Agujita, Palaú, and Múzquiz, I was in the company of our family's Mexican ghosts.

The Guerra family home in Sabinas, Coahuila, across the street from the church and the central plaza, was another matriarchy—ruled over by a *Viejita,* Abuelita Josefina, a widow already for more than thirty years, who was dutifully attended to by her daughters, sons, grandchildren, and a small coterie of India maids.

During one of the first of many visits to the Guerras in Sabinas in the mid-1960s, I awoke with a sudden noise. Outside in the plaza, reservists, bedraggled from long Saturday night cantina vigils, had begun their drills in the plaza at dawn, blowing bugles and pounding their snares as if they wanted to crack the sky open, scaring the grackles and rattling the tin gutters of the house, sounding like clarions of the apocalypse. With the bedroom shutters open to the plaza, I started out of bed, fearing the end of the world had surely begun.

Walking out onto the cold, green malachite floors of the hallway, utterly quiet now, and into the kitchen, old Zulema, whom everyone called "Zule," the longtime head maid of the house, sat quietly on a stool in the early light, knitting her thick gray hair into one long braid, and afterward putting the water on to boil tomatoes for the breakfast *salsa ranchera.* She had the moon-shaped face of the Chichimeca Indians of the region. By then, her eyes were growing misty with cataracts, so most of the chopping she now left to the *muchachitas,* who were diligently at their work. Abuela Josefina, dressed in black with a mantle of starched lace chevrons around her collar, sat at a table with a cup of *chocolate,* sorting beans and chiles through her bifocals while orchestrating from across the room as Zule added the portions of salt, cumin, and cracked black pepper to the softly bubbling clay pot of salsa on the stove. She would narrate every step of the recipe to me—first burning the skins of the tomato, using a pumice stone *metate* to grind the spices, and always waiting until the very end for the cilantro—while interspersing stories of a specific overfiery salsa she had made for one of her daughter's weddings thirty years before, or a philological aperçu on the origin of the word "tomato" in *tomatl,* from the Nahuatl tongue of ancient Mexico.

Much of the breakfast came from the courtyard garden, scented with thickets of mint and mottled in the morning shade of lime trees with a nebula of low-hanging fruit. From high up in the leaf-draped branches of a primeval avocado tree there, I watched all of the comings and goings of the morning. The gas vendor who rolled his tanks through the streets shouting "Coahuila Gas!" came through the garden gate looking for one of the girls in the kitchen whom he had a crush on. Meanwhile, the man who sold flowers rang and waited for Zule at the gate, crossing himself every time the church bell chimed in the plaza. Throughout the early morning, with the sound of clapping sandals on the stone floors, grandchildren would appear in small gaggles, looking for their abuela Josefina, who would let each one take a sip from her cup of steaming *chocolate.*

Around the grand dining table, under an equestrian portrait of the family patriarch, Don Alejandro Guerra, Doña Josefina would gently steward the discussion during the meal, beginning by catching up on the family in San Antonio. If her eldest son, Tío Alejandro, was there,

the talk would quickly move to news and politics of Mexico's borderlands, the politics of *El Norte,* a joke about the new Mexican president,
an assassination of a governor in the Yucatán—or about poor Mexico
herself.

Pobre Mexico.

In these mealtime colloquies, over *huevos* and *frijoles,* Mexico was
referred to in tones of pity and exasperation: all the poverty, all the corruption, all the dust. The idea of annexing Coahuila to Texas would receive a jubilant toast of watermelon juice.

And I worried to myself secretly: *What would be the destiny of
Mexico?*

Once they arrived in Texas during the revolution, maybe the Santos and Garcia families simply wanted to forget their past in Mexico—
the dusty streets, broken-down houses, and hunger. They wanted to
burn away the memory of when the families came north across the Rio
Grande. Northern Mexico became one of the most violent and chaotic
battlefields of *la Revolución* of 1910, a revolution that was to last eleven
years. But for the first years, the revolution was only distant thunder,
more of a concern to Mexicans well to the south of Coahuila in states
such as Guerrero, Puebla, and Mexico City. The family's flight from
Coahuila was in 1914, the year Pancho Villa, along with a myriad of
other revolutionary bands, rose up to occupy the bare constellation of
towns across the parched high Norteño desert where they had made
their homes. San Antonio provided them a convenient escape from the
fighting, and—despite other intentions—a shelter for memory, instead
of its negation.

For my cousins, as for my brothers and me, the homes of *las Viejitas* were sanctuaries where Coahuila was still alive, and places where
the inhibitions and proprieties of the Gringo world of San Antonio,

Texas, outside did not apply. Those were days when the taco and the tamal were stigmatized in public, and Spanish was seldom heard on downtown streets. The old tíos had to speak English, often haltingly, to get along in the working world. Most of *las Viejitas,* staying in their homes, spoke only Spanish, or at least pretended not to speak English. When Uela spoke Spanish, her sentences moved in one steady arc, like a bow across a violin, and her words were delicately pronounced, so that you could hear every tinkle of an old chandelier, every gust of a Coahuila wind falling to a hush, and the grain of a rustling squash blossom.

The migrations continued through the century. In the 1960s, my parents moved us from one of the old neighborhoods of the city to a new suburb at the city's northwestern edge, in order to get us into the better public schools in San Antonio. We were the first Mexicans in the neighborhood, in a two-floor house with a two-car garage, a built-in dishwasher, central air-conditioning, and intercom consoles in every room. We spoke English to each other, and Spanish to the old ones in the family. When the mariachis played in our backyard, the rapid plucking of the bajo sexto and the shimmering trumpet lines echoed off the neighbors' houses and drew them out to listen. Out there in that virgin neighborhood, it always felt as if we were closer to the iridescent Texas sky, stripped of the protective canopy of sycamore, wisteria, china berry, and live oak that arched over so many of the streets of our old, secret Mexican city, San Antonio de Bejar.

That old San Antonio was part of the hoary earth of the ancestors. Out there in the suburb at the edge of the city, following the early Gemini and Apollo space missions, I read books about space and prepared for the day in the future, which would undoubtedly come, when I would leave this planet in a rocket of my own.

Today, in New York City, I live in a world *las Viejitas* never visited, very far from the land they knew well. I have been to places they never imagined, like England, Europe, Turkey, Peru, and the Sudan. Yet, wherever I go, there is a ribbon of primordial Mexican night, the color of obsidian, snaking in a dream through the skies high over my head. Sometimes it is easily visible to me, like a burning galaxy, sometimes it is not. Sometimes it drizzles a fine rain of voices, images, and stories. And *las Viejitas* are here now, too, as they have always been, invisible yet abiding. They are keeping a vigil over the stories they told to me as if they are a *compromiso,* a promise that has been handed on. I have always felt connected, oriented, and imparted to by them, but unsure how I fit into a story that was never meant to be told.

Tía Pepa has an old polished silver pistol with a pearl handle which she often brings out when she's in the mood to tell her stories of Mexico. It was given to her by her father, my great-grandfather Jacobo, as a wedding present. Her husband, great-uncle Anacleto, was the foreman of the large coal mine in Agujita, Coahuila, which in those days, could be a dangerous place. Anacleto, who later served as mayor of the small cluster of towns that included Cloete, Sabinas, and Barroterán, is still fondly remembered as the only man to serve in that office without ending up a rich man.

According to la tía, she only had to use that sidearm once, when some bandidos tried to rob their modest house and steal a week's payroll. Hearing them outside, Pepa yelled a warning to them, then fired one shot through the front door, and the *hombres malos* fled. Years later, when she and Anacleto came to the United States, the pistol was confiscated in its metal Gamesa cookie box by the American customs agents at the border town of Eagle Pass, and it took my mother a year of legal wrangles to help Tía Pepa to get it back.

Along with Uela, her sister Tía Pepa, and several aunts, Mother drove to the border after submitting all the required gun-permit papers and notarized letters of reference necessary to establish the weapon in the category of an "irreplaceable family heirloom." After a morning of shopping in Piedras Negras on the Mexican side of the river, visits with cousins in Villa Union, and bowls of *caldo de pollo* at a restaurant in the marketplace, they crossed the international bridge and kept their appointment with the chief Immigration Service officer. After receiving from the ladies a gift of tamales, along with the required documents, yet still puzzled by this delegation of nattily dressed Mexican, and Mexican American, women, the agent warily opened the vault and brought out a cloth bag that contained the pistol. Pepa thanked the agent and put the gun in her purse. As she tells the story of its return today, Pepa looks down at the old gun on her lap as if it were the last talisman of all the old Mexican time.

For years after arriving in Texas, Madrina missed their home village of Palaú, leaving her feeling perpetually displaced and homesick. She had brought little from Mexico, and today she has few things that go back to that time. In her room in Aunt Connie's house she shows me a photograph of her father Jacobo and his twin brother Abrán, taken in a studio in Palaú, with a map of the Santa Rosa sierra in the background. It sits on top of her 27-inch television, which she keeps tuned to one of the Spanish channels at stentorian volume. Another portrait, of Uela, looking stern, yet consoling, hangs over her bed.

Year-round, she bundles up now like an Inuit elder, with a furry wool stocking cap pulled down around her ears, a pink and turquoise flowery house robe, and embroidered slippers made of blonde Scottish lambskin. With one gloved hand, she clutches the dainty glass of beer she takes every day with lunch.

In those long-ago days of the revolution and the migration, she knew a part of old Mexico was dying in the lives of all those who were displaced. That life the Garcias had known in Palaú was soon to be vanquished, and with it a way of living that had been changeless since no one can remember when. It was a way of life that had carried them out of the past like an undetectable current through all the plantings and harvests, the births, marriages, and deaths.

Madrina remembers how many of the families that had left Mexico with them arrived in Texas with nowhere to go and no one to help them. They were los perdidos, the lost ones. If there was nobody to vouch for them at the border in Piedras Negras, they were put on federal freight trains manned by Army soldiers and Texas Rangers, bound for the sprawling desert refugee camp at Fort Bliss, which quickly became known among the Mexicanos as "Fort Misery."

"We were always going to go back when things got better—but then they never did. So we stayed in San Antonio," Madrina recalls now.

Yet, there wasn't much homesickness among the old Garcia brothers. They were not much given over to sentimentality about anything, even Mexico. They simply kept to their practical ways, and by doing so, they remained connected to the feeling of that old Mexican time inside of them. Where *las Viejitas* maintained something of the knowledge and meaning of that time, their brothers kept and passed down the practices, the daily routines of tasks and chores. Uncle Frank helped me plant a patch of watermelon plants in the beige sand of our ranch in Pleasanton, Texas—moving slowly around the plot, stringing a network of twine from an elaborate frame he had constructed to hang cheesecloth to keep out the greedy dark purple grackles. In that garden, we planted both the round watermelons and the longer, dirigible-shaped ones. Uncle Frank pursued his gardening as if he had done the same thing a thousand times, anticipating the evenings when we would stand over the same garden, spitting watermelon seeds into the bright moonlight.

Despite Madrina's early unease, the family gradually became anchored in the ancient soil of Texas and in the streets of San Antonio. But all of those ghost geographies in the family: the Mexico de Mexico, the Mexico de Tejas, pulled at me like an invisible magnet whenever I spent time with the Garcias.

Where their brothers were all good with lathes, gears, and engines, the three Garcia sisters, Margarita (Uela), Tomasa (Madrina), and Josefa (Tía Pepa), were more inclined to the immaterial realm, where the saints could intercede with God on behalf of humans—*seres humanos*—and from where humans could draw the power to heal, or, to hurt one another. Many of *las Viejitas* in the family knew these things, and the Garcia hometown of Palaú in Mexico has always been known as a town of gifted healers.

This was the knowledge that had been handed down, usually mother to daughter, since the time of the conquest, cloaking old Indian *sabiduría*, or wisdom, in the trappings of a pious Roman Catholicism. If someone possessed these arts and wanted to, they could do harm to you with *el mal ojo*, a gaze so jarring your soul would be shaken, leaving you listless, desperate, or crazy.

Most illnesses were believed to be carried in the winds, so you had to take precautions that unfavorable breezes did not enter your mouth, your ears, or the top of your head. And then there was *susto*, a kind of supernatural fright, that ensued when you inadvertently allowed yourself to be invaded by unfriendly spirits. Above all, spirits were real.

Pepa was with Uela when she went to a medium in Monterrey, and they watched the old Indian man pass slowly into a deep, slurring, closed-eye trance. Suddenly, in a distinguished voice, speaking in the crisp, proper Spanish of a *metropolitano*, he called out to my grandmother by her first name.

"Margarita! Margarita! How I have looked for your across the centuries!" The medium's face was pursed in a grimace. Uela was terrified.

"Who are you?" Uela asked, gripping her sister Pepa's hand.

"It is I, Juan de Dios Pesa."

It was the spirit of the nineteenth-century poet of Mexico City, whose verses Uela adored. When she was young in Palaú, she had wanted to be an actress, and she used to recite one particular poem of Pesa's about a rose pleading for rain from a cloud that was always in too much of a hurry to grant the wish. One day, when the cloud finally returned looking for the rose, it was already dead and dried up. Many years later, in San Antonio, she still recited that poem for her grandchildren.

The ghost of the poet promised Uela it was written in the annals of heaven they would be together someday, and that occult prophecy became a secret the sisters kept until my grandmother's death.

"And what would you do with your husband, Juan José?" Pepa asked her sister, leaving the medium's studio.

"Don't even ask such a question, hermana!" she answered, full of consternation.

As the youngest daughter, Pepa was devoted to all of her brothers and sisters, but especially to her eldest sister, Uela, my grandmother, and in subtle ways she shared some part of each of their powers, the earthly and the ethereal.

Tía Pepa had been there when her middle sister had gotten the *susto* that changed her forever: Madrina hadn't always been so ethereal, so helpless, so pampered as we knew her when we were growing up. As a child and a young woman in Mexico, she had been mischievous and quick to anger. Then, suddenly one day, she changed. It was on a ranch where the family was living in Marion, Texas, near Austin, when Madrina was about fourteen years old. It was a beautiful, clear Texas day, but it had been raining for days before, and everywhere puddles reflected the yellow sunlight, making the whole landscape shimmer like a mirage.

That morning, a young Anglo woman had died of tuberculosis at a nearby ranch, and the body was being taken to town to be prepared for burial. Pepa and Madrina were playing together on the porch in front of the house when the small buggy carrying the body passed by. The dead woman had been seated upright on the bench, supported by her two sisters, when they hit a bump crossing a small creekbed that sent the corpse flying forward. The shroud that had covered the deceased fell away and the young woman's ravaged body was revealed, with all her hair gone, her face shrunken, and her raked cheeks painfully contorted with teeth showing, her arms clutched tightly to her chest.

The sisters in the buggy screamed and cried out her name, "Adelle!" cradling the body as they sobbed.

According to Tía Pepa, she looked away but Madrina kept staring. At that very instant, Pepa says, Madrina saw the poor woman's spirit leave her body and spiral upward like smoke toward the morning moon, which caused her to fall into a violent seizure, writhing on the floor of the porch and foaming at the mouth. It was the first of many such spells she would have for the next twenty years.

Pepa says the seizures made her sister extremely attentive to others, grateful for how they, in turn, took care of her. Madrina was also highly regarded for her intuitions. She didn't have to think about a problem. She just told you the answer that came into her mind, which was usually good counsel. This power, too, was said to come from the seizures. If Madrina was able to endure the driving emotional storms of her fits, everyday feelings must have appeared to her as if they were in slow motion. She was able to see deeper into the patterns of fleeting moments, to feel faint currents of the phenomena that shape our future. Now, Tía Pepa simply says that you must be extremely careful when the spirits are walking among you.

In *la Tierra de Viejitas,* I always knew the ghosts of the ancestors—the Santos, the Garcias, and all the others—are *still* with us. If not prepared, one could be frightened by the sight of them. Dressed in their downtown Frank Brothers vintage suits and Joske's department store dresses, they still stroll the wide sidewalks of San Antonio's Houston Street, taking long, slow steps past the blue, yellow, red, and green tile walls of the old Alameda Theater and the brightly painted walls of El Tenampa Bar.

The spirits stand dazed in front of the statue of the Virgin of Guadalupe inside the door of the San Fernando Cathedral, exhausted and dirty from a long day of picking tomatoes. In pairs, the wraiths sometimes float on flat barges down the San Antonio River, past all the tourists, preparing for a long journey south, smoking hand-rolled cigarettes and pouring yellow tequila into shot glasses. *Los Muertos* do not give up their homelands. We call it Texas. Some of them knew it as Tejas, or part of *la Nueva Extremadura* of New Spain. Others refer to it secretly as Aztlán, the mythical birthplace of the nomadic Mexica people who were to become the fierce Aztecs of central Mexico.

Along with the ghosts, their old gods—from the time before the Europeans—still whisper their prophecies in the ageless sunlight that falls on the ancient earth of Texas, severed so long ago from its Mexican roots. Their old, abandoned calendars, already well spun out, are still counting off these years in the churning mill of the stars, in this, the age of the fifth sun the Aztecs called *Cuatro Movimiento,* Four Movement.

"You will find your home," says Huitzilopochtli, the Aztec god whose name means "Hummingbird of the South"—just as he told the Mexica centuries ago when he sent them off to the south in search of a new home. On his instructions, they left behind their birthplace, where

they had lived for so long—Aztlán—"the place of whiteness" in the ancient Nahuatl tongue.

"You will receive many signs, and you will find the kingdom I have promised. But first you must make a very long journey."

All of these movements, north and south, follow maps left drawn in the blood, and the family stories carry their echo, from deep inside the past. The Mexica, who would become the Aztecs, were nomads across sprawling deserts, river plains, and mountain cordilleras for almost three hundred years before they saw the prophesied sign of an eagle consuming a serpent over a cactus. There, in the lake basin of the Valley of Mexico, they built the great imperial city of Tenochtitlán. Soon, though, they did not remember where Aztlán was—only that it lay to the north. They longed to abandon the memory of their centuries of hardship and wandering, replacing it with a glorious chronicle of victories, conquest, and oracles of a vast empire.

Mexico was always an empire of forgetting. After the cataclysm of conquest in 1521, when Tenochtitlán fell to the army of Hernán Cortés, Mexico was cut off from the wellspring of its Indian genesis, a place forevermore of fog and mystery. For decades, as the stories tell, night skies glowed with Spanish bonfires burning the codices, parchments, and totems that preserved the sacred knowledge of the Indian past. José Martí, the Cuban patriot and writer, said that the *conquistadores* "stole a page from the universe."

Spain was just as distant and ineffable, try as the conquistadors might to build a "New Spain" on Mexican earth. For better or worse, all the progeny of the conquest, Indios, Españoles, and mixed-blood Mestizos alike, shared the destiny of being irreversibly separated from their origins. That was the beginning of the Mexican Diaspora. To be Mexican American, Chicano, is to be further removed from those origins.

As a *raza*, a "nation," we are a *Diaspora within a Diaspora*.

Yet, something miraculous happened that marked the destiny of every Mexican to be born out of the crucible of the conquest. Ten years after the fall of the Aztec empire, on a hill outside of Tenochtitlán where the Indians had worshipped their goddess Tonantzín, a brown-skinned woman dressed simply as an Indian appeared to an Aztec man, Juan Diego, and told him in Nahuatl that she had come to be Mother to all the peoples of this land. By legend, she appeared in a shimmering cloud and made a field of roses bloom in the middle of winter.

Later, her winsome, cloaked image mysteriously appeared in a painting on Juan Diego's cloak. She would come to be known as *la Morenita,* the Virgin of Guadalupe, part Indian, part Spanish, a living emblem of the union of opposing worlds in the new Mexico, and the supreme Mother whose spirit forged the watchful presence of all of the generations of *Viejitas* who were to come.

Las Viejitas were born in the Virgin's magic.

They grew up in a twilight time and geography, poised between those ancient Indio origins from the south, Spain's grand utopian designs, and our Mestizo future in the north. The world they remember from their youth is not the modern Mexico ruled over by a rough-trade priestly elite of Ivy league, pedigreed technocrats, orchestrating Mexico's extreme slow-motion collapse. Their legacy is from the time that the Spanish language, theology, and science were first thrown across the Mexican geography like an enormous net, from a vision of the land enmeshed within the cosmos. That vision, with all of its mystical powers, has been almost lost.

When Madrina asks now if all of the Santos have died, she's really wondering whether a whole time has passed, *her time, her age*—and a generation with it—a generation with a living memory of the deep family bonds into Mexico's past.

All of the Santos have died.

I am one of their survivors.

2

Códices
de los Abuelos

Grandfather Codices

 *Just past dawn at the hilltop church in San Juan Tzompántepec, the morning in Puebla is already bright. Garlands of silvery fog left behind after a heavy storm the night before are still visible in the valley below, running sluggishly along the creeks, tattered in the treetops, swaddling other hills in the distance. I am here looking for faint traces of the grandfather no Mexican wants to admit to: Hernán Cortés.*

On its march to the Aztec capital, his army had fought a bloody battle with fearsome Tlaxcaltecan Indian warriors here. The Spaniards were nearly defeated. Legends tell how Cortés himself only survived a likely fatal chase by hiding in a hollow Tzompantle tree on this site. I came here to find a painting of the conquistador and his Indian consort, Malintzín, that is thought to be the only one painted by an Indian artist in Cortés's lifetime. But it is inside the church and the church door is locked.

On my father's side, Madrina and Tía Pepa had always said the Garcias had Spanish blood, though no one remembered exactly how, or from where. The Santos knew still less of their heritage, Spanish or Indian. In my mother's family, in the Lopez and Vela lines, Uncle Lico had found the deeds of Spanish land grants that had given our ancestors title to lands in Mier, Texas, near the Rio Grande, in the eighteenth century.

Most Mexican families are Mestizo, mixtures of Spanish and Indian heritage. But, after the Revolution of 1910, after three centuries of Spanish disregard for the indigenous world, the Mexican soul became Indian. Officially, the revolution sought to exorcise the influence of all things Spanish. Monasteries and convents were closed. Royal land deeds were nullified. Monuments to conquerors and viceroys were destroyed. Artists, with government support, painted epic murals of the pre-Columbian world that had been wracked by the Spanish. Poets and writers celebrated the Mestizo world of the new Mexico, a fusion of Indian and Spanish cosmologies. Gradually, the Iberian light cast on us by our Spanish past was further eclipsed.

But, I am back in Mexico, looking for traces of those first days in the age of Nueva España. From the doorstep of the church, I see an old man, unshaven, wearing two weathered denim jackets, meticulously shoveling soil into a bucket in the small cemetery that lay inside the walled churchyard. When he tells me his name is Ramón Lopez, I joke that we are parientes, or relatives, as Mexicans often call each other when they share a common family name. He asks me where my mother's family came from, and when I reply, "Cotulla, Texas," he whistles in amazement.

"I don't think any of my Lopez ever made it that far north!" Cotulla is only one hour north of the border.

The heavy rains of the day before had sunken the dirt in the grave of his third wife, and Ramón has come there to fill it in for the third time *since her death a month ago, at age seventy-eight. His earlier two wives are buried together in another grave, nearby. As to his age, Ramón says only he is older than the dirt, laughing with a coarse rasp through a toothless grin.*

"I don't remember Cortés," he says, "but I remember Zapata! My mother gave his soldiers chickens and avocados when they camped nearby, unknown to the dictator Porfirio's army."

After I tell him of my morning's quest, he says there is no such painting of Cortés in this church, and he should know. He has been the care-taker there for sixty-eight years, during which time he has dusted off the noses of every saint, scrubbed every chipped mosaic, and cleaned the gilded frame of every painting.

"Maybe the padrecito has it in his bedroom, I don't know, because I never went in there. Or maybe they took it to la Capitál. They take any-thing that's worth money."

But there is something he wants to show me. Ramón wipes his hands on his pants and asks me to follow him to the rear of the church building. After we walk through the scrubby brush at the edge of the churchyard, Ramón stoops down on one knee and pulls away the high, grassy weeds near the bottom of one wall, exposing an old, elaborately carved stone disc, slightly larger than a garbage can lid, set into a circular niche in the wall. Ramón wipes it with his jacket sleeve.

"You know what this is?"

At first, the carved miasma I see there makes it hard to focus on any details. It isn't one of the old stone calendar discs of the Indian time-keepers, calibrated and segmented in glyphic language, like the great Aztecan sun wheel of Tenochtitlán. It is exquisitely carved with inter-locking stems and flowers, coursing around a central tree, and all around it are thistle heads, rabbits, frogs, scorpions, bees, conch shells, and an arc of stars and their rays. Around the entire border, the sleek,

curved glyph for wind appears in an unbroken chain, making the whole
circle look radiant and in flux, as if the stone were meant to capture the
churning energy of a creation where all things are connected in a single
great motion.

While the wall has clearly been whitewashed hundreds of times, the
stone is pristine, cherished, hidden away, and guarded by the people like
a secret treasure. The Spanish often chose to build their churches over the
Indian pyramids, as they did over the great ceremonial pyramid in
Cholula, not too far away from here. Here, this old Indian disc is imbed-
ded in the church wall like a cornerstone, anchoring the Christian sanc-
tuary in the dark Mexican earth of the ancestors' time. Perhaps the disc
might have had some ceremonial function. It looks like a vision of the sky
wrapped around the great tree of the world, alive with the spirits of fa-
miliar plants and animals of the region. Ramón says no one really
knows what it means, but the parishioners of La Parroquia de San Juan
Tzompántepec nonetheless regard it as an heirloom, fighting over the
years with priests who sought to extract what they considered a pagan
abomination.

"Who put this here?" I ask Ramón.
He shrugs his shoulders. "Pues . . . ," he says, "los Abuelos."
The Grandfathers.

By the time I was born in 1957, my grandfathers were already long
gone. When their names were mentioned, once in a long while, by parents or aunts and uncles, it was always with great ceremony and formality. There were never disparaging words of any kind. My mother's
father, Leonides, owned a dry goods store in Cotulla, Texas, and my father's father, Juan José, with the same name as my father, was a gar-
dener and laborer in San Antonio. Both were remembered as men of
few words, prone to meting out family justice in swift and unwavering
fashion. I hadn't seen pictures of Juan José, but in an old photograph of

Leonides, taken when he was already in his early fifties, he is sitting next to a great desk in his store, stacked high with papers weighted by horseshoes. A big man with a bald head, and light-complexioned for a Mexicano, he is dressed in a suit and vest, with a shiny watch fob hanging, and his demeanor is serious, with a forceful gaze as direct and unyielding as an old judge's. If the stories are to be believed, both grandfathers were exemplars of virtue, honesty, and integrity, beloved by their families and communities alike. *Los Abuelos* never indulged in alcohol. Both Juan José and Leonides were said to be teetotalers who rarely drank, even at weddings or during holidays. There are no tales of drunkenness or recklessness among them. Yet neither lived to meet a single one of their scores of grandchildren.

Did they leave anything behind? Was there anything of the memory of *los Abuelos* left for us, their progeny, to share? It felt as if their legacies had been completely extinguished, perpetually lost to their descendants.

Perhaps the answers lay in the words of Tundama, the powerful Chibcha Indian *cacique*, or king. In 1541, in the part of Latin America that is present-day Colombia, Tundama rejected a peace overture made by Quesada, the Spanish conquistador, with a warning that prophesied the invincibility of the past, even in the face of imminent defeat and death:

> *You desecrate the sanctuaries of our Gods and sack the houses of men who haven't offended you. Who would choose to undergo these insults? We now know that you are not immortal or descended from the sun. Note well the survivors who await you, to undeceive you that victory is always yours.*

Grandfather Leonides used to help people in Cotulla by using his horse-drawn wagon to transport corpses from their homes to the undertaker to be prepared for their final rest. Many of the Mexican families of the town would ask him to speak at the funerals since he knew everyone and, as one of my aunts put it, "He always spoke so pretty."

Once, just before he died, Grandfather Leonides awoke Uncles Leo, Lauro, and Lico in the middle of the night. Without telling them where they were going, he put their jackets on and led them down a side street until they were just out of town, where the railroad tracks passed through a large, flat, dry pasture. There were other people there, holding candles, singing and praying softly in the moonlit indigo evening. Uncle Lauro remembered how it felt as if hours went by before everyone heard the sound of a slowly approaching train, heading south for Laredo. The three-car procession was decked with brass torches and great ribbons of black bunting that waved in the warm night breeze like banners.

"It is the body of Anfitrio Mendiola!" Grandfather whispered to my uncles, who struggled through the crowd to get a clear sight of the funeral train.

Mendiola was one of the most acclaimed Mexican stage actors of the time, and Grandfather had seen him perform in classical Spanish plays on buying trips to Monterrey. He had died while working on a silent movie in California.

Now his body was being taken home to Nuevo León, and all along the route through south Texas his fans had come out to the tracks to offer their *despedida.* The glass-walled car, like a traveling shrine, passed them, and the candlelit, draped coffin was visible to the small group of the devoted from Cotulla who had been keeping vigil half of the night. They crossed themselves and waited until the train fell below the horizon. Then they made their way back home as dawn was coming on.

"Within a month, he was gone, too," Uncle Lauro said, speaking of his own father.

"An ordinary day, working in the store, talking to everyone, then, in the afternoon, a massive cerebral hemorrhage, and he was gone.

"He was in his underwear, on his bed, and there was silver froth on his lips. And not a doctor to be found."

Even in our own homelands, our traditions were fragile, and without *los Abuelos* to serve as their guarantors, many of them have been lost in the translation between the worlds of Mexico and Texas, Mexican and Anglo. Great-uncle Frank, Uela's eldest brother Francisco, was like a grandfather to me. He lived with my grandmother for many years before her death. If *las Viejitas* showed me how the world of spirits worked amidst the world of the living, Uncle Frank, a naturally gifted inventor, engineer, and metallurgist, tried to teach something to all of us about how to act in the world, how to conduct ourselves in the proper Mexicano way that his father, great-grandfather Jacobo, had taught him.

He told me that Mexicans born in the United States were different from the Mexicans of Mexico. They acted differently. Uncle Frank felt they had lost the long-held Mexican traditions of courtesy and love for others. Worse, they had lost respect for their elders, and for the dead. If he was on a sidewalk in the middle of town and a chain of cars in a funeral cortege passed by, he would stop, even if he was the only one doing so, to stand erect, take off his hat, and cross himself, waiting until the procession went by. Uncle Frank worried that, once lost, these traditions would never again return.

"When we were on the other side, in Mexico, they taught us to respect the older ones. This is gone now. No one respects the old people."

Whether we're born north or south of the border, rich or poor, proud or contrite, we decide whether we will continue to abandon the often beautiful, sometimes terrifying stories of the past by small degrees, or, against the drift, to remember, to salvage—to conjure and resurrect them anew. Every Mexican lives this destiny out by either embracing, or falling further, from the sources of hidden light left behind in the past with *los Abuelos*.

Great-grandfather Jacobo Garcia, Uela's father, was a perfect twin, absolutely identical, except for a large brown mole, a *lunar,* in the middle of his brother Abrán's cheek. A hand-painted photograph of the two hangs on a living room wall in Tía Pepa's house, with the two of them looking like a mirrored reflection, their hands to their hearts, and crabbed expressions on their mustachioed faces. They looked so much alike that it is said that Jacobo once found himself holding a conversation in a full-size mirror when he thought he was talking to Abrán. And they stayed identical, until their deaths in their nineties.

In addition to Jacobo and his twin, there were twins in the next generations—Jacobo's sons, Manuel and Valentín, now dead, and my brothers, George and Charles. There were other twins, elsewhere in the family, as if there was a regular doubling pulse in the bloodline. As the Garcias moved through time, this pulse resulted in the presence in every generation of people who lived with their mirror image. With so many doubles around the tribe, it made the rest of us more aware of our own solitariness.

Uncle Frank, like most of the Garcias, lived into his late nineties. His long, lanky frame and enormous hands could make him seem like an intimidating old gentleman, but his limpid eyes and gentle mien showed a tenderness that he shared with the rest of his siblings. He remained lean, disciplined, and active to the end. When Uela died, Frank was already in his late eighties. But on the way to the cemetery, we spotted him along Colorado Street, with his thumb out, hitchhiking. Somehow, everyone had left the funeral parlor without him.

By then, he had been alone almost twenty years. In the 1950s, his only son had died young, suddenly and mysteriously, in a motel in Laredo where he was on business. Uncle Frank's wife never got over that loss, and she also died a few years after their son. As the eldest of the Garcias, Uncle Frank had been the one who came alone to Texas and eventually helped to bring the rest of the family north. The Garcias had left their life in Mexico behind. He saw his two greatest inventions—a dump truck and an industrial pecan sheller—stolen by dishonest business partners. Yet, despite all the sadness that he had experienced in his life, he was content. Years later, after being blind for nearly twenty years, he had a cataract operation, and suddenly he could see again. Living with Madrina and Uncle Manuel, he spent the last several years of his life reading historical novels about the time of Jesus, mowing the lawn, making drawings of new inventions, such as motorized drying racks for clothes and garage doors that opened sideways. When we frequently talked together, he saw all of the lives in our family as part of one continuous story, one mission, one journey.

Great-grandfather Jacobo's father, el abuelo Teofilo Garcia, had lived to be one hundred years old, and Uncle Frank remembered him vividly from his youth in Coahuila. As a young child on a farm outside of Palaú in the middle of the nineteenth century, Teofilo was kidnapped and raised by the Kikapu Indians in the Coahuila sierra. By then, the Kikapu had been roaming in the nearby mountains for decades, occasionally raiding the Mexican frontier settlements when food was scarce in the wild. It was said they had once been a part of the Cherokee nation, but in the nineteenth century, when Texas Republicans expelled all the Indians to the nearest border, the Kikapu were repelled across the Rio Grande. President Benito Juárez later granted them a rich piece of territory on the headwaters of the Sabinas River high in the mountain range called the Serranía del Burro. The land was named *el Nacimiento,* "the birthplace," where the Indians remain to this day.

Uncle Frank recalled that el abuelo Teofilo had grown up with the Kikapu, under the name Tibú. "*Qué curioso,* for a name, no?" he always began, as he prepared to tell the story again.

It was years later, on a dawn raid against the town of Múzquiz that Abuelo Teofilo was wounded and left behind. According to Uncle Frank, he was rescued and cared for by a couple who found him, shivering, hysterical, and bleeding from a gunshot wound to the leg, by the banks of the Rio Sabinas. While his wounds healed, he stayed in their home, eating and sleeping "like an animal" on the floor in the corner of a room, unable to speak Spanish or to communicate in any way.

Then, there came a day when the woman who had rescued the young man heard him singing after breakfast while he lay on the floor looking at the ceiling. It was a lullaby that she remembered teaching her own child eleven years before, when he had been kidnapped by the band of Indians. She began to sing along with him. Suddenly, from deep inside of himself, he recognized her voice from where it still burned for him as faint as starlight.

Uncle Frank relished telling the end of the story, sitting upright in his chair.

"And from this moment on, Abuelo Teofilo was reunited with his parents, and stayed thereafter in town with them, later bringing home a Kikapu woman he had already married, with whom he later fathered Jacobo, my father, and Abrán, my uncle—absolutely identical twins.

"Abuelos can be lost and found," Frank would say about his grandfather Teofilo.

"*Somos de los abuelos perdidos y los hallados.*"

We are of the grandfathers lost, and of those found.

❦

It was late afternoon one May day in 1974 when the distant voices of *los antepasados* were in the parched Texas scirocco wind that blew through San Fernando Cemetery, feeling like a breath the planet exhaled thousands of years before. It was the same wind that had always been blowing through our lives and the lives of all those we had brought there in so many long, slow automobile corteges down Culebra Street, past barrio *taquerías* and hubcap shops, to the great Mexicano necropolis of San Antonio. A wind of story, a wind of forgetting, a perpetual wind, through storms and droughts and *calorones* that is a blessing from our ancestors.

It was Mother's Day and we were visiting Uela's grave. In San Antonio, Mother's Day is like the *Día de los Muertos* in Mexico. It is a day when it is necessary and honorable to revere all of *las Viejitas,* whether living or departed. Earlier that week we had driven to Laredo, on the Texas border, where my mother's mother and father were buried. We washed the cracked headstone, clipped the overgrown Bermuda grass, and pulled the weeds with dull flowers. I remembered a sunny autumn day many years before, seeing Grandmother Lopez, with a wry, almost pathetic little smile, standing proudly in a great caramel-colored fur coat next to that headstone with her name already etched into it, as Mother snapped her photograph. In that picture, Grandmother has an almost haughty expression on her face, as if to mock the death that awaited her, and to show that she had no fear about her destiny in that place.

Back in San Antonio, standing by the graveside of my father's parents at San Fernando Cemetery with my parents and two brothers, one scraggly mesquite tree offered sparse shade, and the scent of Mother's Day chrysanthemums wafted across the grounds like a narcotic spell.

It had been only nine months since "the great *despedida,*" as we all came to refer to that season of the sudden exodus of the family's grand-mothers. *Despedida* means a "fare thee well." The September before, in the space of sixty days, just as if it were a scheduled embarkation, most of the remaining grandmothers from around the extended tribe took their leave from this world. Both my mother's and father's mothers. Uncle Richard's mother. Aunt Minnie's mother. For decades, they had known one another as *comadres,* sharing tamales and a discreet cerveza or two at Christmas parties—polite, regal, but aloof from each other.

They left as a departing chorus would, each one carrying off their own veiled and unspoken secrets from the past with them. Their pass-ing on left us that much further from all the Mexican stories, a little more engulfed by a world increasingly taken up by expressways, shop-ping malls, and the news of Vietnam and Watergate. In the end, re-silient and fierce as each of them were, they had been vexed by this caterwauling century of revolutions and wars, and most of them died in fitful sleep, exhausted and confused by much of what they saw around them in their final years. In this way, they had joined *los Abuelos.*

That afternoon, looking at the headstone on my grandparents' grave, I noticed for the first time the dates of Abuelo Juan José's life:

$$1890-1939$$

I was seventeen, and I thought I knew all there was to know about the family's past in Mexico and Texas. I had gone to the dusty *pueblitos* in the Coahuila foothills of the Sierra Madre. I knew the stories of la Tía Fermina Ferguson, Mother's clairvoyant albino aunt. On my fa-ther's side, there was el Tío Santos Garcia, the evangelist, who had prophesied the end of the world would begin with a great tidal wave in the Gulf of Mexico. There was the Lopez dry goods store in Cotulla, where a young schoolteacher had listened to grandfather Leonides's jokes and accepted gifts of cabbages and potatoes in exchange for giving Aunt Lydia English speech classes. The teacher was Lyndon Baines Johnson.

All the faces, the few keepsakes, the shoeboxes of sepia-tinted photographs, were a Mexican Book of the Dead, with the shards of a story that had remained untold. Yet, the stories had always seemed to fit together like a brightly colored mural that, taken collectively, might tell the saga of a family. But I had never known that my father's father, among so many others who lived to virtually biblical longevity, died at age forty-nine.

I rehearsed what I knew.

Abuelo Juan José was one of six children in his father's second family. He had crossed the imaginary threshold of the Rio Grande, heading into Texas in the time of the revolution. Like the Garcias, he had come from the Serranía del Burro in the northwestern mountains of Coahuila. Settling in San Antonio, he had tended a network of subterranean floral greenhouses connected by tunnels on the large estate of Col. George W. Brackenridge, the onetime prince of the city's business, social, and military gentry. Later my grandfather had worked in one of the local foundries, Alamo Iron Works, from which we still have two exquisitely crafted metal bookends in the shape of the Alamo and a polished bronze sculpture of two hands clasped in prayer, both of which he made.

That day, I realized that no one had ever spoken about his death.

I asked my father how his father had died.

He fixed me with a quick, hard stare, strange for his usually gentle temperament. "He died too young," he said, with a conclusive snap that told me he wasn't going to say anything further.

My brothers darted their eyes to me, and Mother gave a stern look. We had just come from a long *Misa de las Madres,* a "Mass for the Mothers," and we were already getting uncomfortable in our church trappings in the bright Texas heat, but I asked again.

Growing more exasperated, my father promised to tell me some-day. His voice trailed off, indicating that this was the absolute last word on the matter, and burying the first secret we openly held from each other. I could tell he wasn't really angry, though. It was more a feeling of a hidden sadness and fear, as if the act of forced remembering might bring with it an uncontrollable rush of despondency.

I had seen this before in him.

My father, usually a quiet man, often decorated his silences with his guitar. He could retreat into it for weeks. In the evenings, after din-ner, off on his own, he sometimes strummed in a dream, staring dis-tantly across the living room. At night, against sheets of cascading cicada song from outside, he leaned forward and down, with his head bowed, wrapping his arm around the instrument, throwing flamenco curls off the battered face of the guitar. In those evenings, he seemed to draw his breath from deep out of the lost world of his own past. Daddy slowly drew his hand up, backward against the strings, singing slowly.

Ma-ala-gue-ña-a Sal-e-rosa-a-a . . .

Days later, I still felt a gnawing curiosity about Grandfather's death. Maybe it was a hunting mishap, I thought, or maybe an accident during one of the days I had heard about when the whole Santos-Garcia family had worked as pickers on one of the farms surrounding San Antonio.

Then, Mother told me. She closed her bedroom door behind her, and spoke in a hushed, whispered voice. She wanted me to know my father's outburst at his parents' grave had come from a very deep place.

Abuelo Juan José had committed suicide.

She said that on one morning in 1939, Abuelo had been missing, and everybody was out looking for him. Uncles and aunts, even neighbors. Apparently, it was Daddy, along with his uncle Chale, who found him dead, floating, drowned in the San Antonio River where it crosses Roosevelt Park, near the old Lone Star brewery, on the south side of town. My father was twenty-two years old.

Standing there with Mother, the windows bright with Texas sunlight, the air of the house chilled with air-conditioned calm, all the decades seemed to telescope into a moment. Perhaps my father, along with the rest of the family, felt it was their *encargo* to bear the story in silence, as if we might vanquish something dark in our hearts by breaking the webs of telling and retelling that told us who we were, where we came from, and why we were here.

In that moment, I felt a pang of the fear of drowning I had always had deep inside of me. Suddenly, it swept through me like the shadow of an unknown memory. The first time I had felt it, I was swimming in the Guadalupe River, in New Braunfels, north of San Antonio. My legs had gotten tangled in the long, undulating plumes of weeds in the green water by the bank. I felt myself falling and falling, as if from an enormous tree that stretched up into the deep blue ether of the sky. I saw ribbons of vivid colors coming out from every part of my body, the faces of family members, Padrino Julín who saved me once from choking on a gumball, friends, and some faces I did not recognize.

The Aztecs believed there was a separate part of paradise, Tlalocan, that was reserved for the souls of those who died by drowning. Now I was falling into that ageless heaven of the drowned. It was as if this trace of my grandfather had been left inside of me—a flash of lightning behind my eyes, my brain hungry for air in the murky water. And before a friend pulled me out of that river, I had a glimpse of a borderless fog as old as night.

I did not know then that Grandfather had dwelled there, that inside the fog was also a hidden time, a lost song, a secret archive of the soul of our family.

Abuelo Juan José, like many others who were compelled to come north during the revolution, never seemed happy with life in the United States. He missed the dusty sierra towns of Coahuila, and he didn't particularly like raising his children in San Antonio. He seldom allowed them to play with other kids anywhere but at the house. If he took his kids to the movies at the Texas Theater on Houston Street, with money short, he would not join them for the film, but he would wait on a bench outside until the film was over.

He never spoke more than a little English, he felt awkward showing affection, and he generally communicated with his gaze. You always knew whether he meant approval or fury by the way he looked at you.

There is a story of another time, just after coming to Texas, when he became deeply quiet, introspective, and *preocupado*. He had always been very serious and reserved—now he was grave. Great-uncle Gilbert remembers a conversation with him when he said, "I will die soon. Someone wants to kill me." At first Gilbert though he was joking, but his eyes were fixed and steely. Then he gradually got better, and the family passed it off as a passing mood or distemper.

In the last two years before his death, it seems he had grown quiet and sullen again, his attitude toward the world increasingly remote and fearful. Through those days, he would stand in front of the window at the house on Parsons Street, looking out across the *calle,* as if he were expecting someone.

Uela and her sisters had taken him to see *curanderos,* Mexican faith healers, who treated him with teas, poultices, and prayers. They took him next door to see Doña Lupe, a spirit medium who performed healings when possessed by the soul of "el hermano Guanares," a Coahuilteca Indian healer from north Mexico who had died several years before. On a backyard covered porch, hanging with drying herbs, and with the assistance of her daughter, Inez, she began the *curación* by projecting her own spirit into a large crystal goblet made of maroon and green glass. This left her free to receive the spirit of the healer, who would offer remedies to the sick and the troubled. On that day, el Hermano would not manifest himself for Grandfather, despite Doña Lupe's tearful pleas.

With another healer named Agustín, he sat in a chair in a hot, dark shed next to the San Antonio River, just outside downtown, as the old man brushed him with fragrant cedar branches, blowing tobacco smoke, and feverishly whispering the names of saints over him, complaining to Uela that he was suffering from a very bad case of the *susto,* the same kind of supernatural fright that had afflicted her sister, Madrina, years before.

A heavy veil of forgetting has gradually fallen over much of what happened next. Over the years, from aunts and uncles, from some older cousins, a tale as confusing as a hall of mirrors has emerged. According to one of my aunts, weeks later, on the January morning of his death, he woke up, as he usually did, before dawn. The petroleum company where he worked as a manager was nearby. Uela watched him as he went to the front window once again, pulled the curtains back, and peered out onto the empty dark street. Then he went room to room, according to what Uela later said, as if he were taking one last look and giving the *despedida* to each of the children. As he left, the sun had not started to rise, and that morning there was also a *niebla del año nuevo,* a thick "New Year fog," common in San Antonio at that time of the year. Then, he left the house.

Later, the family learned that Abuelo never made it to his place of work, which had never happened before. What were they expecting? The younger children, an uncle and an aunt, were left next door with the *curandera* Doña Lupe, and the rest of the family went out to look for him.

As another version of the story goes, it was Uncle Frank who first found him, after he had heard reports of someone jumping from a bridge and a body in the San Antonio River where it ran through Roosevelt Park. Aunt Margie remembers hearing Uela's screams from next door as Doña Lupe watched through a crack in the curtains as police, relatives, and neighbors began to gather in the front yard, under the great sycamore tree.

All of the city's newspapers—Spanish and English—covered the story, but no clippings were kept. Uncle Roger, just a boy then, recalls seeing a newspaper account of his father's death. Beneath a photograph of the body, he swears he remembers the caption read tersely,

Well-Dressed Body Found in San Antonio River

He was found in the knee-shallow waters of the San Antonio River. According to one of my aunts, his clothes were soiled, his hair disheveled, but his eyeglasses were still on his face. Among the family, some saw in these spare details incontrovertible evidence of foul play.

Others said there were no signs of a struggle, no blood or abrasions. His face apparently wasn't even fully submerged in the water when he was found. Uncle Roger believes there should have been a murder investigation. Aunt Connie wonders whether, in a daze of deep depression, he walked and walked until he found himself on the banks of the creek. "I think his little heart just stopped, and he fell into the water. *Mmm-hmmm.* Already dead, that's right."

As she describes her vision of his death of "a homesick heart," I see the Mahasamadhi of the high Hindu yogis of India, or the practices of the Tolteca sorcerers of Mexico, who are said to be able to choose the transcendent moment of their death. Could Abuelo have chosen the moment of his death in this way? Why was there no water in his lungs? What about his long despondency? Where did it come from?

I have had times of large, deep quiet and darkness in my own life. Despite a host of blessings that have come to me, I have nonetheless steadfastly expected some shapeless, postponed doom. I have seen a silence the size of an invisible continent overshadow aunts and uncles. Can the same old *melancolía* be handed down, wordlessly, through numberless generations, inscribed onto the helical codex of the DNA?

After Abuelo Juan José's death and prompt burial, he was rarely spoken of. The story became a family secret, held so close for so many decades that it faded and elapsed in the hearts of all those he had been dearest to. Uela became stoic. She was always noble and erect, but also guarded away, somber, and hidden to us. Though she wasn't the pious type, she nevertheless gave you the feeling of seeming to be in silent prayer. Every week, she made her legendary fist cookies, baked with *pan volador,* which got its name—"bread that flies"—from when the family used to toss it to each other when they worked in the tomato fields of western Bexar County, where they once had a farm. Uela made them by tightly squeezing a dollop of the dense pecan-flecked dough until it carried a perfect imprint of her clenched hand, with every line and wrinkle of her palm etched into the toasted, crescent-shaped cookie. We bit into these ambrosial *galletas,* and in this way, we received the communion of all her buried grieving.

The dead are always with us, but the dead can be lost, too.

When a family secret emerges, it can come forth like a great island emerging from the sea, all its cliffs and mountains cascading salt water—and you realize you are confronted by new, uncharted geographies. But a secret can also appear like whispered fragments you've heard many times before, but never understood.

Suddenly, the words become clear.

3

Valle
de Silencio

Valley of Silence

 *His perfect, radiant grin scares me at first, when I remember the last time I had seen him six months before, dressed in a brown pinstriped suit with overly large lapels, looking tightlipped and uncomfortable with his arms folded across his chest inside the brushed copper coffin. As a ghost, he seems utterly content now, like a child, and the anguish and gravitas of his long illness has been lifted from his bones.*

The skin on Uncle Raul's face is supple, the color of dark Mayan honey and as smooth as a mango. He looks like the neighborhood ice cream man, in a pair of white work pants and a well-starched white work shirt. He is wearing the old black round-toe lace boots he always wore. They are beautifully shined, and they look as soft as kidskin.

When I discover him, he is standing in the bright amber afternoon light of my new study, looking out the window at the two giant bridges into Manhattan—the garish Triborough and the medieval stone bridge at Hellgate on the East River—that are visible from my window.

"It's a good thing to live some place where you can see a bridge—but two! That's pretty damn good!" he says, with his cackling laugh.

In life, Uncle Raul had the energy of a south Texas remolino, or whirlwind, and jokes rushed out of him as if they were being carried in fierce gusts, punctuated by an ear-piercing, rapid-fire laugh—part eagle shriek, part coyote song—that could shake the air. There was something about this energy that gave him enormous power over animals. He could exhort his dog, Stupid, to chase his tail until the terrier was in full churn, spinning like a proton, almost levitating over the patio. With the same powers, he taught his neighbor's parrot Güero to sing "Volver" while wearing a tiny sombrero.

As we stand in my new study, it grows quiet. The room is still empty, freshly painted the color of sand. I am speechless, still amazed to see my uncle, who had never visited New York City while he was alive. Time slows to a murmur as we sit down across from each other in the unchanging light. When I ask him first what he remembers of his life, his eyes close, his lips move in a whisper, and he reaches over to touch the back of my hand.

Then together, we remember.

It had been raining all morning in San Antonio on the day of Uncle Raul's funeral, but the sun was breaking through as the afternoon Mass began. When my cousins and I first picked up the coffin as pallbearers, it seemed almost weightless, and it possessed its own orienting force, like a gyroscope. As we carried him down the aisle and outside across the plaza of Little Flower Church, a triple rainbow arched over Culebra Street, marking the way to San Fernando Cemetery. "That's a sign!" Aunt Connie said. No purgatory for el querido tío. He would dwell forevermore with el Padre Jesucristo, el Espíritu Santo, la Virgencita, and all the saints.

Maybe now, I thought to myself, my uncle has returned to earth as an angel.

When I open my eyes, he seems to be praying, and periodically crossing himself.

"Mariposa. Canela. Atole. Huisache. Tortilla. Deseos. Enamorados. Alameda. Azulejos. Enemigo. Nubes. Terreno. Vaqueros. Granja. Arroyo. Acequia. Concepción. Tranquilidad. Bendiciones y bendiciones. Siempre. Siempre. Siempre."

The Spanish words hang in the air: Butterfly. Cinnamon. Porridge. Huisache. Tortilla. Desires. Lovers. Boulevard. Tiles. Enemy. Clouds. Land. Cowboys. Farm. Creek. Aqueduct. Conception. Tranquility. Blessings and blessings. Always. Always. Always.

"This is a prayer against our forgetting," Uncle Raul says, with uncharacteristic seriousness. "But the prayer is as long as time, so you can never be done with it. It just goes on and on, forever."

Raul, my father's elder brother, had died of cancer, and he was among the many Santos I never had a chance to ask about the family's past. Along with Uvaldino, Chita, Andrea, Nela, Paulita, and all the others that had gone before. I wanted to ask him now—about the stories he had heard of Mexico, about the family's early life in San Antonio, and about his father, Abuelo Juan José.

"There were memories in the familia before there was anyone around to remember them," he said, before I had a chance to ask. "So where do we begin?"

Uncle Raul looks at me now with tears in his eyes, "There were the stars and the planets in the sky, the earth, the fire, and the wind. Why not ask them, John Phillip? Why not ask them?"

The Tarahumara Indian priests of northwestern Mexico say we are meant by the Creator to walk twenty-four miles a day, and that this is why our feet are shaped like a bridge. We are meant to walk through the lands that surround us. If we stand still, we become spiritually sick, and eventually, whether in the space of one life, or over the span of several generations, this sickness will overwhelm us.

The Aztecs and their descendants have always been sorcerers of the earth. They know the land is alive, a place of magic and awe that connects us to the panoramas of the unseen worlds, to geographies within geographies. This invisible topography of the dead is called *el Inframundo*. It includes Tlalocan, the place of the underworld, and the paradisal Tamoanchan. *El Inframundo* is not like Hell and Heaven, set apart from the world. It is more like a portal out of history and into eternity, encompassing all of the gradations of darkness and light, where all of the dead dwell, simultaneously beyond, and among, us. In the *Inframundo*, you communicate with the spirits of the dead, with the spirits of animals and all created things, and sometimes with the gods themselves.

You enter the *Inframundo* by several paths. There are places spread across the land that are like gateways into this dimension: caves and hills, streams and charcos, gorges and cañones, buttes and valleys.

The old brujos, or sorcerers, the fierce geomancers of the *Inframundo*, could enter directly, through a trance, looking without blinking at old maps or paintings of revered sacred places. Gradually the masses of color and lines would begin to undulate and swirl, spinning like a maelstrom, accelerating past north, south, east, and west, until whole continents were pinwheeling in the movement, fiery at their extremities, consuming everything—stone, cactus, wind, and sunlight—in a perfect equilibrium of chaotic energies. By these means, you could reach the place that lies at the end of the seen world, the lands that await beyond the walk of one thousand years. The whole landscape becomes a bridge into the empire of the spirits and the time of the ancestors.

This is the story I was told about the first journey.

El Tío Francisco, Uncle Frank, the eldest of the Garcias, made the trip, taking a train to the *frontera* and walking across the Rio Grande on a high, creaky swinging wooden bridge at the border with Texas which connected the towns of Eagle Pass on the American side and Piedras Negras on the Mexican. The only people there to greet him were some Kikapu Indians selling balls of white *asadero* string cheese and deerskin shoes and purses.

It was a cold February that year, and he remembered making the "four-day walk" to Uvalde, where he'd heard you could catch a freight train heading north to San Antonio. On those chilly nights he slept warily in the open country, having heard stories of Texas ranchers shooting Mexicanos they found on their property. To him, it all looked like high Coahuila desert land. There weren't many fences then, so you could walk long flat stretches of the parched land with only bird shadows for shade in the daytime. It looked like home, only, he pointed out, there were more stones on the Texas side.

When Uncle Frank sent news back to Mexico of a big dam project on the Medina River near San Antonio, the rest of the Garcias followed the pilgrimage north. He had written to his brothers, all of them naturally gifted workers of metal and steel,

> *Queridos Hermanos, there are pipes to fit in Medina,*
> *pipes to fit in Medina!*

Abuelo Juan José and his brother Uvaldino came north with the Garcias, though my abuelo was reluctant. The revolution was making everyday life in Coahuila a struggle. The roads between towns were often blocked either by Villistas or Maderistas or Federalistas. And they sometimes conscripted the men of the region, young and old, to join their ranks on threat of death. Young women were in constant danger of assault and rape by the same roving bands, who didn't seem to be under the control of any officers, and the troops, often without any provisions, looted supplies, food, and livestock, from the citizenry at gunpoint.

The Garcias didn't particularly care for any of the warring factions. In fact, politics seemed to them little more than chicanery in fancy trappings. The brothers—Francisco, Santos, Juan, Jesse, Gilbert, Manuel, and Carlos, whom we called Chale—gravitated toward rectitude, simplicity, and things that worked, as evidenced by all of the machines and tools they would build throughout their lives. Abuelo Jacobo wasn't going to wait until he saw his adored sons fighting each other across barricades for the benefit of good-for-nothing *pelados* and *charlatanes* in Monterrey and Mexico City.

They had heard that in *El Norte,* Mexicanos were needed for the demanding work of building the new Texas. Frank and the other Garcia brothers knew their talents as inventors, machinists, and engineers would be needed. Abuelo Juan José, like his future father-in-law, Jacobo, wanted more than anything else to work with the land, and he had heard there was rich sharecropper's farmland in the Texas territory between the Colorado and Guadalupe Rivers, beginning north of San Antonio, stretching south into the San Fernando Valley. The time had come to leave Mexico and its *revolución de locuras* behind.

Madrina remembers how the train the family rode with all their belongings was attacked by Pancho Villa's army as they approached the border town of Piedras Negras. The blistering volleys of bullets ricocheted off the sides of the cars, leaving all the passengers, goats and chickens included, scrambling inside for cover. Tía Pepa recalls a peaceful daylong ride to Piedras Negras, staying overnight with cousins in Villa Union, where they cooked a dinner of chicken with mole sauce and calabazas.

Once they were all in Texas, without even thinking about it, they began to cast their spells of forgetting across the new landscape. Many of them would not see Mexico again for many years. Others never returned again. The land of their birth, the *nacimiento,* seemed to become a memory of a dream of a lost world.

Mexico, to which some of us would later return and return, was gradually engulfed by the *Inframundo.*

Old Abuelo Jacobo's instructions had been simple. As my father remembers, they were to follow a small road north out of Jiménez, Coahuila, until you could not miss a big cliff on the right side that had the shape of an old man's face. Then you leave the road there, walking to the left onto what looked like a boundless sierra plain, following the river for about an hour and a half, all the way back to the foothills, until you come to the place called *la Loma de los Muertos,* "the Hill of the Dead." There was gold in that hill, Abuelo Jacobo had said. Lots of it.

"¡Esa fregada loma está bien llenita de oro!" he had told them often back in San Antonio. "That damn hill is full of gold."

Great-grandfather Jacobo and his twin brother, Abrán, were perpetually prospecting for gold, whether following legends of buried Spanish treasure and digging secretly in the middle of the night under the plaza in Palaú, or prospecting for the raw ore itself, using divining rods, seeking telltale "golden mirages" that were said to emanate from a deposit, or, in one case, an old swoop-backed hound from Palaú named Pipo, who was known to have a nose for the precious metal. It was with Pipo's help that they had actually seen those veins of gold, as thick as rope, running through the stony outcroppings in *la Loma de los Muer-*

tos. Without picks, they had left markers, but somehow, over the years, they never returned to prospect for the ore. Or so they said.

Now, decades later, Uncles Raul and Rudy and my father were back in Mexico, looking for the treasure. They were traveling in a new beige 1947 Hudson, with a massive glistening chrome grille and a pair of fenders that were polished like platinum, immaculate and inspiring awe from the Mexican onlookers. In one neighborhood in *la Villa de Juárez,* they had to park the metallic behemoth on a side street because it was wider than the pavement on the block of the aunt they were visiting.

Once they left the highway, the car's oversized whitewalls handled the hardscrabble Norteño terrain well enough, occasionally scraping the oil pan on the lip of a gully, or scratching the enamel finish on the passenger's side with low-hanging branches of thorny huisache. Cactus and mesquite dotted the otherwise wide open plain, which seemed flat in all directions. After an hour of untroubled roaming with the river in sight, with the afternoon growing late, the Hudson and its trio of would-be prospectors stalled in the middle of some railroad tracks. The only railroad tracks for two hundred miles. Since the invention of railroads, it has been like a supernatural curse. Mexicans walking, sleeping, or in their stalled cars are perpetually getting hit by trains after being unable to get off the tracks.

A solitary hill off in the distance might just be *la Loma de los Muertos,* but the Hudson would not turn over, and the machine was so heavy the three together could not push it off the tracks. El Dorado was in reach, and their engine was flooded. Then, just before nightfall, when Uncle Rudy and my father walked off a mile and dug a few holes looking for gold, they found a giant geode. When they cracked it open, it took their breath away. It looked like a bowl full of light blue stars, glowing in the crimson sunset.

They ended up camping there for the night, eating two rabbits

Rudy shot with his .22 caliber pistol, listening nervously for a train whistle on the horizon. But the only sounds were the warm wind and a few far off cattle, wearing bells, grazing on the grass that grew between the trestles of the railroad tracks. When the night sky came out, they lay awake for hours, staring upward counting the galaxies that dotted the heavens like archipelagos of frost.

In the morning, the three were able to dislodge the Hudson from the tracks with the help of two *vaqueros* passing by on horseback, and they walked back to the main road for help. Watching the whole landscape recede in the rearview mirrors as they were towed by a pickup truck back to Múzquiz, the two brothers and their cousin resigned themselves to reporting back to Great-grandfather Jacobo and his brother, Abrán, that *la Loma de los Muertos* had been spotted, but remained unexplored.

Madrina told the story of a valley in Coahuila, somewhere near their town of Palaú, in the Serranía del Burro. She said that in this valley, in a clearing by a large mesquite tree, there were places where no sound could penetrate. If you stood in particular clearings, or specific gullies and hills, no sound of birds could reach you, no sound of wind, no loud, coarse donkey's bray. She remembered playing with her cousin Narciso in that valley, and watching him climb a tree and shout down at her—and she could see him screaming at her, but she couldn't hear a thing.

The world was deaf there.

Because of this strange phenomenon, the place was called *el Valle de Silencio,* "the Valley of Silence." As to where it lay exactly, she could only say that it was near *la Loma de los Muertos,* where my father had gone prospecting. Madrina said she was told by her grandfather Teofilo that this was one of many such places around the world that

God had, for some unknown reason, left unfinished at the time of creation. For some reason, there were many such places in Coahuila. These were places, often completely unnoticed, with no sound, without color, dark places where no sunlight could penetrate, places where the world had no shape or substance.

Just like us, Teofilo had explained, creation itself was incomplete. And forevermore, until the end of the world, there would be no sound in *el Valle de Silencio*.

Breaking free of their Mexican past wasn't as easy for the old ones as they thought it would be. The landscapes of south Texas, the chalk cliffs, the sandy river plains, the crystalline Rio Nueces that was once the border, the hill country, the abiding fertile river valleys; all of them crisscross a spiritual home that has no boundaries. The family maintained its calendar of the sacred year, the fasting at Lent, the feasting on the day of *La Virgen de Guadalupe,* Easter, Christmas—and the *Diez y seis de Septiembre,* the Sixteenth of September, celebrating Mexico's independence from Spain in 1821. In late October for the *Día de los Muertos,* we visited the cemeteries to pay homage to the ancestors. Beneath the increasing Americanization of San Antonio, many Mexicans kept the red glass votive candles burning on the old altars.

In 1968 San Antonio hosted Hemisfair, which included everything from continuous performances of Czech avant-garde theater to presentations of the delicate protocols of the Japanese tea ceremony. With a high-speed, elevated monorail encircling the downtown fairgrounds, the Hemisfair was meant to be a celebration of humanity's technological future, with the eight-hundred-foot-high Tower of the Americas as its centerpiece, which featured a rotating restaurant and bullet elevators that shot up from the ground like X-14 experimental rocket planes.

Down below, the Mexican Pavilion showcased a troupe of Indian dancers dressed in crimson spandex outfits with feathered wings who performed the ancient ritual of the *Volador,* or flyer. It was said to be one of very few religious dances once performed across Pre-Columbian Mesoamerica that has survived into the present. As a booming Spanish-accented man's voice narrated the ritual from scratchy loudspeakers, every top of the hour the five dancers marched like wrestlers into a gladiatorial arena:

> *"To appease their Gods . . . since the beginning of time . . . the people of the Sun, ancestors to all the children of Mexico, had to offer the hearts of young maidens to postpone the destruction of the world!"*

On an altar set on a dais, two barrel-chested priests in loincloths and sequined capes enacted a terrifying mock sacrifice of a young, bare-breasted woman to the fierce god Tezcatlipoca. As the priests lifted up the dripping fake heart to the sky, the five *Voladores,* themselves dressed in loincloths and plumed headdresses, climbed up a one-hundred-and-twenty-foot-long pole that had been braided with heavy ropes. At the top, in the strenuous heat, four of the Indians sat on the edges of a pivoting wooden frame attached to a rotating hub appended to the top of the pole. Then the leader, or *caporal,* would slowly stand up on the pole, poised in the gusting wind between the other four. As his *compañeros* watched while shaking their rattles, he blew into an eagle bone whistle while beating an old hide *tambor,* dancing on the narrow diameter of the pole, gradually saluting and bowing to each of the four directions of creation. Then, while all of us in the crowd leaned back, gripping our seats, we watched the other four Indians lean off with a slow backward arch into the air, with the ropes tied to one ankle and threaded through the pivoting wooden frame they had been sitting on.

Slowly, hanging upside down with their arms outstretched toward the ground, they began to spin earthward around the pole, gradually disentwining their tethers with each revolution, moving closer to the ground. I was hypnotized as the *Voladores* flew over me in giant descending circles, their graceful shadows dancing over the crowd, coming gradually nearer to us, in great, swooping, widening spirals. The fifth Indian always stayed on the top, his back against the rotating hub, staring upward at the sky, singing all the way through the ritual. The whole dance took forty minutes to perform.

The *Voladores* had the power to make time stop, to make the rest of the world around me fall away. Staring up at the flyers, silhouetted against the silvery Texas sky, it was one thousand years ago, before empires and conquests, revolutions and borders. The *Voladores* were guardians of the old time, the time of the Maya, the time of the Aztecs. That summer, they unleashed it in San Antonio, reconnecting the city, and all of the Santos who lived there, to our most distant past.

I did not know, then, why I always found the pageant of the *Volador* dance so magical. I did not know, then, what any of it meant or how to pronounce the names of the *Nahua* gods. It was said to have come from the mountains of Puebla, in central Mexico, far from any place my family had any memory of living. Maybe it reminded me of childhood tales of winged gods and angels descending to our world. Who had imagined such a dance in the first place, and what was it meant to signify? Was it a dance left behind to remember that we are descendants of the sky? Or was it just a dance to evoke the irresistible beauty of dynamic, balanced symmetry, effortlessly churning a small galaxy of synchronous movements?

I saw the *Volador* ritual performed many times that summer, imagining myself in all the falling spirals, the flying, the feather costumes, and the exquisite, silent speed of the flyers. The primal sounds of the old Mexican flutes and drums wafted out across the other pavilions of the sprawling fairgrounds. And after every time I saw the ritual, I felt as if I had been chosen for this blessing, as if this dance that came from deep in the Mexican past was harboring some secret intended especially for me.

One place I have felt the ineluctable pull of old Mexican time is at the Guerra ranch, Rancho Los Generales, in the Serranía del Burro, near where the Garcias and the Santos come from in Coahuila. As a child, when I went there, I would gather sticks and stones in the woods near our house in San Antonio and take them with me to leave out on the ranch. When I returned, I'd bring back some rocks and twigs and flowers from the ranch to toss out of the car windows onto Texas earth as we entered San Antonio. In this way, I thought I could begin to sew the two worlds together again.

To reach the ranch, you drive five hours south from San Antonio. At the mining town of Nueva Rosita, with its landmark towering sooty brick chimney bellowing black smoke, you turn off from Highway 57 and head west for the mountains, already visible in the distance. Passing the old Rosita Cemetery, *el panteón,* and the rushing turquoise water of the Rio Sabinas, the dusty road begins a slow steady climb into the sierra.

Rancho Los Generales lies along the road that runs first through Palaú and Múzquiz into the mountains, going all the way to the Texas border, and the remote fluorite mines called Las Boquillas del Carmen at the southern tip of Big Bend National Park. I would discover later it was territory my family had traveled for generations. Along that same road was the Nacimiento de los Indios, the land where the Kikapu Indians had lived for one hundred and fifty years, and where my kidnapped great-grandfather Teofilo had grown up among them more than one hundred years ago. When it was still unpaved, Tía Pepa remembers walking with her grandfather west out of Múzquiz along the road, picking the healing herb *la gobernadora,* wild mint, and oregano.

The land around Los Generales is a mix of the landscapes of many places. From the ranch, you can see distant grizzled gray peaks of the sierra, cleaving the clouds on the southwest horizon. To the east, the faintest blue apparition of the mountain pueblo of Las Esperanzas can be spotted flickering on a clear night in the notch of a nearby canyon. Alejo, the *vaquero* foreman who ran the ranch, once found the fossil of an old conch shell in one of the high prairies there, which he said meant the whole region must have lain at the bottom of an old ocean. Now, a palm tree sways next to a stand of pines and cedars at the top of one rocky hill. There are narrow gorges and hidden valleys that I spent those summers exploring, learning their secrets.

One morning, Alejo and I rode out together through three pastures to reach a long, deep gorge that descended from one of the big hills down to the floor of the valley below. Taking a path off from one of the pasture roads, cutting a swath through the scrubby bushes up the hillside, then taking several turns farther toward the mountain, we rounded a smooth stone wall and looked down into the deep blue shadows of the long dry notch. The rains usually create a flume of water here that washes everything into the valley. But after the recent rains, the gorge bed was overgrown with thorny saplings and cactus, a cascade of chipped stones that glowed like oyster shells in the half-light of early morning that filtered down through the thick brush canopy and the overhanging rock outcroppings.

In this cool, secluded sanctuary, Alejo said we would find the chile piquín, the wild Sierra chile, the size of a berry, that grows green, yellow, and red on the same plant and is prized across Mexico for its unforgiving burn. Uncle Beto used to carry a breast pocket full of the chiles when he went to restaurants, pulling one out and popping it in his mouth before biting into his barbecued brisket. The Kikapu say that it was in the tiny piquín chiles that God hid away the first fire that created the world, leaving it with us to remind us where everything came from.

As we cut and gathered large bundles of the shrubs, their branches speckled with gemlike chiles, the peppery smell of the capsaicin filled the air around us, as we moved slowly down the gorge. Along the cliffs on both sides, the water had carved out scalloped caves here and there where animals, *gatos de monte,* "mountain cats," pumas, maybe even bears, had made their lairs. We stepped gingerly around each of the rough chambers, peering warily in from behind first to make sure no animal was sleeping there, though such beasts rarely linger in their dwellings during the day. With their beds of dirt and twigs, paw prints crisscrossing in all directions, but not hurriedly, the places seemed like private sanctuaries from the outside world. If the *gatos* began attacking cattle, as they sometimes, usually in drought, would suddenly begin to do, it was near this gorge that the *vaqueros* would hunt for them. More often, they lived unto themselves, rarely seen, almost in a parallel space and time.

Just above the last tier of the gorge, with the valley already in sight through the trees, Alejo stopped and crouched down on his haunches. Holding his fingers up to his lips to keep quiet, he pointed down the ravine to where a dark cloud appeared to be hovering around a stand of persimmon trees. As we fell to quiet, a low, modulating hum echoed along the walls of the gully. Through the undulating cloud, I could make out the shape of one, then two, then maybe five large beehives, hanging from low branches, loaded with honey. From a distance, the hives seemed to be glowing with an amber light, as if they were awaiting the daring harvest, which was about to begin.

Late in September, when summer's *calorón* heat still made a desert of every day, and everyone at the rancho sought shelter from the oppressive sunlight indoors, the clear air would suddenly be filled with thousands of monarch butterflies, wafting dreamily south to Michoacán.

It was on one such day that I rode out alone, along the trail through the five pastures in which the herd of ivory Charolais cattle were spread out to graze. It was late afternoon, and I rode down one of the hills into a great valley on the rancho that is shaped like a perfect bowl. There, along the rock walls, the layers of epochs were exposed. An age of limestone. An age of ash and pumice. An age of alluvial pebbles and river sand.

Once we had descended to the valley floor, Pinto, the horse, broke into a full gallop, driving through the scattered, drifting clouds of monarcas, until we reached the center of the basin.

Alejo had called this valley *El Valle de los Ancianos,* "the Valley of the Ancestors." All around the valley, the dozen or so hills were the same distance from each other, some massive and dignified, others ragged at the top, with cactus and mesquite dotting their peaks. From the middle of the valley, the halo of hills looked like a council of elders, sitting in quiet deliberation.

The light was familiar. The everlasting wind. The slow, far-off clanging of a few cow bells. Numberless shoals of pink clouds were tracing the edge of the western horizon. The entire scene felt like a memory of a time that was older than me, as if it were the memory of the land itself. My father taught me how to see places like this. He taught me awe, watching him silently looking out across the landscapes we were in together, almost overwhelmed, whether it was Texas or

Mexico, by the richness, the intricate beauty, of what he saw before him. His gaze would grow distant, his breaths long and slow. Maybe he had learned this from his father, Abuelo Juan José, whose family was always said to have been *ranchera,* "of the ranch life."

Maybe Abuelo Juan José had taught all of his children. In one photograph of my uncle Raul, he is standing on a craggy peak over a desolate Mexican mountain canyon, and a maguey cactus is at his feet. Unshaven, dressed in khakis and a cardigan, with a wool stocking cap on, he is wearing the telltale expression of Santos awe. The barely perceptible smile. The contemplative mien. With one leg perched on a stone, he stands with his arm outstretched, pointing into the hazy expanse of the canyon's maw, like a veteran scout who has discovered his long-sought destination.

The Mexican earth is alive, but mute. Yielding its fruits, it clings to its secrets. All of the calendars that have ever been used across these lands were keeping time out there in the open pasture of the valley: the Julian, inside the Gregorian, the Mayan inside the Toltecan, inside the Aztecan—all of them overshadowed by what the Nahua Indian people of Mexico called the Fifth Sun, our time, which they called Four Movement. This age, it had been foretold, would end in famine and a violent shaking of the earth.

In the lulling summer breezes of that afternoon, I felt small, abandoned, waiting for the arrival of some wild wisdom in the same Coahuila silence that had nourished my ancestors. We can return and return to the places of our family's origin and never hear the voices of the lost *ancianos,* never know the place in the great count of days they bequeathed to us.

But they are there.

Mexico
Viejo

4

Cuento
Mestizo

Mestizo Tale

My mother's brother, Ludovico, whom we called Uncle Lico, kept a private study that was an improvised archive of the Lopez and Vela families. That's where he kept his curios and personal genealogical research. There were bricks from some of his favorite buildings that had been torn down over the years around downtown San Antonio, a collection of barbed wire, and oddly shaped stones from the Rio Grande Valley. He stored yellowed documents inside rotting ledgers, the deeds and county plat maps from the two families, going back to 1767, transcriptions of interviews with old relatives, and the many drawings he made over the years of his father Leonides's grocery store in Cotulla. And in two large boxes he kept his lifetime supply of San Judás Tadeo prayer cards, of the patron saint of lost causes whom Uncle Lico had long ago adopted as his personal saint.

This study was also where he had his magnificent, ultra-modern, stereophonic reel-to-reel tape and record player, with speaker cabinets recessed into the wall and decorated with crisscross beveled woodwork that looked like it had been copied from furnishings of the Alhambra. With the air-conditioner chilling the room to an arctic cool, he would sit in matching burgundy pajamas and silk robe in his motorized recliner, listening to those Esquivel, space-age Muzak versions of mariachi standards, poring through the clippings and papers that made up his collection of the Lopez and Vela family chronicles.

To be invited to sit with Uncle Lico in his study was a rare privilege. He liked to read his genealogies out loud to me, which could sound like the litanies of lineages in the Book of Genesis.

"Antonio Lopez Bermudez, married Gertrudis Garcia, legitimate daughter of Don Bartolome Garcia and Doña Maria de la Luz Zamora, who had six children: José Julián, José Maria, Ana Maria, Maria del Pilar, Maria Rosalia, and Maria Yñes, all of them Lopez Garcia." Then a long pause, staring at the document. And finally,

"The five children of Santos Lopez de Flores all died without family. Very sad."

After Grandmother died, it was Uncle Lico who oversaw the tax payments on the parcel of land the viceroy had given to one of our ancestors, a dutiful scribe, near what is now the U.S.–Mexico border in south Texas. Lico used to say it was probably bursting with oil or uranium. It was probably full of buried treasure, since there had been a Spanish fortress nearby in Mier.

Over the centuries, the original land grant of four hundred acres had dwindled by parcel sales to eighty acres, and it had come to be landlocked by a large ranch. Now, the remaining Lopez patrimony was a plot of desolate scrub land, marked at its perimeter with ragged orange flag stakes, and the only evidence of our homestead claim was the beat-up trailer Uncles Lico and Lauro had left out there to reinforce the family's deed. *They used to joke about dressing up a caretaker as a conquistador and having him live in the trailer.*

According to Lico, the original deed, which Grandmother had given him before she died, had been written in a fancy longhand script on stiff sheepskin vellum, and it was marked with the golden seal of Don Fernando de Palacio, viceroy of Nueva España. But years ago, Buster and Tito, Uncle Lico's two Mexican pugs, had found it on the floor next to his desk and mauled it to tiny bits, thereby earning their banishment, forevermore, from his icy inner sanctum.

"You realize most of those first Mestizos—the ones with Indian mothers and Spanish fathers—didn't know who their fathers were," he said, looking up from his recliner in the middle of one of his recitals of the family marriages and births.

"That's just the way it was then. But I tell you, your grandmother wouldn't let us forget," he muttered, pushing the bifocals up on his nose to begin the recitation where he had left off.

"That damn land in Mier wouldn't let us forget."

Many years later, as I sit in a silent, dark, cold room in New York City, the faces are floating silently in midair. Their deep brown skin is as smooth as *leche quemada,* like caramel among the young, creased and coarse in the old. They are crowded at a bus stop on St. Mary's Street, leaning against a stone bridge over the San Antonio River, walking in slow motion in front of the Alamo. Some have the broad, flat faces of the Maya, with profiles familiar from the stelae and friezes of Palenque. Some look like elders in an El Greco painting, carrying a Spanish weariness that seems ages old. I am watching them all, over and over for days, piecing together a montage of them for a film about how the Mexican Americans of San Antonio celebrate Easter.

In slow motion, an old man with a wispy goatee silently stares forward, unblinking. Chicano break dancers cavort in front of the statue commemorating Don Tenorio Navarro, one of the Spanish governors who ruled over that part of Nueva España. Then, in one long take, a Mexican kid stands in the mercado plaza playing the theme to *The Godfather* solo on his trumpet.

Looking at the rushes, you can see that the Mexicanos of San Antonio carry in their very bodies all the details of the long, forgotten history of those lands. It is ingrained in the way they hold their heads, almost imperially. In their flat, wide shoulders accustomed to heavy loads. In their dark-eyed gazes, focused faroff, lost in thought. Their faces shimmer in the electronic glow of the video monitors, and the spectacle takes on the feeling of a complex ceremony in some science fiction tale, a ritual to remember the last of the Mexicans of San Antonio.

The Franciscan Friar Bernardino de Sahagún was one of the most dogged chroniclers of the vanishing Azteca culture in the immediate aftermath of the conquest in 1521. Working with groups of friars whom he had trained, he interviewed the old priests, philosophers, and historians of the Azteca people, compiling the stories he gathered into both pictographic and written codices.

In the Florentine Codex, Sahagún tells us how the old Indian grandmothers he spoke to prized their lineages, yet also described the human body as a great unplumbable abyss, an opening into the infinite. Each body, they believed, was a crack in the universe, an infinite chasm that contained the entire *Inframundo:* the thirteen heavens of Tamoanchan and the nine underworlds of Tlalocan. When the Spaniards arrived in the New World, they brought their own Heaven and Hell with them. Since then, these two universes have been colliding and collapsing, one consuming the other, then being consumed anew in a whorl of endless creation.

At the time, if someone came from a noble Azteca family, it was said of them, "From someone's entrails, from someone's throat, he came forth." If someone brought infamy to their family, it was said they were "of the garbage heap, of the crossroads." The bones of the ancestors were believed to be part of the Mexican soil beneath their feet, and the dust contained this sacred essence of the *antepasados*. A family carries within itself this hidden memory as old as dust. The Azteca priests told Sahagún that the dust was to be as revered as *familia*.

My body, my brothers' bodies, the bodies of parents, cousins, uncles, aunts, great-uncles and -aunts, grandparents, are all vessels of the same ancient dust, exquisitely charged, polarized along the meridians of lands in the New World and the Old, destined always for some unnamable target further on in future time. For the Spanish, the Conquest of Mexico was another triumph on the irreversible path to the eventual reign of Christ on earth. For the Aztecas, whose voices are preserved in the Florentine Codex, time was circular: "What used to be done a long time ago and is done no longer will be done again. It will thus be once again as it was in the past. Those who live today will live again, and they will be anew."

Mestizos carry both of these stories in those Mexican chromosomes that are inscribed on tightly braided corn husks, painted in vivid cochineal inks by the ancestors who handed these bodies down through an unimaginably vast cascada of time. Did our forgotten ancestors— Indio, Español, Mestizo—walk with the same dignified and upright carriage of the old Garcias I know? Where did the almost Asian lineaments of the Santos come from? How far back toward the beginning of Mexican time? Is there a meaning to all of our shared talents, our affinities, our vulnerabilities and repulsions? We carry these messages from the past about we know not what, marking out destinations in our own lives while our families make circles through an oceanic immensity of time.

"Just be honest," Uncle Gilbert, one Garcia great-uncle, said, standing in his impeccably tidy garage workshop. "Uh-huh, that's what we were taught—just be honest, work hard, and you'll do all right. It's that simple." But no one taught the Garcia brothers to be inventors. No one taught them how to dream, like the old pyramid builders of Mexico, in 3-D, allowing them to build their own cars, to make furniture and boats and machines.

In Mother's family, Grandmother and her albino sister, Fermina Vela Ferguson, held the world at a studious distance, allowing them the time to gather a judgment so potent that when it finally poured out it was like a soporific aged brandy. Once pronounced, those judgments were meant to have almost divine authority. One time, after being quiet and lost in concentration for a while, Grandmother stirred in her big living-room La-Z-Boy chair, one arm held high, to announce her violent dislike for a Muzak version of "Hey Jude" that was playing on the radio, as if she expected the broadcast to suddenly stop short and fall silent.

Since she was a child, Grandmother's sister, Tía Fermina, loved to memorize lists of numbers and then recite them proudly, as if they described some underlying, unchanging mathematical understanding of the world—that only she was privy to. "Twenty-three. Seventeen. Eleven. One hundred and one. Sixty-eight and forty-seven," she proclaimed, holding up the list with great pride for us to see over her cup of coffee, from across a blue Formica kitchen table in our old house in San Antonio on Eland Street.

All of the Lopezes carried this stillness about them. Uncles Lico and Lauro were perpetually on the frantic verge of breaking a big deal, a land buy in Poteet, an investment in a downtown restaurant, or a big real estate contract with the city of San Antonio. Yet, underneath, there was unmoving Zen-like tranquility, sometimes aided by a couple of icy scotches, even when the deals, as they often did, went sour. Their smiles took up their entire faces, arching the cheeks, focusing the eyes in a sweet pout, and showing all their teeth, sideburn to sideburn. Uncle Lico once sent me a photograph of himself from 1946. He is wearing the classic Lopez Buddha smile, dressed in crisply pressed army khakis, and sitting on the edge of a Mexican fountain decorated with a mosaic of blue and white Poblano pottery.

SUNNY MONTERREY! it is captioned, HOTEL BERMUDA—ON VACATION . . . and signed, LUDOVICO!, in an autograph framed with flowery serifs.

Of the Santos lineage, some of the old Garcia uncles, suddenly growing very serious, will say the same thing.

"There's some kind of weakness in that family."

"It's a weakness in that line," Uncle Jesse says more gravely.

Among the Garcias, there was a deeply practical way of seeing the world. What needed to be done? What kinds of tools would be necessary to complete the task at hand? Among the Santos, there was a restlessness, perhaps an exaggerated sensitivity, by turns taciturn and chaotic. In some of them it could be corrosively comical, as in my grandfather's elder half brother, the wandering José León—who is said to have always slept in his boots, and who regularly told people with whom he was quarreling that they would be unwelcome at his funeral. In others, like my grandfather, the same inward quality could cast long shadows into their lives. Everyone knew there was depression in that family, even if it were never openly discussed. And rumors of other suicides besides my Abuelo Juan José's.

For the Santos, apparently, it wasn't enough to leave Mexico. Some sought further refuge from the world itself. One of my grandfather's half brothers hanged himself with an electrical cord in the basement of a bank in Hondo, Texas. One of his nephews leaped out a library window in downtown St. Louis. And my aunts think there may have been one other, a Santos relative who was living in Chicago, who had used a gun. These suicides were never openly spoken about, so I would ask about them, every once in a very long while—about Abuelo Juan José and "the weakness in the line."

After Abuelo Juan José's death in San Antonio in 1939, the Spanish padre from San Fernando Cathedral came to visit Uela to offer his condolences, and he was deeply moved by her piety and resoluteness. After reading the Bible together through the afternoon, spending some time in quiet prayer, he told my grandmother, along with some of her gathered brothers and sisters in the house on Parsons Street, that Juan José's had been an "ambiguous" death, with no suicide note, no eyewitness to testify conclusively that he had done himself in.

Spanish Catholicism was unyielding in condemning the souls of suicides to Hell. Through the ages, those who took their own lives had been forbidden from being buried in Catholic cemeteries. In parts of Europe in the seventeenth century, their bodies were not buried at all, but had been left at the side of a crossroads, outside of town, as if to consign their souls to be forever lost *en camino*. If the circumstances had deemed it an indisputable suicide, the padre would've been compelled to banish my abuelo's soul.

An "ambiguous" death would mean he could be buried with a Mass at the Cathedral. From all the padre had heard—of the lungs without water, the absence of abrasions on the body—in the eyes of the Church, the mystery of Abuelo's death would remain unsolved until Judgment Day. The Church funeral was allowed to go forward.

Mexico is a land of Indian mothers. It always has been. Before the arrival of los Españoles, before the great Indian civilizations of the Maya, the Toltecas, and the Mexica-Aztecas, the mothers were already there. These ancestors who are most remote from us in time, the ancient Olmeca people of Mexico, *Abuelos de los Abuelos,* carved exquisite pear-shaped earth goddesses out of dark jade. They had folded arms, swollen breasts, and pregnant wombs, with implacable expressions, traced with three lines to create jaguarlike faces of stoic strength. These small stones are still being unearthed throughout the hills and plains of southern central Mexico.

Indian mothers gave birth to the new race of Mestizos. *Mestizos,* literally meaning "the mixed ones," combined the blood of the Old World and the New. Indian and Spanish, Indian and African, Indian and Asian. With the emergence of the Mestizo world, Mexico became obsessed with this mixing of the world races, finding exotic names for each racial combination. The child of the union of a white and an albino Indian was called a *Saltatrás,* or a "leap backward." The child of the union of an Asian and an Indian was a *Tente en el Aire,* or "blowing in the wind." The child of the union of an Indian and a Mestizo was a *Coyote.* There were more than fifty such names, a taxonomy of miscegenation.

It was the mothers who created *Mexico Mestizo.* And long before the conquest, the Mexica priests of Tenochtitlán, the Aztec capital, had prophesied that this would be an age in which all the people of the world would mingle their blood. There are stories of the *presagios,* series of darkening augurs the Mexica wrestled with before the conquest, which were told to Padre Sahagún by Indians who had personally witnessed them.

Ten years before the arrival of the Spanish, in the year Twelve House of the Azteca calendar, people saw fiery signs in the heavens for an entire year. Sometimes they were shaped like a spike pointed down, sometimes like a flame hanging from the middle of the midnight sky, sometimes like a tear. They said then that the sky was *weeping* fire.

And then the fire fell to earth.

At the Templo Mayor, in the center of Tenochtitlán, the House of

Huitzilopochtli, the god who had led the Mexica on their long migration south, burst into flames and would not be extinguished.

A swift, silent bolt of lightning is said to have destroyed the temple of old Xiuhtecuhtli, one of the most primeval and revered gods of the Mexica. His temple had always been made of straw. They would say later that it was struck by the sun.

Then, one day, the sun reversed its course, streaming a tail across the sky like a comet coughing flames, rising in the west and rushing to the east, raining bright red sparks with the sound of thousands of tiny bells.

Eventually, phantasmagorical beasts and men appeared in a mystical array among the Mexica.

There was a two-headed man.

Finally, an ash-colored bird was caught in a maguey net and taken to the House of Magic Studies, so that it could be shown to the supreme ruler, the *cacique,* Motecuhzoma. In the crown of its head, there was a mirror that seemed to be turning like a spiral. In that mirror, Motecuhzoma first saw a pageant of all the stars in the night sky, turning around the North Star. When that scene dissolved, in the distance he saw a vision of an approaching legion, raising battle against a herd of running deer.

After the *cacique* had beheld the marvels that were brought before him, they are said to have disappeared before the attending priests could witness them. When they looked, they only saw themselves in the mirror. By then, Motecuhzoma had come to believe that the Aztecs, who spent so much of their lives doing rituals to keep their world from being destroyed, were now being warned their world would soon come to an end.

This, too, had been prophesied.

But of all these mystical *presagios,* these long-remembered premonitions of doom, the one that is most Mexican is the report that people had often heard the sound of a woman's voice, crying, letting out great peals, and screaming in the darkness. Fretful and plaintive, they heard her speak the words,

My little children, now we must go far away!
My little children, where will I take you?

My mother's family are Tejanos from the deep time of Nueva España, when San Antonio represented one of the northernmost outposts of civilization in the sprawling desert wilderness that reached all the way south to Querétaro, the colonial town to the northwest of Mexico City. The long history of the Lopez and Velas in south Texas and the borderlands left them with that aloof quality that comes from seeing many nations come and go as would-be masters of the land. The United States of America was only one incarnation. They knew there had been other worlds before this one, even if they might not be able to name all of them.

When my grandmother Leandra drove her polished ebony Buick through the streets of San Antonio, it felt as if we were on a slow promenade through the shady boulevards of an ancient capital. She drove so slowly, always with her lights on, that a few old Mexicanos would stop along the streets, dip their heads, and wait for us to pass, thinking we were part of a funeral cortege. We were out collecting her rents, stopping at the curbside in front of the little tree-lined houses where her tenants called her Señora Lopez.

Despite my pleas, Grandmother would honk the horn repeatedly until one of the occupants of the house would come out with an envelope full of cash, or with a sheepish look that led to an elaborate explanation of why the rent would be late again that month. And Grandmother never seemed to mind.

She had started out in Laredo as a teacher, so she would always want to know if the kids were in school, if they were doing well in their studies, if they were eating well. Never budging from the driver's seat of the enormous car, with her gloved hands on the steering wheel, she would then shut off the idling engine and ask about other members of the family, if she knew them—a husband whose leg had been badly mangled doing ranchwork, a brother who had been deported to Mexico the week before by the Immigration Service agents, who periodically swept through the neighborhoods looking for "wetbacks."

And then there would be a long silence. Grandmother and her tenants would wish each other well, and we would set off.

On the way home, we drove past Mission San José, the largest of the old churches that date back to the late seventeenth century, when the Franciscan Fray Damian Massanet first offered a Mass in a cottonwood arbor on the banks of the river the Payaya Indians called Yanaguana. It was after that Mass, which celebrated the feast day of Saint Anthony of Padua, that the river was renamed Rio San Antonio.

From the road, you could see through the massive arched entrance to the mission and see a sprawling open courtyard and the little church in the distance. Grandmother said the church had been there forever, and where she came from in south Texas, missions were a common sight, forming a galaxy of ruins of the empire of Nueva España that stretched southward all the way to Mexico City.

The trail that links the five old San Antonio missions and their network of aqueducts connects the city to that nearly forgotten past when the first Mestizos were still coming to terms with having been born of a Spanish father who came from one ancient world and an Indian mother who came from quite another. On cliffsides in the woods around San Antonio, there are petroglyphs where the Indians recorded their first impressions of the missions, los padres, and the Spaniard *vaqueros* on their horses. Drawn in thick lines with dark vegetable inks on stone, churches appear as little arched sanctuaries, crowned by a cross. A stick figure is recognizable as a priest by an exaggerated mitred hat, just as the *vaquero* can be distinguished by his cocked sombrero.

But if it hadn't been for the river, the Yanaguana, the Rio San Antonio, thickly lined for miles with palmettos and yuccas, willows, oak, and huisache, there would have been no missions; and if there had not been missions, there might never have been a city.

By these threads, we could find our way back to the beginning.

I used to sit silently with Grandmother in her bedroom, when she was already nearing her death. She received all of us from her bed with the expression of an exhausted, world-weary south Texas duquesa. She had virtually given up speaking by then, not due to any ailment, but simply because she seemed to believe she had spoken everything already. She seemed incessantly fatigued by our chatter.

The room smelled of Grandmother's Mexican talc and eucalyptus oil, which Grandmother's maid, Maria Moya, left in a pan on the radiator to "purify" the air. With the television going in the background, Grandmother wielded her remote control like a whipcrack, continuously changing the channel before you could focus on an image. Then we would sit for long, tranquil pauses in the draped afternoon light with our gazes locked on one another, until she would eventually become annoyed and look away. Hers wasn't a gaze of dearness. She had the indomitable mien of a witness, a grizzled bearer of knowledge which she had long ago left behind any particular need to pass on.

Looking at Grandmother, who held her old quiet with such unyielding gravity and determination, I wondered how far back she thought we went in that long story whose ruins surrounded us in San Antonio, Texas. Through Uncle Lico's work, we knew hers was an old family, and we could count generations of her family like rosary beads, as far back as 1767. But there are families that trace their lineage to ground zero of the conquest, like sacred genealogies of a second creation time.

There are living descendants of Cortés and descendants of Motecuhzoma, and even descendants of la familia Cortés-Motecuhzoma, as Cortés fathered a child with Tecuichpotzín, the daughter of the defeated Aztec *cacique,* and who later came to be known simply as Doña Isabel. In this way, the Spanish set out to dissolve the royal Mexica bloodlines. New dynasties would not be allowed to form in their place.

The conquistadores destroyed the pyramids and temples, stone by stone. They burned manuscripts and smelted basketfuls of golden idols in the flames. In this great carnal maelstrom, fathering children with Indian women was another way to break the tradition, to place fatal caesuras in the transmission of the Indian mind and soul through time. The children of these unions, these rapes, these romances, were mainly illegitimate, outsiders to the two worlds that had given them birth.

Indian memory is Mexican memory. Their history is our history— implicit, silent, inevitable.

Uncle Lico's excavation of the Lopez and Vela family catacombs showed no trace of Indian ancestors. But such things are rarely recorded, as with my great-great-grandfather, who married a Kikapu Indian. No one now remembers anything about her Indian family. The Mestizos, with Spanish names and outward appearance, and Indian hearts, usually gave their allegiance to New Spain. They dropped their indigenous names and became *Zeferino, Guillerma, Leocadio, Crescencio, Perfecta,* and *Ruperta.* They became *de la Garza, Reyna, Areval, Treviño, Adame,* and *Saldaña.*

In the time of the conquest, one of Motecuhzoma's grandsons, Juan, the youngest son of Doña Isabel, and another Spanish officer left

Mexico for Cáceres, Spain, where he married a Spanish woman and built the Motecuhzoma Palace, which allegedly still stands. According to their family history in the archives of the Indies in Seville, his off-spring became titled nobility. The Count of Enjarada. The Duke of Abrantes. The Duke of Linares. Then, late in the sixteenth century, in the court of Philip II, the heirs of Motecuhzoma agreed to renounce all their natural rights in Mexico as descendants of the Mexica emperor in exchange for vast lands in Spain that would be theirs forever.

Uncle Lico once signed a letter to me with a description of himself as "your *Very Hispanic* Mexican Uncle," followed by his characteristi-cally flamboyant signature that grew more filigrees as he grew older. Uncle Lico explained the meaning of that signature one day, while hav-ing lunch with me in a diner in downtown San Antonio called The Mexican Manhattan. He took off his powder blue straw porkpie hat, drew his hand across his balding, gray-haired head, and declared, "I'm gonna find the grandfather that got off the boat—the one related to the King of Spain," recalling one of his own genealogies of the Vela family that began with an unnamed Spanish monarch.

Long ago, Lico had interviewed Dionisio Alarcón, one of the older residents of the Lopez-Vela hometown of Cotulla, Texas, who told him the Velas were descended from the King of Spain, thereby igniting my uncle's genealogical fever. As a child, Dionisio had known my great-grandfather Emeterio Vela and reported having once been shown a sil-ver goblet with the name of some king or other inscribed on it, though he could not exactly remember which. It was also rumored, according to Don Dionisio, that when the family first came to New Spain, they were, in Dionisio's words, *"maranos, conversos"*—Jewish converts to Christianity. And perhaps this wasn't untrue. In one family portrait of Grandmother Leandra from the late 1940s, with all of her grown chil-dren, they look Basque, Andalusian, or North African. Their deeply set dark eyes, dark hair, their long features and limbs, carry a look of faces of the Pyrenees and of the Mediterranean littoral.

But Uncle Lico never found that first ancestor who made the Atlantic crossing. He was never able to put all of his research together into *"La Cronica de las Familias Lopez y Vela de Cotulla,"* the title for the historical book he spoke of writing of the families. He brooded over his research as if it were a disintegrating family relic that had been left uneasily in his care. It was, as he put it, "my calling in this world." He knew and was in contact with others like him, dispossessed Mexicans scattered all over the United States, all of them piecing together the evidence of a south Texas world that had been lost in time.

He imagined what the ancestors might've looked like, how they might've spoken and dressed, where they lived. But for all the names that he had recovered from oblivion, he had never found a single photograph of any of the distant relations. The charts and discs he made of the family's descent in time were always being reworked, sometimes in italics, sometimes in thick pencil, with a new name added here and there. He made numerous copies of his manuscripts and charts, bound them in legal size plastic loop binders with manila covers, and sent them in packages out to his nieces and nephews.

I received them repeatedly as a university student in Indiana. The packages always appeared as the telltale fruits of his obsession—the same charts, transcripts, and copied letters, perhaps newly annotated—with breathless greetings on carbon-copy, pink onion-skin stationery. They usually ended with a question like,

Circa 1750, Father of Capitán Antonio Sanchez:
1st Royal Governor of Tamaulipas???

And always included was a single, pristine San Judás prayer card.

◈

In Cotulla, Texas, when the Lopez family was young, my mother had a sister, Lily Amanda, who died as a child of two, and that experience left both of my grandparents, Leandra and Leonides, with a fascination with death and the spirits of the ancestors.

On each of those expeditions with my grandmother to Laredo to visit the family graves, she would insist on yet another picture of herself being taken in front of all the headstones of her father and mother, and, of course, my grandfather's grave, which would also someday be her own. Over the years, she kept a time-lapse image of herself against this timeless backdrop. She would regard the stones with careful attention, circling around the graves once before asking us to give it a sweeping and a good wash, while she arranged some newly purchased plastic irises in a vase.

When Grandmother died on my birthday in 1974, she left detailed instructions to bury her in the grave in Laredo, alongside her husband, Leonides. Laredo, on the Texas-Mexico border, had also been her birthplace. Grandmother had stipulated that her burial would take place after a Mass in the downtown cathedral, during which a singer was to perform traditional funeral dirges in Latin with an accompanying organ.

After setting out from San Antonio with Uncle Lauro early in the morning, following the black Cadillac hearse south down Interstate 35, we eventually entered Laredo. We went to a house near the cathedral to hire an old woman dressed in black whom the padre had told us could sing the songs Grandmother had requested.

"You need one of the old-time professional mourners," he said. "You need la señora Rosa, Queen of the *Pésames*."

Doña Rosa's living room looked like a chapel, with an altar full of candles burning in votive jars and hundreds of small photographs of all the souls at whose funerals she had sung over the years. Many were already yellowed and cracked.

"Of course I knew of your mother. I saw her sweet picture in the paper. How sad," she told my uncle, touching his arm.

"The Velas are a very fine family. A very great lady, your mother."

She pulled a large black cotton rebozo over her head and began moving more slowly, as if she were getting into the proper frame of mind before the funeral Mass. Her fee was to be thirty-five dollars, and she would play the organ herself.

"Such a great lady, how sad," she kept repeating and shaking her head, as we walked across the plaza back to the cathedral.

Once the Mass had begun, her unfettered caterwaulings startled all the relatives and friends who had gathered in the church. Doña Rosa rattled the keys of the small electric church organ, singing "Te Deus" with an intensity that made her voice crack and her body shake. As sad as grandmother's passing was, none of us could keep a straight face through Señora Rosa's performance. The priest offering the Mass even lost his composure during the Communion as she wailed hallelujahs until the whole church reverberated in her doleful, piercing ululations.

"Not quite what Mother intended," Uncle Lauro said, dryly staring at the professional mourner.

Later, most of the funeral party was diverted from the cortege when another uncle mistakenly followed a dark limousine off the expressway and took most of the line of cars with him. Only a small number of us in Grandmother's family found the cemetery where the priest completed Leandra's last rites on that wet, gray morning on a hillside overlooking the Rio Grande. She always liked *serenatas,* going back to when my father used to sing through an open window to my mother and her friends. My father stepped forward and sang her one last song, "Ave Maria," with the rain beginning to fall.

We left Grandmother there on the border, ate *caldo de gallina* on the Mexican side, and headed back for San Antonio.

"All the old Mexicans are dying."

That's what Uncle Lico said, shuffling through a pack of the funeral prayer cards of departed friends, which he kept together with a rubber band on the top of his desk. The walls of his study were crowded with photographs of the family. Tía Fermina, radiant with her ivory skin in bright sunlight. A newspaper clipping about Grandmother's having sent the lone floral tribute that made it to the grave on the occasion of LBJ's death. There was also a picture of LBJ, signed and dedicated to Grandmother, "WITH MANY HAPPY MEMORIES OF COTULLA." The president is in a cowboy hat, holding his beagle under one arm while leaning on a cedar post fence on his ranch in Stonewall, Texas. And there were pictures of Henry Cisneros, and Congressman Henry B. Gonzalez, autographed for Uncle Lico.

Holding up one faded prayer card of San Miguel, the archangel, Uncle Lico announced, "Gus Garcia. 1965. Greatest Mexican American attorney ever. First 'Meskin' to argue and win a case before the Supreme Court. A brilliant speaker. This cat had green eyes, man, just like a movie star."

My uncle turned the card over and looked at the picture of the archangel, from which most of the gold glitter had flecked off over the years.

"Died a drunk in Market Plaza, under a bench, wrapped in newspapers."

That day, the last day I saw Uncle Lico alive, I told him the story of Gonzalo de Guerrero, the Spanish officer who had been shipwrecked in the Yucatán in the early sixteenth century and chose to remain with the Mayans after being found by Cortés at the beginning of his military campaign against the Aztecs. Guerrero had married a Mayan princess and they had four children.

When he was discovered by his Spanish compatriots, he was tattooed and adorned with stones hanging from pierced earlobes. He had studied the sacred practice of Mayan astronomical timekeeping in the priestly schools of Chetumal, where he was living. He told Cortés's delegation that he would stay and fight with his new people, which he did, dying in battle some years later battling against his own Spanish brethren.

"You know, there were Guerreros in the Lopez family, back in the 1780s," Uncle Lico remembered, opening one of his long wooden filing drawers to look for his eighteenth-century annals. "It could be we are related to that guy," he added.

In his diary, Guerrero confessed to never being anything but appalled by the bloody sacrifices to the Mayan god Kukulcán, which were at the center of Mayan ceremonial life. He had witnessed some of his comrades having their hearts pulled out, and laid, still beating, on the gory Chac Mool altar of the temple at Chetumal.

When one of Guerrero's children, a daughter, was going to be sacrificed, he stood up before his father-in-law, a Mayan *cacique,* and the gathered elders and made a speech to try to dissuade them from choosing her. Yes, it was an honor to be sacrificed, to give your life so that the world would not be destroyed. But he told them that in his own visions he had been told the old gods wanted only the pure blood of the "old" tribes—the Spanish and the Indian. These new children, born a part of both worlds, would serve new gods. Their blood was distasteful to the old gods who had ruled for ages and ages.

It meant that, as more and more Mestizos were born, the old gods would go hungrier and hungrier. Eventually, the old gods would be abandoned.

They, too, would die.

The elders nodded resolutely and Guerrero's daughter was spared.

"Sounds like he could've been a Lopez," Uncle Lico said, laughing. "Very, very crafty. *Puro Lopez.*"

5

The Flowered Path

El Sendero Florido

*Uela was a Rosicrucian.*

From the time she was a young girl in Palaú, she had been a follower of the Via Rosae Crucis, *the mystical Way of the Rosy Cross, an allegedly ancient occult movement that had nestled within the traditions of the Catholic Church since the Middle Ages. She never told me about it. It was Tía Pepa who remembered how the three sisters, Uela, Pepa, and Madrina, had all studied the Gnostic teachings of the Christian secret society by correspondence. The Rosicrucians sought to reconcile the pre-Christian traditions of magic and esoteric studies with the revelations of Christ. Madrina had left her studies very early, Tía Pepa much later. But Uela had reached the highest level of initiation, the Adeptus Major, which is said to involve powers of prophecy, tongues, and healing.*

Their study books and pamphlets, still advertised in comic books and occult magazines, identify the origin of the Rosicrucian tradition of natural magic in "the ancient Egyptian Mystery Schools of Thoth." Central to the teaching is the knowledge of a hidden wisdom in the world through which it is possible to learn, and live by, the secret essences of things:

How the three spheres of paradise are contained within the head.

How the heart is the seat of a universal blazing sun of love.

How everything in the universe is inscribed with mystical invisible letters that could be read and understood.

Uela held her secrets very close, whispering the rosary, praying silently with her lips moving, as she sat in her rocking chair in the front room of the house on Cincinnati Street in San Antonio. She was sitting in that rocking chair on a rainy Saturday morning when I read some of my first poems to her, explaining them to her afterward in Spanish. They were awful poems about lightning storms, first love, an adolescent's dialogue with God. Uela was fond of poetry. She adored being read to or recited to, but she never told me she had searched for some of the same things—that both of our compasses had been set to the same imaginary direction.

Before she died, she called my aunts into her hospital room and asked them for their promise to burn all of her Rosicrucian books and papers. They were to sign a certificate of witness that the material had been destroyed, and then send it to the Supreme Temple of the Ancient Mystical Order Rosae Crucis in San José, California. The day she died, as Uela had instructed, my aunts burned two trunks full of Rosicrucian effects in the alley behind Uela's house, on a bier of mesquite twigs and dry pecan tree leaves.

All that survives of her library is a copy of the 1602 Valera Spanish translation of the Bible, which she gave to Madrina as a wedding present in May of 1944. Today, its spine is reinforced with silver duct tape. The worn blue-fabric cover bears the hermetic Rosicrucian insignia of a rose superimposed over the cross. Inside, on the title page, in her graceful handwriting, in Spanish:

Hermana Tomasa   5/29/44
Cherish this Holy book as a remembrance.
You will find peace and tranquility in reading it,
just like the divine balm which sweetens and strengthens
our tired and hurting souls.
Its words of wisdom show us
the flowered path which leads us straight to the truth.
Words of consolation from which
Sister, comes all that is holy, good and just—
the Divine love of God.

Su hermana que te quiere,
Margarita G. Santos

"What were you searching for?"

The question sounds awkward even as I ask it, and Tía Pepa looks confused.

"What was your father looking for?" I asked.

Tía Pepa is busy in her kitchen, making *masa* for tamales in two clay pots while preparing a compote of herbs for her renowned medicinal JTV suppositories in a third. "JTV" for her name, Josefa Talia Valdes. She makes the suppositories in stainless steel molds that her brother Gilbert designed and fabricated for her. She then packs them in boxes shaped like cigarette packs with her initials stenciled on the outside.

La Tía tosses a handful of finely chopped leaves into the bubbling pot of herbal paste with a flick of her wrist, saying that at ninety-three, she must concentrate or she will confuse the ingredients, with unsavory consequences. Then she steps back from the stove and wipes her hands, front and back, on her apron.

"We just wanted to live in peace, nothing else," she says, starting to churn a large dollop of lard into the sandy-colored *masa*.

"Mexico. Texas. It didn't matter to Papá. He would've taken us to Chicago if he had to."

What was it that he wanted to be left in peace to do?

"We really didn't think about those things, *hijito*. In those times, it was enough to keep tortillas and frijoles on the table."

I have just returned from a long trip in Mexico and I have brought Tía Pepa an obsidian arrow point, dug up from pasture land around the ruins of the ancient city of Tula. I explain to her that Tula had been the capital of the Tolteca Indian empire, which preceded the Aztecas, and, at one time, had been ruled by the man-god Quetzalcoatl.

The ruins of the city include pyramids, plazas, murals, and ball courts, and they lie forty minutes to the northwest of Mexico City. Long before the Aztecs arrived in the valley of Mexico, it was in Tula that Quetzalcoatl is said to have banished human sacrifice and cultivated a society devoted to creating ornately decorated monuments, learning, and feats of rhetoric and poetry which they called "the scattering of the jade."

His brother, Tezcatlipoca, jealous of the esteem that people bestowed on his sibling, conspired against him by getting him drunk at a fiesta. In a delirious state, Quetzalcoatl made love to his own sister. Scandalized, humiliated, and broken, Quetzalcoatl and a group of his followers went into exile, prophesying that he would return someday to throw down all the kingdoms of Mexico. Tula was abandoned, and as fate would have it, the date that had been foretold for Quetzalcoatl's return, the year known as "One Reed," was the year that Cortés arrived in

Mexico, leading Motecuhzoma, emperor of the Aztecas, to believe that the banished god had returned to fulfill his ominous prophecy.

Tía Pepa listens to the story while she cradles the arrow point in her hand.

"You are not like us," she says, with a mischievous grin. "You are an adventurer."

I describe for her the four massive Atlantes warriors, clutching butterfly-shaped shields, who stand as sentries, looking south from atop the great step pyramid in Tula. Like a host of other large ancient cities on this continent, at some point, the people of Tula just moved on. They abandoned the noble city they had taken generations to create. They disappeared into the ether of the past, leaving Tula behind like a relic with only the Atlantes to keep vigil over the sacred precinct through the ages.

What were they searching for? Why were all the old Mexicans always abandoning their cities, from Teotihuacán to Chichén Itzá? How much of that old wanderlust was left among us Mestizos, leaving behind Mexico, Coahuila, and the Texas that had been forged in the crucible of ancient Mexican time?

"There was nothing that ever scared me like when we left home," Pepa remembers now. "Everyone in Texas looked different, like the Americanos who used to run the mines in Palaú. The Mexicanos were all poor, like us, and we kept to ourselves. For a long time, it didn't seem like home at all."

Uncle Frank remembered coming to San Antonio several times, as a child, around the turn of the century. He said the trip took five days each way, crossing the Rio Grande at the old Paso de Francia, near the present-day Piedras Negras, before there was a bridge there. His father, Abuelo Jacobo Garcia, had been traveling to San Antonio from Palaú,

Coahuila, all his life. He had represented the miners of Palaú there at the 1888 International Fair. The event was inaugurated by Mexican President-for-Life Porfirio Díaz, who pressed a telegraph key in Mexico City that lit up the newly installed street lamps in Alamo Plaza.

"It didn't really feel like we were leaving Mexico," Uncle Frank told me once. "Except most of the streets were paved, and they were wider. And there was less dust."

In those days, the Rio San Antonio was wider and messier than the regulated river and manicured tourists' riverwalk of today. When Uncle Frank first saw it, it divided the city in a winding, muddy meridian. Branches of old oaks hung out over the water, draped with Spanish moss, mixed in with stands of bamboo and elephant ears. The water ran so sluggishly that lilies grew along the bank. Uncle Frank says he remembers how the San Antonio River was wider than the Rio Grande—fifty yards at its widest mark—and that the wealthy *patrones* had their houses right along the riverbank, with white picket fences encircling their property.

There were iron arches with gas lamps over the downtown streets, illuminating the city center at night as if it were the seat of a grand empire. Along with his father and his brother, Frank was dazzled by the first electric streetcar he had ever seen, hypnotized by all the clean, rapid movements of its perfectly synchronized, silent working parts. On that trip, he and his brother Manuel traded drawings of the streetcar and how they thought it worked; eventually Uncle Frank did work on train engines in Texas.

It seemed everyone, even many of the Gringos, spoke Spanish. Just as they had since the time of the missions in the early eighteenth century, the famous "chili queens" of San Antonio had their busy open-air food stands in Market Plaza and along other streets downtown, selling fresh tortillas, moles, and bowls of rich, spicy ground beef *picadillo,* the original Mexican dish from which Texas-style chili is

derived. Just as in Mexico, there were religious processions and celebrations taking place around the downtown cathedral. On one of their
trips, Uncle Frank remembers seeing a man crucified—for real, he
insisted—in Main Plaza during easter observances, with a large crowd
looking on.

Coahuila and Texas were a single state of the Mexican republic,
and the viceroy who ruled the state sat in Monclova, Coahuila. San Antonio had always been a distant northern settlement, increasingly embattled as more and more Americanos settled there. Eventually, the
Anglo Texans broke away from Mexico, and Texas formed their own
republic, later becoming a state of the American Union. All the Mexicanos who had lived as Tejanos, as the longtime Mexican residents of
Texas were known, became Americans overnight.

Visiting San Antonio in those days, Uncle Frank said, was like going to a museum. They city had been there almost two hundred years
already. The missions, with their fallen walls and collapsed limestone
aqueducts, or *acequias,* were just landmarks that they passed on the
road north into the center of the city.

There, the modest limestone "palace" of the Spanish governor,
with its cool, tree-shaded courtyard and fountain, was still standing
from colonial times, when San Antonio and parts of southeastern Texas
had been settled by los Canarios, eighteenth-century homesteaders
from the Canary Islands. There had also been a wave of settlers from
Cáceres, in the high plains of Spain. Also, many of the Indian tribes
who had allied themselves with Cortés against the Aztecas, like the Totonacas and the Tlaxcaltecas, had long ago been given land in the
northern reaches of Nueva España, in places like Monterrey, San Diego,
in the Rio Grande Valley of Texas, and San Antonio.

On those early visits, Uncle Frank and Abuelo Jacobo stayed with
my great-grandfather's boyhood friend Tacho Carvajal, who had been
a foreman at the Palaú mines and who moved north to supervise one of

the quarries that were cutting stone to build the state's new capitol building in Austin. Tacho and his family had a big house near the quarry, which stood on the northern edge of town.

Abuelo Jacobo would arrive bearing gifts, *piloncillo* and *rollos de nata,* sugar cane candy and goat's milk caramel delicacies, from the sierra country where Tacho had been born. Tacho complained that nothing like that was available in San Antonio. Uncle Frank said it was also hard to find real *barbacoa,* made from the head of a cow, fire-roasted for hours, buried underground. And it was harder still to find decent *cabrito,* the succulent roasted young goat which was a staple of the *cocina norteña.*

Abuelo Jacobo joked with his old friend Tacho about how long it would take him to have his fill of this new American way of life and come back to Palaú. Tacho's mother was getting older, and she had refused to move with her son to San Antonio. His small farm in Palaú lay fallow. His brothers and sisters expected he would return, though as the years passed, several of them eventually moved north themselves, staying with Tacho before finding their own homes in the city. Uncle Frank hadn't ever imagined that they, too, would soon leave Palaú for San Antonio. He never thought they would be anything but Mexican. Abuelo Jacobo was the administrator of las Minas de Hondo, an old mine in Palaú that seemed to be loaded with unlimited amounts of coal. He also owned a *granja,* his true passion. This small parcel of land was where he farmed the vegetables and herbs which his family of eleven children, three girls and eight boys, consumed by the bushel.

According to Uncle Frank, the Garcias were never much taken by "America-struckedness."

But they weren't Mexican nationalists either. Maintaining the unity of the family was their ultimate *compromiso,* their unspoken obligation. The less the world around them threatened that simple ethic, the better. It was 1911 when the clashes began between the local battalion of Federalistas in Allende and dozens of loosely organized militant bands operating between the towns of Nueva Rosita, Palaú, and Múzquiz. By then, the revolucionarios, strapped with *bandoleros* bristling bullets, openly stood on street corners, brandishing their homemade Mexican flags and rickety-looking rifles. Over the next years, as day-to-day life in Coahuila during the revolution became un- manageable and then dangerous, the roads led north, and Mexico lost an entire generation to migration and war. Many went to San Antonio, joining the legions of Mexicanos who had already been there for so long.

The librarian approaches my table with a worried frown on her face.

"I have three hits for Juan Santos or John Santos," she says, trail- ing sheets of perforated computer paper across the reading room. She has done a computer search of the archive at the Institute of Texan Cul- tures for the original photographs in the San Antonio papers reporting Abuelo Juan José's death in 1939.

"One's a suicide. You knew that? One's a basketball star. One's a Rhodes scholar," she reports. "Now, the collection's a little spotty in some places. The suicide was thrown out, the *Express-News* pitched everything pre-1940s. The Rhodes scholar is missing."

Then, with some satisfaction, she says, "But I've got the basketball star—a glass negative from the *San Antonio Light*—from 1935."

She pulls the plate from behind her back, holding it with fuzzy white cotton mittens. She holds it up to the fluorescent lights of the reading room for me to see. It is my father, all wiry-limbed, crouching in dark silk shorts and tank top, arms cocked back, holding a basket- ball, his eyes fixed upward on the hoop with the transported stare of a solemn, religious devotee. He was an all-city player at Fox Tech High

School in the '35 season, and the sports section of the paper had done a formal athletic portrait of him before the championship game.

The headline read simply, SANTOS TO BE FEARED.

The librarian returns to her computer, thinking the reports of my grandfather's suicide may still be in the institute's microfilm collection of San Antonio newspapers. My father hadn't known that the photograph existed. All three of us—father, son, grandson; two Juan Josés and a John—were a part of the archive, carrying an infinitesimally small part of the history of San Antonio that the library houses, even if my grandfather and I had fallen through the cracks.

In school, we were never taught about the Mexicans in Texas. We were required to study Texas history, but it was history from the viewpoint of the later Anglo settlers from the United States and Europe, beginning with the battle at the Alamo for Texan independence, and later, statehood. There were no lessons about the Indians, the Payaya and Xaraname, who had been there ages before, or the Spanish and the Mexicans who had first built the city by the river. There were no stories, no pictures, of the great migration that had occurred just fifty years before, during the Mexican revolution, which had brought so many of our families to San Antonio. Because of that, I wasn't aware that any part of the story was missing for a very long time. If there was a secret history of those lands, I had to cobble it together out of the stories Uncle Frank and the other *ancianos* had told me, and out of the trips to Mexico and to those small south Texas towns, built around a plaza and a church, that still felt like Mexico.

The Spanish language was a reservoir of memory. In English, we had become Americans of Mexican descent. But in Spanish, we were still *la raza,* the chosen people. And the tales of *la raza,* that ongoing saga of the family with its myriad cast of characters, were by turns tragic, hilarious, bittersweet, poignant. *Las Viejitas* were always aware of the goings-on in the countless swirling lives of relatives and friends. These were the chronicles of *la raza*. As if through a sixth sense, they kept track of every episode in these ceaseless, improvised dramas that were as gripping as any *telenovela:*

Uncle Beto had cooked a *cabrito* that was so tough it pulled another uncle's dentures out. A *comadre*'s charming son-in-law, a perfect *hijito,* had gotten seduced by bigtime money, and now he was off to jail. In Monterrey, a distant niece was ordered to remain motionless in bed, dressed in silk nightgowns for the last eight months of her pregnancy, unable to move even her pinky finger. A ne'er-do-well cousin, a *sinvergüenza* who had already squandered his father's life savings, had now disappeared with his elderly dad and hadn't been seen in three weeks.

The unstoppable carousel of stories was our parallel history of San Antonio, part of another history of Texas, another history of Mexico. We sat in kitchens, living rooms, and backyards across the city, listening to episodes from these always incomplete annals. It seemed every family carried a larger story it was telling to the world over time. Though no one could say exactly what that story was, the Spanish language carried a feeling of it in the way Mexicanos always referred to themselves with the diminutive suffix *-ito*. We were Mexican-*itos* in a world of giants and monumental forces.

We were the meek who would inherit the earth.

We were the poor who would be welcomed into the Kingdom of God.

Just as a family possesses within itself these enigmatic, almost untraceable lines of destiny, so can two families' destinies become closely intertwined, each changing the direction of the other, as happened with the Santos and the Garcias, the families of my father's parents. They had lived close to each other in the small town of Palaú, and both families were large. Uela had two sisters and eight brothers, and Abuelo Juan José had two brothers, four sisters, and four half-brothers from his father's first family by a wife who had died very young.

According to one old Mexican adage, *"Pueblo chico, infierno grande,"* or, "Small town, big fire." It was just before the revolution, and life had been unsettled in the northern Mexican *frontera* for some time. Out in the state of Sinaloa to the west, there had been sporadic uprisings among the Yaquis and the Mayo since the 1890s. Many of the dissidents who sought to topple the thoroughly corrupt and autocratic regime of the dictator Porfirio Díaz, who was half-Indian, had been driven into exile and were operating from places such as Nogales, El Paso, and San Antonio.

In Palaú, most of the people worked either on the surrounding farms and livestock ranches or in the deep, rickety coal mines that still honeycomb the region. The summers were very hot, the streets cursedly dusty, and the only relief seemed to come on the Saturday nights when *conjuntos* and *bandas* would play in the gazebo at the plaza. It was there that Uela first met Juan José, when they were still in their teens. She was already possessed of a certain regal attitude, in high collar, long dress, and buckled leather boots. His thick black hair well combed off to one side, he was dark-skinned, with large brown eyes, and, it is said, the way he looked at someone, he seemed to never blink.

When a group of traveling thespians came to the village from Mexico City, they recruited Uela to play a maiden in one of the productions of old Spanish plays that were part of their repertoire. She did so despite the fact that her father, Jacobo, was incensed and scandalized by the idea. According to him, the wandering players were nothing more than vagabonds, *charlatanes* and misfits, aiming to deflower all the virtuous young ladies of Palaú.

"Those men wear dresses, and the women smoke pipes! They are out to do the devil's work, for sure," he told my grandmother.

But everyone was quiet when young Margarita acted out her death scene in the play, which was performed under a tent in a harvested corn field just beyond the edge of town. Juan José had come to the play with his brother Uvaldino, who was falling in love with Madrina Tomasa, my grandmother's sister, so he was distracted through the entire show, trading glances with his paramour.

Following the play as it took Margarita through soliloquies, romantic liaisons, and poetic plaints, Juan José finally could not bear to watch his beloved pantomime her own death in the arms of someone else, so he left the tent early, disconsolate. When Margarita did finally die at the play's end, her brother, my Tío Jesús, was grief-stricken, thinking his cherished older sister had truly died.

Uela was such a success in her acting debut that she was invited to join the company and return with them to Mexico City, to cultivate her talents as an actress. She was torn because of her professed love for Juan José, but those who saw her perform or heard her recite her favorite poetry said her voice had a rare balance of delicate timbre and volume, frailty, and power. And she had the ability of the rarest actors, to *become someone else*. She could draw you into her imaginary world with the smallest gestures, the tone and resonance of her voice, and the unpredictable way her lips would move and pause around the Spanish words.

One of my aunts says Uela always saw acting as the true destiny she would never fulfill. Abuelo Jacobo was not about to surrender his daughter to a pack of dilettantes. After all, where would she be left after her beauty and youth faded? How could any of the family see to her needs if she were as far away as Mexico City? Hadn't she been raised to rear a family and live close to the earth's cycles of planting, farming, and harvest, just as he had been taught? And what of Juan José, whom my great-grandfather adored as a son and had often said that they would someday start a farm together? Would she abandon him and the family their union promised for the fleeting glory of a life on the stages of traveling tent theaters?

Daily, there were more and more signals that the revolution was coming to Coahuila. There was banditry on the roads between villages and no authorities to turn to for help. Anyone who tried to make things better in the little towns of the north, without allying themselves with either the Porfiriato government or one of the myriad of opposition political camps, was assassinated. Abuelo Jacobo's job as a manager of the Palaú mines was imperiled by frequent strikes and work stoppages. It was growing harder to get to the market to keep the family fed. After the letter arrived from Uncle Frank, offering hope and news of jobs, preparations were begun for the family to move to Texas.

"*¡Basta ya con Mexico!*"

"Enough of Mexico!"

Abuelo Jacobo decided the Garcias would start their new life in *El Norte,* and Margarita would soon forget these devilish exotic notions.

And as for Tomasa being courted by Juan José's brother Uvaldino, this, too, would be brought to a close. Abuelo Jacobo was a frank man who liked to attend to family matters on Sunday afternoons, sitting at the dining table, smoking loose, fat cigarettes he rolled in corn shucks. One Sunday Jacobo pronounced the dashing, courteous, and well-spoken Uvaldino a womanizing *gavilán* who would come to no good end.

Aside from the questionable appearance of two brothers romancing two sisters, Uvaldino Santos was very different from Juan José. He was known to frequent the cantinas where he loved to talk *tonterías,* to sing, and to play the violin. Worse, he was meant to be off soon to study at the university in Monterrey, so what use would he have for a wife? And that was that.

Feeling their first great disappointments, Margarita and Tomasa both grew anxious to leave Mexico with all its intricate sadness behind. The three sisters shared one bed, and la Tía Pepa remembers both of her sisters crying late into the night that year. To make them feel better, she would ask them each to take a bite of her taco, because, she said, it made it taste better. Then, she would ask them to take a drink of her water, because, she said, it made the water taste sweeter. She remembers that was the summer they learned to pray together, that the three sisters began to study the *Via Rosae Crucis.*

From Palaú, the nearest junction to the road leading north to Piedras Negras on the border was a long day's ride away to the east, in Nueva Rosita. For months, the dusty carriage track from the bigger town of Saltillo to the south had been crowded with horseback riders, covered wagons, and buggies with flatbeds, as Mexicanos set out by the thousands for Texas to flee the mounting tumult of the revolution.

All of Mexico seemed to be there in the long caravan heading north. There were Lebanese Mexicans from Saltillo, Jewish Mexicans from Querétaro. The day the Garcias and Santos left Palaú they joined up with a group of Mexican Chinese families who had lived for generations in Monclova, to the south, where they had helped build the railroads in the 1890s.

One of my great-uncles made friends with another young man among them who was a prodigy in feats of illusion and magic, which he performed at fairs in the region. All of the Mexicanos from the mountain towns stared at him in his bright turquoise silk outfit and monk's cap. After they had talked awhile, the young magician described a trick called "the great Mongolian escape" he someday wanted to perform. My tío remembers making a drawing for him of a box he could have constructed to do the act, and for a long time, he wondered whether he ever achieved it.

Under the blistering canopy of Coahuila sunlight, the repetitive grinding sound of the axle had a lulling effect on the young ones riding in the buggy. But Abuelo Jacobo was nervous about traveling with the Chinese. Over their wagon flew a ragged banner that bore an image of Porfirio Díaz on it. The embattled president had been the *patrón* of the Mexican railroads, undertaking an epic building project that had managed to connect tracks from Mexico City with *la frontera*. The Chinese might be rightly grateful, Abuelo thought, but the banner would make them an easy target on the open plains ahead—easy valor for a Villista sniper or a Maderista border guard. Old Jacobo, above all else, did not want to get caught in the crossfire. After a few hours' riding, he pulled the two family wagons off the trail at Villa Unión and let the Chinese move on.

The Rosicrucian studies the Garcia sisters had done over the years taught them a way to live with proper attention to the signs and visions by which the unknown meaning of things could be discerned. Since all creation was part of the same manifestation of God, everything the world presented was part of the story of something larger taking place, revealing the ultimate meaning of the world. It was each initiate's obligation to be able to discern the messages underlying whatever they saw.

A hawk seen in flight in fog was a warning: Your greatest efforts will be useless in the present web of circumstances.

A jug of wine with a drowned butterfly? The drunkenness of a loved one.

A silver halo doubled around the October moon was a sign of childbirth, probably twins.

Everything was connected. *Mal aires*, the evil airs, might enter your body through your uncovered mouth or head, wrapping themselves like a treacherous smoke around your bones. This could leave you with a rheum, *la gripa,* a life-threatening flu. As Madrina knew well, a frightful sight could paralyze you with *susto,* a fright that could freeze your emotions and leave you quivering and blank like a zombie. Worse, a malicious look from a stranger, *el mal ojo,* could kidnap your soul forever.

These ways of seeing had been second nature in Mexico. In the United States, even in Texas, which had been that part of New Spain known as *la Nueva Extremadura,* they began to feel like superstitions, especially to the men in the family. Yet, for the women, the power to see behind the face of things was even more important in this new world where the *pan dulce,* the universal sweet bread of Mexico, tasted so different. The pumpkin-filled *empanadas* tasted like mud. The roasted almond cookies, decorated with a pentagram, crumbled like dust in your mouth. It was the women who kept vigil over all of the knowledge that had been gathered across generations. In their blood was the book of the past. In their visions, they could read the book of the future.

It was years, Tía Pepa says, before she felt the family was finally safe and settled on the American side of the border. Great-grandfather left his work in the mines behind in Palaú and set out, with the help of his sons, to be a farmer. After arriving in Texas, the Garcias changed farms several times, in one case having to lose an entire crop after a quarrel with the farm owner. As Tía Pepa tells the story today, it was in those troubled days that she received a sign that she was where she was meant to be, and that the Garcias were on the right path.

It was a hot night in Creedmoor, Texas, and everyone had moved their beds outside onto a small grassy hill near the house, which always had cooling breezes, even on the most uncomfortable days. With her sisters asleep next to her, Pepa heard from far off the bass vibrato of her father's snore, wreathed in the steady whistling of thousands of crickets. The mosquito netting drawn over her bed kept her from seeing many stars that night, but Venus and the moon were as bright as polished ivory.

"Then, as I watched, the moon seemed to open up, like a yucca flower throwing out its seeds."

Pepa raises her hands above her head, spreading out and moving her fingers like a rain gently beginning to fall to the ground.

It was a slow-moving cascade of numberless luminous pears, glowing bright green against the midnight sky as they made their way down toward earth. As she watched the pears descending, Tía Pepa looked from bed to bed and saw her brothers and sisters sleeping, scattered across the small hill. The crickets and her father's snoring had fallen silent.

The pears filled the air around them, bringing a sweet scent of the fruit as they drew closer. Then, one pear passed with a whisper through the netting above her, and when Pepa put her hand out to touch it, it passed through her hand as well. The immaterial fruit seemed to rotate slowly as it passed through her nightshirt and into her chest above her heart. She looked again to see her sisters and brothers, and the pears were descending out of the sky and passing into each of them as well.

"For a while, I just counted the pears as they passed into my heart. Some were bright green. Some were riper, with a little bit of red on them."

Eventually, Tía Pepa says, she lost count near one hundred.

That was the night she slept her first real sleep since leaving Mexico.

6

From Huisache to Cedar

De Huisache a Cedro

 *Among the Garcias, several uncles and aunts, along with my father, tell the same tale as if it were their own, as if each had lived it and drawn from it their own unmistakable conclusion. It is a story* about returning to Mexico, after the family had already been many years in the United States. Maybe it really did happen to each of them at different times, like the same vision, given to many, as a talisman for navigating the new life in El Norte.

Invariably, the scene is an isolated road in a Coahuila town. Sometimes it is in Nueva Rosita. Sometimes Palaú. Or San Felipe. Or Ciudad Juárez. The time is the 1940s. It is an unbearably hot, dusty day, which is everyday weather in the desert highlands of Coahuila. It is a visit to the house of one of the few relatives who stayed behind.

The car is stalled. It has a flat tire. The travelers—and usually there is more than one family member present—are stuck, trying to push *their big American car up a steep, unpaved, and rocky hillside road. As they noisily work to make the car go, a Mexicano walks by, offering a quiet saludo, leading his heavy-laden burro down the road.*

"He was an old, old Mexicanito farmer," my father recalls, "like a scene in an old Mexican movie. Wearing a sombrero, white pants, and blouse, and a beat-up pair of huaraches, with tire treads for soles. The burro was loaded with bags of dried corn cobs. His feet and his clothes were filthy."

"He was a Kikapu Indian," Uncle Rudy remembers in his version. "In those days, they used to come through the towns, selling their gamusa deer skins, dried comino seeds, and the hot chile pequín from the sierra."

In Uncle Gilbert's version, the man and the burro walked with several children at his side. While most of the onlookers in the village had been fascinated with his car, peppering him with questions about how fast it went and how long it had taken them to make the long journey from San Antonio, this man just kept his eyes down and walked past in silence.

"He was very, very quiet," Uncle Gilbert explains.

As the story goes, they all watched after the Mexicano as he slowly made his way down the road, and the same thought went through all of their minds. In each tale, they end by turning to one of their traveling companions, whether brother, sister, cousin, uncle, or aunt.

"If we hadn't moved to Texas," they say, pointing at the old Mexicano, "that would be you!"

"There but for the grace of God, go the Garcias."

"Esto, también, pasará."

That was Uela's favorite proverb, of which she had many.

"This, too, shall pass."

"Esto, también, pasará," she said quietly to my uncle Raul who sat, with a distant expression, next to her. The room was warm and

moist from the squat gas heater purring in the corner. The only light came from two oil lamps that were on the mantle, illuminating a ceramic Nativity scene. The whole house smelled of oil, orange rind, and brown sugar from the kitchen, where my aunts were making stacks of *buñuelos,* fried batter pastry florettes. These would be brought out and placed on the dining room table with all the rest of the Christmas delicacies—tamales, chiles rellenos, steaming hot *capirotada,* with its burnt, sugary scent.

Uela was dressed in a dark cotton, floral-print dress, with crisply pressed white scalloped collars. She was in mourning that year, and her starched posture was even more formal than usual. My cousin René had been killed some months before in a helicopter crash in Vietnam. Uncle Raul and Aunt Clara's son had been eighteen years old. It was the first Christmas since his death and all the elders seemed morose. Uela knew that feeling well.

As his younger cousins, we had been aware that René had left to fight in the war, and before his death, whenever the television news had shown footage from Vietnam, we would compete to see who among us might be the first to spot our elder cousin warrior. He was part of a tradition of soldiers in the family that we regarded with awe. The hand-colored portraits in green, red, white, and blue of soldiers, living and dead, were a fixture of Mexicano households all over San Antonio. Most of our fathers had been in the army during World War II, and Uncle Raul, who had seen combat in Italy, had also been sent to Korea after rejoining the reserves to make a little extra money for his growing family.

At first, no one told us of René's death, and our peals of delight at seeing Vietnam footage on TV were now met with an edgy silence. By the time we were told, months afterward, it already had the feeling of distant history, of a life arrested and taken back into the farthest recesses of time. I struggled then to remember my cousin's face and his gangly Santos-Garcia body.

"It's more than we should be asked to give, but it is just so, and we must accept it," Uela had said quietly in her impeccably pronounced Spanish. Then she shrugged her shoulders and let out one of the characteristic sighs that used to issue slowly from her like the final note of a song, held pianissimo until the last vibration fell from the air.

"Esto, también, pasará."

As usual that year, Uela's house was crowded with *viejos,* the old ones, for a Christmas fiesta. All of her brothers and sisters were there, along with my aunts and uncles. Most of my cousins were playing in the large backyard, lit up by a streetlamp Uncle Frank had installed just for the occasion. At these family *pachangas,* these gatherings of the tribe, I was always attracted to *los viejos* and the slow quiet that seemed to revolve around them.

Whether we were in one of our houses or encamped for an afternoon in one of San Antonio's thick-gladed parks, their presence, confident and wise, made it feel as if we were all denizens of a secret Mestizo city, a world that existed parallel to the apparent physical lineaments of the city everyone else saw. There was a sense of ceremony around them: Uela; Madrina; Tía Pepa; Uncles Frank, Jesse, Manuel, Chale, and Gilbert. Plates of Aunt Minnie's fresh Christmas bean and chicken tamales were especially prepared and set before *los viejos,* along with a Negra Modelo beer, poured into freezer-chilled fountain glasses. The tamales were delectable corn *masa* dumplings, some pork, some bean, some chicken, wrapped tightly in pale corn husks. A bowl was passed around with fresh jalapeños to be bitten raw, along with a mouthful of tamal. Among that generation, they ate chile into their nineties, impervious to the stomach ailments that force many middle-aged Mexicanos these days to renounce the "fire of the earth," as one uncle calls it. The room was quiet, except for the sound of them eating and gently sipping their beers.

Time took on a different quality around them. There was never any alarm. All could be witnessed. Everything could be endured. Elsewhere in our lives, we were careening through a century of accelerating atrocities and wonders. The bombs of Hiroshima and Nagasaki, the tremors of the 1960s over civil rights struggles and the Vietnam war, even the Apollo landings on the moon passed before the Garcias as if they were watching a long movie.

"We have to admit we like things to be easier than they were before," Uncle Frank once told me. "But there will always be pain."

Around *los viejos,* it seemed time was spiraling in cycles that eventually brought us around the same curving nebula of tales and trials. The grief of a new widow. An uncle leaning heavily on the tequila. Famine brought on by war, revolution, or a change in the weather. A grandchild crazed on drugs, with no respect for anyone. They gave you the sense that the story was always longer than just the tale being told. It didn't matter how desperate these times appeared to be to others. They knew how the world could spin through long spells of grief and solace, need and succor.

That Christmas, the Garcias had a message drawn from their long years of witness:

This too shall pass.

Abuelo Jacobo and the whole family, Madrina and six of her brothers, traveled from their sharecropping, hill pecan farm where they had lived since 1914. It was late in the afternoon and they arrived by train at the Missouri Pacific Railroad Depot downtown. The station was an aging majestic, Moorish temple–like structure with massive arches and a giant burnished bronze dome. As the train slowed to approach downtown, it loomed like a Spanish caliph's palace over the city's modern skyline. San Antonio had a rumbling sound Madrina had never heard before. Almost a roar. The street cars rushed alongside the train as they passed through town. Throngs of Mexicanos were busy buying produce and eating at taco stands in the mercado square, where the iron post gas lamps had already been lit.

As the train braked and squealed into the station, with bellowing gusts of dust and steam swirling around her window, Madrina looked up and saw the statue of a lone Indian perched on the peak of the dome of the train station. He wore a small headdress of feathers and a loincloth. He stood in perfect balance on one foot, with his other outstretched behind him. With his arms, he grasped a bow and arrow at the very moment of release, aiming east toward the city.

She knew it was a statue, but it reminded her of the Kikapu she used to see in the mercado in Múzquiz, selling their leather crafts and dry shredded beef for *machacado*. It seemed such an odd place for an Indio, as if his arrow was aimed at her, bringing forth a torrent of memories of the Mexican home they had left behind. He was a sentinel of memory, greeting every visitor as an emissary of a vanished world. It gave San Antonio the eerie feeling of a city frozen in time.

"*Y el pobrecito, tan solitario,*" Madrina adds—"Poor thing, so alone up there."

The poor Indian had been abandoned on the dome, keeping a lonely vigil over San Antonio de Bejar.

The whole Garcia family moved to San Antonio because Uela and Juan José had found a house big enough to reunite the whole familia. From the days in Palaú, when they had first worked together on the family *granja,* my grandfather and his father-in-law had nurtured a dream of starting a commercial produce farm closer to a city, giving them access to bigger markets than they could find in the villages or towns of north Mexico. Abuelo Jacobo treasured his son-in-law's honesty and tireless labors, and the old man was one of the few people with whom my otherwise taciturn grandfather could pass hours talking. Now, it might be possible to realize that long-held dream. Uncle Frank, Abuelo Jacobo's oldest son, had been married and living in San Antonio for several years. Two of his brothers, Santos and José, who had their own families, worked with him in a machine shop he had opened on Guadalupe Street. Slowly, the Garcias were making their new home in the south Texas city.

The new Santos-Garcia home on Burr Road was just beyond what were then the northern outskirts of the city, near where the stream of the Rio San Antonio grows into a wider river from a large network of underground springs. The sprawling wooden house, shaded with big furry-leafed Chinese elm trees, was part of Fernridge, the large estate of Col. George Brackenridge, a prominent banker, city father, and scion of an old family of early San Antonio settlers. The house, big enough to accommodate several families, came with Juan José's new job as caretaker for the complex of submerged greenhouses that were the colonel's passionate amusement.

The Santos and Garcias remember the house on Burr Road in San Antonio as the first real home for the family since Palaú. Mexico was still swept up in violent whirlwinds of bloody change. Presidents changed with the seasons. Local government officials were more corrupt and vengeful than ever. Tía Pepa, who had moved back to Mexico with her husband, Anacleto, wrote them often of the politically motivated hijackings on the roads of Coahuila. As a foreman of the mines at Barroterrán, Anacleto had been threatened several times by various unionists who sometimes wanted the mines closed in strikes, sometimes wanted them kept open to draw out coal to sell for arms.

"Puras locuras mexicanas," old Abuelo Jacobo would say with disgust, listening to Pepa's letters read aloud to him by Uela. "Pure Mexican madness."

But finally, here was a lasting respite from the revolution and all the wandering it had cost them. The daily calendar of the household revolved around an interminable pageant of meals, all of which were served in two sittings, for the young ones first and the elders last. My father woke up to the same sound every morning. With a rapid battery of ear-piercing slaps, Uela's hands patted the flour *masa* into dozens of tortillas for the dawn breakfast that sent her brothers and Juan José off to their work or school.

The house slowly filled up with the soothing roasted-flour aroma of tortillas on the heavy iron comal. Breakfast was tacos with egg and potatoes with chile. Usually, dinner was *fideos*, a spicy Mexican pasta cooked with cilantro, cumin, and, once or twice a week, some cuts of beef for extra flavor. Today, my father cannot bear the sight of *fideos*.

There weren't many Mexicans in that part of the city. They were mainly downtown and on the west side. Many older Anglo families, along with a new and growing business class, had long ago settled in the verdant north side neighborhoods of Alamo Heights, near the Fernridge estate. Most of the Mexicans to be seen in the streets there were domestic help.

Uncles Jesse and Gilbert began the new academic year at Alamo Heights Public High School and they were the first and only Mexicans enrolled, which Uncle Jesse remembers helped to toughen them up early in life. "We didn't even speak one word of English," he tells me, laughing, as we sit together in his living room in San Antonio, decorated with laminated homages to some of his most memorable catches: a red snapper, a bass, a marlin.

"We couldn't understand a single thing the teacher was saying."

There were fights. Their bicycle tires, already patchworks of plugs, were slashed. Once, Uncle Jesse found the word *Meskin* scratched into his school desk.

"But he made friends with all the girls!" my aunt Fela says of Uncle Jesse, her husband, speaking of a time long before they met. "That's how he got through that school!" Uncle Jesse runs his leathery hand through his short-cropped gray hair, smiling.

When I ask, Jesse says Abuelo Juan José loved to spend early evenings on Burr Road in the greenhouse, when the tea-colored light from the lamps cast webs of shadows and made the whole glass enclosure glow green. From down the hill on the porch of their house, you could see Juan José's shadow moving across the glass, which looked pearly because of the condensation.

In sepia-colored pictures of the greenhouse from the estate archive, long braids of orchids hang like garlands in a column in the middle of the room. Great palms line the sidewalks like standards. There are Japanese plum trees in full flower, ivory-barked persimmon, miniature china berry. Taped to the back of one photograph of a stand of lilies is a sketch in my grandfather's hand of where those flowers were to be planted that year. *Plano de azucenas,* it says, tracing a cross that went from one end of the frosted glass walls to the other, connecting the two doors in the middle of the hall with purple irises mixed in with the lilies.

Abuelo wore a suit and tie to work in the garden, a suit that my aunt remembers smelling of loam and plant resins. While he was clipping and trimming, he scrutinized every branch and leaf with a chemist's deliberation. My father said Abuelo usually stayed extremely quiet and concentrated while he moved from plant to plant, looking for the smallest blemish, gathering clumps of cuttings and petals in a bag hanging from one arm as he went along. As he watched his father from behind a large potted cactus, the sound of Abuelo's steady breathing, of his boots rasping and echoing against the moist soil on the paving stones, was calming. Playing throughout the greenhouse with my uncle Raul and aunt Connie, it smelled of mint, camphor, lavender, and eucalyptus, unless they ventured too close to the acrid ammonia cloud that hung over the compost box. In the middle of a game of hide-and-go-seek or tag, they were always dazzled anew whenever the pipes that ran along the high vaulted ceiling would begin first to rattle, then hiss, and then the entire greenhouse would rumble and fill up with fog so thick that my father could hold his hand in front of his face and not see it.

Everything that surrounded them—palms, lilies, ferns—was gradually shrouded in an opal-colored neon haze, and they wondered to each other if this was what heaven looked like all the time.

Good wood is like a jewel, Tío Abrán, my great-grandfather Jacobo's twin brother, used to say. Huisache burns fast, in twisting yellow flames, engulfing the log in a cocoon of fire. It burns brightly, so it is sought after for Easter bonfires. But it does not burn hot, so it's poor wood for home fires. On a cold morning in the sierra, you can burn a whole tree by noon. Mesquite, and even better, cedar—these are noble, hard woods. They burn hot and long. Their smoke is fragrant. And if you know how to do it, they make exquisite charcoal.

"La leña buena es como una joya"

Good wood is like a jewel. And old Tío Abrán knew wood the way a jeweler knows stones, and in northern Coahuila, from Múzquiz to Rosita, his charcoal was highly regarded for its sweet, long-burning fire.

Abrán was one of the last of the Garcias to come north. Somewhere around 1920, he finally had to come across the border with his

family. He was weary of the treacheries along the roads, from robbery
to rape, that had become a part of life in the sierra towns since the beginning of the revolution ten years earlier. Most of the land near town
had been deforested and the only wood he could find around Palaú
was huisache. To find any of the few pastures left with arbors of mesquite trees, he had to take the unpaved mountain road west from
Múzquiz, along a route where many of the militantes had their camps.
Out by the old Villa las Rusias, in a valley far off the road, there were
mesquite trees in every direction as far as you could see. He made an
arrangement with the owner of the villa to give him a cut from the sale
of charcoal he made from the mesquite. But many times, the revolucionarios confiscated his day's load of wood, leaving him to return
home, humiliated, with an empty wagon.

Aside from Tía Pepa and Tío Anacleto, who had returned to
Mexico by then, he had been the last of the Garcias left in Mexico, and
he had left reluctantly. On the day he arrived in San Antonio with his
family, he had told his brother Abuelo Jacobo, "If there was still any
mesquite that was easy to get to, we would've stayed."

He said he had come in search of the legendary Texas cedar
stands. And he found them sixty miles north of San Antonio. Here was
a broad swath of hill country that had been rocky grassland until the
middle of the nineteenth century. That was when the charcoal industry
based in Austin had planted miles of cedar, from Kerrville to Buda, to
support the growing demand for fuel, as more and more settlers arrived
from the north. Eventually, that part of Texas became a cedar forest, a
forest which is still growing, pushing farther south past Austin and
closer to San Antonio. Jacobo and his family went there despite the *sen-
tido* among some family members that this was "Gringo" country,
where Mexicans were not welcome.

And perhaps they knew this to be true, for it had been in cedar
country, growing pecans and corn and raising goats, that the very first

Garcias to come out of Mexico had first settled. Abuelo Juan José's brother Uvaldino Santos had settled north of Austin, in Elgin, a town that sat at the edge of the forested hill country, looking north onto the vast Texas flatlands that ran all the way to the Red River.

Like these early settlers, I have always been drawn to the ridges and canyons of the Texas hill country and its infinite cedars. The silence of the cedars seemed familiar to me. Along the road from Sisterdale to Grapevine, a two-lane, farm-to-market highway that runs like an artery through the middle of the hill country, I have heard the wind slowly wrapping itself around the draping flat branches of the cedars. Even the birds seem to fall quiet there. Uncle Gilbert remembers how he walked with his father and his uncle through hills full of cedar on the land Abrán had found to make his charcoal in Spring Branch, Texas, northwest of San Antonio, "It always seemed chilly up there, like you were up in sierra country," he says now.

On one of those days, the whole tribe made the journey from Burr Road, and Juan José, Abuelo Jacobo, and his sons all helped Tío Abrán on his first large order of charcoal for a buyer in Austin. A pit the size of a small house had already been dug when they arrived. Abrán had meticulously lined it with chalk and lime, and then everyone helped stack the cedar in precise rows, alternating directions, until the pit was nearly full. Making charcoal involves an alchemy of dirt, wood, fire, patience, and prayer. If all of these are not in impeccable balance, the final result is a pile of ash.

As the wood was being stacked, Tío Abrán moved around the pit in slow circles, sprinkling droplets of kerosene from a paint can onto the cedar with his fingers. After the wood was anointed, Abrán, already in his early sixties, stepped gingerly across the latticed cedar trunks, dusting them with handfuls of what he called his *polvo mágico,* or magic powder, a combination of sulfur, coke, and other secret ingredients. The pit was lit with long branches, flaming at their ends, which were pushed down as far as they could to the bottom of the pile. When the smoke began to be visible at every corner, but before flames engulfed the wood, the whole pit had to be covered with a large mound of soil, shoveled quickly from every side.

Then, Tío Abrán would forget about it and walk away, saying it was bad luck to watch too closely. For days, the mound smoldered and shifted as the earth around it grew warmer with each hour. Uncle Gilbert sat near the mound while my grandfather cleared the area of twigs and dry brush, as if he feared the pit might explode and rain fire on all the surrounding terrain. After all, there was an enormous ball of fire consuming everything just beneath their feet, sucking in air through the dirt.

Maybe the fire they had started would never be put out.

"That was the first time I saw him nervous, afraid of something, *preocupado,*" Uncle Gilbert recalls today. "We couldn't convince him it was all under control."

Two days later, the air took on a subtle scent of embers and Tío Abrán announced the partially collapsed mound was ready to be uncovered. As my great-uncles helped him shovel the dirt off from the top of the pit, just beneath the surface they saw the glistening ebony chunks of fresh charcoal, smelling sweet of cedar and crackling like black ice beneath their feet. Juan José stood off from the pit, furtively looking on from beneath a lone oak tree. There was no explosion and the invisible fire had subsided. But he had already told Uela he was ready to return to San Antonio.

And he didn't want to take any of Tío Abrán's new charcoal back to town.

On the morning after Madrina arrived in San Antonio to stay, she went out for a walk on Burr Road after breakfast. It was astounding to her how little dust there was. So much of her life in Mexico had been lived in a world of swirls and eddies of infinite dust. In the mornings, you could wet down the ground around the house with water drops from a full bucket, but within an hour, the scirocco haze of dust would return. In San Antonio, the streets were paved and the ground alongside the road was planted with grass that held the dust down.

As she went through the gate of the yard in front of the house, she saw a small truck parked across the road, about twenty yards down the hill. As she walked closer, she could make out the shape of a large cage, with thick bars, that sat high off the cab bed of the truck. Along the side of the truck were painted the words: WOLF BRAND CHILI. As Madrina got right up to the truck, she took a quick step back in fright.

Inside the cage, a lone wolf, crazed and panting, circled the small space so quickly that, at first, he looked like a smudged, bluish blur.

When he stopped for a moment, Madrina saw where he had nervously bitten the fur off his hind parts until the wounds were raw and red. Elsewhere along his long, emaciated body, the hair was falling off in patches. His gray eyes had the piercing look of a mute scream, and the cage smelled of old food, feces, drool, and spoiled blood. In Palaú, the whole family used to pause on the nights when they heard the packs of wolves howling from the sierra. Madrina says it was less like singing and more like talking, like a conversation in an old language of the mountains everyone but the wolves had forgotten to speak. She knew the ranchers and goat farmers battled with them as their greatest nemeses. But the wolves were a part of God's wild creation that always seemed beyond human control.

As she looked into the eyes of the animal, it felt as if the wolf was looking back at her, like it knew her, she said later. In the quiet morning air, the animal's panting was the loudest noise until she heard her own heart beating, accelerating like a hummingbird's. And then the world went black.

When Uela saw Madrina from the porch, she was still quivering stiffly in the midst of her seizure in the middle of the road, while the wolf looked on from inside its cage. As the seizure gradually began to subside, there was a small lace ribbon of spittle falling to one side of Madrina's mouth. Her head cleared and she opened her eyes to see her father, sister, and brother-in-law gathered around her. They seemed to be floating in a silky, coffee-colored light.

The morning air was clear and there was a faint scent of newly cut grass. She could hear the paws of the wolf scratching against the iron floor of the cage, but she did not want to look at him. It did not seem like Texas or Mexico anymore. It was as if all of that had been left behind. She felt she had been transported even farther north, to where the sky looks silvery and the sun seems farther away than she had ever imagined possible. She felt lighter, as if she had been returned to the body of a child. The three stood over her, wordless, waiting for Madrina to make her own way out of the fit.

A strange thought came to her in that moment. Time seemed to be moving more slowly, and her body was covered in a cold dew.

We have been taken to Purgatory, she told herself. And soon the chastisements would begin.

Peregrinaje

7
Zona
de Niebla
Fog Zone

 *Uncle Sid had been living on Black Cows—frothy highballs of root beer and vanilla ice cream—for three weeks already. Dressed in cream-colored paja- mas and a paisley silk gown, he had stayed in bed* since his doctor had told him the liver cancer afflicting him was inopera- ble. I had just flown into San Antonio, heading for Mexico again, so I gathered three aunts and my mother in her vintage Cadillac to drive to Austin for a visit with my uncle, the eldest son of my grandfather's brother Uvaldino.

For generations among the Santos, there had been an undeniable dichotomy within the clan. There were those among us whose destiny it was to carry what seemed an indelible sadness not of their own making, while there were others who carried a reservoir of ceaseless laughter. As a kind of filial Yin and Yang, it was as if we had been guaranteed that consolation would be always close by for the confounded.

Along with Uncle Raul, Isidro, or Sid, was one of the family's un-wavering emissaries of laughter. His laugh quaked the whole girth of his body, rolling out like a rapidly gamboling Pavarotti tremolo, hitting all the high notes, gathering all of his face up around the bushy Santos eye-brows that would shake in tempo with his guffaws. He laughed with a rhythmic, breathy lisp that gave his booming belly chuckles a cartoon glow.

When he had been well, he told his stories like a jeweler etching on a stone, careful to set up his lightning bolt punch lines. He said he had been trained by the best. Growing up, he had spent a lot of time in Nueva Rosita with Abuelo Juan José's sister, la Tía Chita, who was famous for her ability to tell jokes for hours; whether in the afternoon while she was making hundreds of tortillas for a quinceañera *fiesta, or late at night, sitting in the cool courtyard of her house with a circle of* comadres *during a lunar eclipse.*

Uncle Sid's bedroom was full of his lavish multi-tiered bowling tro-phies, won over the last fifty years, shining now in the last of the after-noon sunlight. When he saw me standing in the doorway, he gestured weakly for me to come sit on the side of his bed. I held his hand and watched his eyes glisten through milky tears. "I remembered something Daddy said about where they all came from," he said. His face was full of a wistful tranquilidad, a softening fatigue that seemed overpoweringly sweet and contented. His skin was smooth and pearl-colored, as he lay on his side, his head cradled on a bended arm. He took a long weary breath and fixed his gaze on me to convey the knowledge passed down from his father, Uvaldino.

"Before Coahuila?" I asked. Sid knew I had been making journeys back to Mexico, piecing together what I could of the family's lost history in Mexico.

"Hell. They were in Coahuila forever."

"Was it Palaú?"

"*Uh-uhn. It was San Felipe. Las Minas de San Felipe. Near Sabinas. That's where Pop said they were all born.*"

Uncle Sid said he wanted me to have a videotape, and he sent Aunt Mary off to find it. A surprise, he said, that he had lost, and then found. While Mother went off with Aunt Mary, to give her the cheese wheel she had bought at a Czech deli in San Antonio, Aunt Connie, Aunt Bea, and Aunt Margie gathered around Sid's bed and laughed with their cousin about the practical jokes that were his métier as a kid. Like tying Aunt Margie's baby carriage to a goat, or wearing a cape and a flour tortilla mask with the eyes poked out, like the costume of a Spanish count.

His laugh was quieter now, slowed down to a gurgling whir. And then, when he grew silent, we all stared at one another, and we suddenly knew that this would be the last time we would see Isidro alive.

By the time we left, the road between Austin and San Antonio was lit in crisp tungsten blue, and the cruise control carried us all home in a floating reverie. On the highway back to San Antonio, with the earth moving through vast space, I knew we had always left our ancestors' spirits behind, scattered in the planet's wake, through other parts of the galaxy, other parts of the universe. Just as we would now leave Sid's laugh behind, in a December sky that had been lit up by an unexpected comet, recently discovered in Japan.

After we returned home, I looked at the videotape Uncle Sid had given to me that afternoon. It was footage of a family reunion during his father, Uvaldino's, eighty-fifth birthday party in Elgin, Texas. Uvaldino, dressed handsomely in a dark suit and vest, looks much smaller than I remembered him, his thick hair completely white, the dark skin of his face growing ashen—and he is wearing a golden cardboard crown. The party room, festooned with streamers and confetti, is crowded with all of the relatives from San Antonio and Austin who had traveled to celebrate Tío Uvaldino's long life in Mexico and Texas.

From off-camera at one point, someone asks him to name all of his brothers and sisters. At first, he seems confused and disoriented, still slow to speak from his head injury of years ago. But before the question can be asked again, he straightens himself in his chair, takes a sip of his margarita, then, looking straight into the camera, recites,

"Mariano. Francisco. Manuela. Andrea. Jesusa. And . . . Juan José."

I stopped the tape at "Juan José," at the very moment when Uvaldino's gaze fell to the right as if in an instant of forgotten reckoning. At the time, only Uvaldino was still alive. He had already been gone for more than a decade, when I saw the tape.

All of the Santos are dying, I thought.

San Antonio de Bejar wears its glistening halo of creeks, streams, and rivulets like an ageless crown, as if this place at the edge of the arid country west and south has been vouchsafed by time, receiving a long span of years with the grace of a thousand springs and endlessly flowing water. Maybe it is an accidental oasis. To the north of the city, there is a wide swath of impermeable igneous rock, jagged ridges of red Texas granite from Grapevine to Llano. To the west, there is desert, to the east are wetlands, bayous and swamps.

San Antonio lies over an enormous limestone aquifer, a vast earthen filter made from the dense sediment of accumulated eons of fossil remains. Over millennia, the husks and membranes of millions of dead organisms were pressed into rock that was porous enough to let the rain wash through, ever more cleansed as it went. And the earth became hollowed out like a honeycomb. As a result, a half mile beneath the ground, there are rushing crystalline rivers and a seemingly infinite reservoir of sweet water.

Agua dulce. That's what the old Mexicans called fresh water. Sweet for drinking, like a *néctar de mango* in the withering hot Mexican summers. Sweet for the crops, for the furry okra vines, the blood-red stalks of sorghum, all the bristling cotton and bright yellow chayote squash.

The Santos and Garcias were river people. Wherever they lived, they had always been close to *agua dulce.* They didn't really know oceans, and there weren't any lakes where they had come from in Mexico. But for some, the Gulf of Mexico held a certain mystique. Uncles Jesse and Gilbert, who built an amber-lacquered wooden boat, would fish in the Almagorda Bay, expressing something else, perhaps some tincture of Spanish mariner's blood left in them.

When you come from a land of wet-weather arroyos where water is scarce, you develop a special appreciation for fresh running streams. Arroyos crisscross all of northwestern Coahuila, and over the years most of them acquired names of endearment, referring back to sometimes only dimly remembered tales. On the road to the Rancho Los Generales, at Arroyo Pato Viejo, or old duck, someone once found a nearly featherless mallard, lost in the high Mexican desert on its migration back to *El Norte.* At Arroyo Papalote de Oro stood a battered, rusty tin windmill that had once drawn so much water it was deemed to be made of gold. These dry creeks run with water only once every few years when gulf storms stall against the eastern face of the Sierra Madre and drop all their rains in one curving flume on the sloping eastern face of the mountains. Then every bleached wash of alluvial gravel and rocks runs opalescent blue and jade green, eventually leaving behind finger-shaped tadpole pools with silvery guppies and perch the size of the palm of your hand.

Back in Palaú, the Rio Sabinas, with its long bank-to-bank colonnade of giant arched cypresses, had run through the pueblo just one hundred yards from the Garcia house. It was the same clear river that rushed past *el Nacimiento de los Indios,* the settlement in the mountains where the Kikapu Indians lived, and further downstream it passed by

Nueva Rosita and Sabinas, and the Villa de San Felipe, where, according to Uncle Sid, the familia Santos had originally come from.

On Sunday afternoons, the Santos cooled their watermelons in the
river and roasted *cabrito* near the bank, while my grandfather's half-
brother José León played the rapid flight of "La Negra" on a violin. On
those later afternoons, their songs and voices went echoing off with the
water, running to the west past Saltillo and Monclova. There, the
spring that began at the Pozo del Centinela high and faraway in the Ser-
ranías del Burro, beyond the Rancho Los Generales, became a wide
river, carrying the scorched ochre dust of Coahuila all the way to the
Rio Bravo, then on out to the deep banks of the gulf. That was their
world before *la Revolución*.

Once the family arrived in San Antonio, they had made frequent
Sunday picnics on the banks of the San Antonio River in Brackenridge
park. Uncles fished for catfish and perch, keeping their beers cool in
the water. They let the children play in the shallow waters of the
streams that coursed through the burgeoning American city.

The rivers give a bounty of fish and long afternoon spells of re-
freshment from the infernal heat of the summers, but eventually the
rivers also take something back. That's just the way of Nature, without
malice, but incontrovertible. For the Santos, it would be the Rio San
Antonio, many years later and farther to the north—across the *frontera*
in the Estados Unidos—that would claim one of their own.

When I was sixteen I pasted the last picture taken of my grandfather Juan José—a stiff, formal Immigration Service portrait—onto the
back panel of the old wooden standup desk my uncle Lico had given
me to write on. The portrait looks as if it had been taken against the
background of a clear Texas afternoon sky, with the rest of the world
stripped away. Abuelo's refugee's stare is ingrained, emotionally ab-

sent, a face already abandoned by the soul, revealing nothing of the man who was once inside, like the spent brown shell of a Texas cicada. The look in his eyes mixes a sullen desperate pleading with a subtler sense that nothing can be changed, that the course of things is fixed and inexorable.

We have only to wait for the inevitable, he seems to be saying.

Many years later, on a trip home, I discover the old desk which had been stored away in the attic of our old house. Next to the picture of Abuelo Juan José, I had taped an old Mexican drawing of the human body, incised and opened as in an antique surgeon's manual, with each of the limbs and organs shown corresponding to a sign of the Zodiac. The legend below describes how the body itself is tied into the panorama of planetary, astrological forces. Aries rules the head. Gemini, the right shoulder. Cancer is the left breast; Scorpio, the sexual organs. The guts, which connect to Virgo, my sign and the sign of my parents, are exposed, with the skin of the belly pulled back in tightly wound scrolls.

While that photograph of Juan José shows him implacable and remote, his gaze was always familiar and strangely beckoning to me. It seems miraculous that the pinstripes of the thick woolen suit he wore on that day should still be discernible, that of all things, he should leave such an improbable detail preserved for eternity. That the peculiar leftward skew, shirt button showing, of the tight knot in his black silk tie should still be as palpable as a broken compass. That one side of his face should seem hurt and sad, the other resolute and untouchable.

Once I became aware of the mystery of Juan José's death, it felt as if the source of the centripetal pull toward the past inside of me had been revealed, as if all of the stories that had been told of the family's past were only meant to distract us from this one memory. After my grandfather's death in 1939, the Santos and the Garcia families maintained their cult of secrets and forgetting around his demise. It was not a conspiracy. It was more a collective intuition.

They did not fabricate tales to make people believe he had died in an accident or a murder or a mishap. They did not say that he had been sick. Many, I have found, were genuinely unsure themselves. Mainly, they simply did not speak of it. When asked, the answers were fleeting. If pressed, the long sighs of exasperation would quickly follow. Then silence. There were stories of much else, but this one tale, a bruised vein, had been extracted. So for a long time, no one asked.

When you seek to forget something, as opposed to gradually forgetting, what is the difference between forgetting and remembering? Whether we remember or forget, we are conjuring around the same ineffable quantity. First, we reveal it. *A suicide. A murder. An ambiguous death in a river.* Then we erase it.

It was as if the exact spiritual valence of Abuelo Juan José had been subtracted from this universe, leaving a cipher, a precise indentation in the shape of his body in the chill esparto grass by the river bank where he had been found. His bundle of years, his every *abrazo* and breath, were rendered a perfect absence, a photo negative of memory, a tear in the fabric of the world, impossible to mend. Sometimes, for me, it felt as if he had taken our entire past with him.

Still, the more I was aware of that absence, and all that it touched, the unanswered questions, the rumors and contradictions—the more it seemed to conjure images and stories out of a mysterious, unnameable place in the past no one had ever spoken of.

The waters of the San Antonio River must have been very warm that cold January morning in 1939, the morning of Abuelo's death. They must have been so warm they were swathed in another river of fog, thicker than the fog that was enveloping the entire city. I've seen that happen before, when there is unusually dense fog, which the newspapers reported that year. The heavy misting conditions, breaking periodically during the day but returning in the evening, had persisted since the last week of December, shrouding the Christmas holidays in gray mists. Traffic accidents were blamed on the fog. A derailed train. And the suicides. In *La Prensa,* the city's Spanish-language newspaper, there was a report that in response to the mysterious *niebla,* as fog is called in Spanish, a Mexican Evangelical church was holding prayer vigils, warning that such an unnatural fog would only aid the devil's work of spreading evil and confusion. In Spanish, *niebla* is also used to refer to mental and spiritual confusion.

Fog in the city is a knowing weather. It turns the traffic lights into ceremonial lamps, refracting the streetlight through the trees into sprays of glowing beams. San Antonio fogs are as old as the place itself, as much a part of the city as the river. Each year, after the Texas earth has been chilled through several months of winter, a strong gulf breeze suddenly gusts to the northwest through the thickly planted orange orchards of the Rio Grande Valley, delighting cattle across the sandy plains, finally stalling over San Antonio like a dome of vapors released from a primeval ocean.

In that foggy weather, with the city shrouded in cloud, it feels as if all the heavens have been stilled, the planets have stopped turning, and the cold, damp atmosphere hangs there, close and opaque. People stay at home. Every sound is amplified, every motion of the body seems laborious and futile. A quiet morning is shaken only by the sound of cars slashing long thin seams of rain along the wet street outside.

Like the sluggish, light-absorbing mists of Britain I witnessed later, these Texas fogs reverse the polarities of the everyday—the body and its senses begin to retreat from the outside world—an unmoving wakefulness, usually unnoticed, is discovered there, overwhelmingly vivid. The smell of freshly cut carpet grass becomes too sweet to bear.

Any light pierces the retina in fiery silk threads. As a child, I thought these fogs, the weather of ill humors, just gave me headaches.

There are other, older fogs that do not roll or diffuse, that do not lift at midday to allow the sun to dry out the saturated earth. Such fogs are the weather of eternity in the world of the ancient Nahua culture, a legacy of the Azteca Indians. The *nieblas* of this world are believed to be gateways to those hidden realms of heaven and the underworld, Tamoanchan and Tlalocan, where the spirits of the ancestors dwell. This image of fogs as the entrance to other worlds wasn't just a flight of fancy. In his account of the conquest of Mexico, Bernal Díaz de Castillo describes how Cortés's army, marching across Mexico during their campaign toward the Aztec capital, was overtaken by a rapidly descending fog somewhere in the gulf coastal mountains—a fog so dense it seemed to transform day to twilight instantly, leaving the army frightened with superstition and cowering against possible attack.

Traveling today through the same lands, these ancient fogs are still present. On my own journey retracing the fateful route of Cortés's army, I stopped in a high-valley farming village called Ixhuacán, in the southern mountain region of the present-day state of Veracruz, Mexico. I was looking for directions to find the ruins of the Great Wall of Tlaxcala, a massive battlement that had been built as a defense by the fierce Tlaxcalteca Indian warriors.

It was a bright afternoon. There were few customers in the mercado, the tiny village market, and the several vendors, who seemed to speak only the Indian Nahuatl language, were in a terrible hurry to close their stands, piling stacks of white corn and yellow squash into boxes they carried off with them. I thought I might have arrived too close to siesta hour.

Then, when I asked again for directions, "*¡Que ya viene la niebla!*" one of the farmers said to me. The fog is coming, he said, pointing up toward the peaks of the hills just to the east of Ixhuacán. There, looking like an army with a sea of white banners, another ageless gulf fog was rolling down the hills in great clouds to the valley floor. I watched the fingers of canopy mist as they claimed every rocky promontory, every spindly stand of tall ponderosa pines, until the fog arrived in the village, filling the streets from east to west, leaving behind an overcast world that was suddenly desolate and abandoned. It was hard to tell what hour of day it was. In the distance, toward the village plaza, voices speaking softly in low tones seemed to hover, disembodied, *en la niebla.*

Sitting down on a bench to wait until some of the haze lifted to continue driving, I thought the fog of Ixhuacán seemed a place outside of time, never ending, a changeless empire ruled by exhalations from the Gulf of Mexico that ranged from the Yucatán, up along Mexico's curving belly in the east, into central Texas, all the way to San Antonio. I expected to see familiar spirits of ancestors walking in those cobbled streets. Uncles and aunts and grandfather spirits. In that domain of fog, dwelling in the old time of the land, we could all move freely between past, present, and future.

I waited for them there in the quietest heart of the cloud.

The year 1939 began under a pall of fear and foreboding.

The Spanish civil war was in deadlock. Headlines spoke of ominous portents in faraway places: EUROPE AWAITS IMPORTANT EVENTS. San Antonio newspapers reported British prime minister Neville Chamberlain's impending journey to Rome to make a peace pact with Italian dictator Benito Mussolini and his Fascist Grand Council, hoping to complete the agreements begun in Munich—and thereby to avoid war. In Mexico, a series of mysterious monumental stone heads of the ancient Olmeca people had been discovered in the jungles of the gulf coast. While, for months, San Antonio had been the scene of numerous strikes that had been met with lockouts and violent clashes between the largely Mexican Pecan Shellers' Union strikers and local police. Pecans were one of the city's chief exports, along with traditional caramel pecan candies that had been transplanted from Mexico. For the Mexicans of San Antonio who still had jobs, the Depression had only worsened their predicament: working long and earning little. That year the pecan shellers complained they sometimes weren't paid at all for work already done.

Those were years of great seething and foment in the city, when the old Mexico that was left in San Antonio was dying, or being snuffed out, and everybody seemed to know it. San Antonio was being electrified, paved, the Texas sky knitted together with telegraph and telephone wires. The English-language newspapers, the *Light* and the *Express*, covered the story of the death of things Mexican with a jaunty, superior tone of labored nostalgia, like a drawn-out elegy for a primitive, antique, and outmoded world that was steadily disappearing. With no real regrets.

In the clinic of the Discalced Sisters of Saint Teresa, an old Mexican Indian scout, Rafael Cantú, who had once guarded south Texas stagecoaches from menacing Comanche warrior bands, was dying. He showed the photographer a moon-shaped scar on his left thigh where he had been pierced by an arrow in a raid near the Frio River, to the south, in 1876. He told the reporter who went to visit him that, at ninety-six, it was enough now. He had seen too much, he was ready to go. When he was born, San Antonio de Bejar was Mexico. Then, for a while, it was just plain Texas.

"We were Tejanos," he was quoted saying, emphasizing the word Texas Mexicans used to refer to themselves. "*Éramos Tejanos,* then all of a sudden, the Gringos really came!" According to Cantú, they shrank the river and widened the streets. They closed the old cantinas and tore down the woods.

"Now it's Estados Unidos. Who knows what it will be next? It's my time to go, I think." In the photograph, grizzled-faced Cantú lies in bed, smoking a pipe, casting his haggard gaze straight into the camera while being tended to by a pair of ivory-wimpled nuns.

The old Mexican mercado was declared a health hazard. The city's new Department of Public Health began a campaign in the marketplace to close the public dining stands of the Chili Queens, the Mexicana street vendors whose homemade *picadillo* had long been one of the famous attractions of downtown San Antonio. The aromatic chili stands once stretched bench-to-bench the length of an entire block, ringing the grand square around Haymarket Plaza. Their long tables were covered in oilcloth, cluttered with bottles of oil and vinegar, wooden bowls of salt and ground cumin, and decorated with plates of tomatoes, cilantro, chiles, and avocados. Uncle Jesse remembers how, in the chilly winter months of January and February, long plumes of steam rose up over the large clay pots, and the women stirred their *picadillo* and beans with wooden spoons.

In one corner of the plaza, on Commerce Street, my father would linger awhile on a curb, listening to Lydia Mendoza, the haunting singer of bittersweet *Norteño* ballads about deceitful men and treacherous love. On weekends, she would sit on a wooden basket next to a stand of tortilla makers, hunched over her guitar, intoning all her songs like dirges in a scabrous voice that sounded as if she had grains of an exquisite sand inside her throat.

The Health Department also banned the noisy funeral processions that had been one of the most visible public traditions of Mexican San Antonio and dated back to colonial times. When a Mexicano died, the body would remain at home for a night or two as family and friends streamed through, bringing tamales or tacos de chorizo, paying their respects, and joining in around-the-clock recitation of the rosary. Then, on the day of the funeral, mourners would be joined by a small band of musicians dressed in the white cotton garments of Mexican campesinos. The trumpet player would lead the way through the streets, followed by a violinist, an accordionist, and a *bajo sexto* player.

In one old painting by the Swiss artist Theodore de Gentilz, who lived in San Antonio during the late nineteenth century, the funeral band is shown in front of the pallbearers. They hoist the coffin aloft on their shoulders as solemnly dressed loved ones trail out of a door and into the street. The small cortege is followed by a lone saxophone player whose brooding melodies are said to have intertwined with the plaints of the bereaved.

Our family quickly established its own traditions in the city. Among the Garcias, simple, deliberate action was all that was required to hold the *tormentas* of the world at bay. You must always keep your word. And it is also good to be punctual. Once they had both settled in San Antonio, the old Garcia twins, my great-grandfather Jacobo and his brother, Abrán, religiously kept their weekly appointment to eat and visit together every Saturday at noon. Accustomed to crossing the plaza in Palaú before, they now lived at opposite ends of a city. Abuelito Jacobo continued to live with my grandparents and the family on Parsons Street on the southwest edge of downtown, and Tío Abrán lived on the near west side of the city on Montana Street.

The weekly rendezvous of Abuelos Jacobo and Abrán was a family *compromiso*. It was carried out in a precise ritual, which was always the Garcia way. On the mornings of one of their visitas, Abuelito would first set my aunt Bea to rolling a pocketful of cornshuck cigarettes made from Cuerno Y Concha tobacco, which Jacobo would joyfully smoke and share with his brother over the course of the day. Another aunt ironed the old man's shirt on a sheet laid across the long wooden kitchen table, making sure later that the top button was properly fastened before he knotted his tie, since his fingers were stiff with arthritis and calloused from a lifetime of manual labor.

One of my uncles remembers how, on those mornings, Abuelo Jacobo would sing a rhyme to them in the high-pitched voice of the famous Mexican clown Don Fito:

Mira la luna! Comiendo una tuna
y tirando la cascara
hasta la laguna!

Look at the moon! Eating a cactus fruit
and throwing the peel
down into the lagoon!

Well into their eighties, they each would still set off from home alone, around ten thirty, bound for the bridge over the San Antonio River at Commerce Street, which started near the circular pink granite tower that looked like a minaret, and which Abuelito called "that Arabic water tower." Sometimes they would have lunch across the street at Schilo's, a traditional German deli where the two old Mexicans always ordered the same thing: the specialty split pea and ham soup and corned beef sandwiches. According to my aunts, who accompanied the *ancianos* every now and then on their weekly *paseos,* people on the busy sidewalks of Houston Street would step to one side and make room for the two staggeringly identical twins, walking with a deliberate, synchronous gait.

Jacobo and Abrán never ceased to relish the awe they could provoke from the city dwellers around them.

According to *La Prensa,* by the ninth day of January there had already been three suicides in San Antonio. Surely, the paper reported, the year's heavy fog was confounding people to their deaths. Then, on the tenth, it carried the banner headline at the top of the front page.

> *MEXICANO AHOGADO EN EL RIO SAN ANTONIO*
> (Mexican Drowned in the San Antonio River)
> *El cuerpo inanimado de un mexicano fué encontrado el lunes en la mañana flotando en el rio San Antonio, cerca de la calle Simpson, en el Parque Roosevelt.*

The story tells how the inanimate body of Juan José Santos was found floating in the river near Simpson Street in Roosevelt Park. It says the body was identified by the deceased's son, my father—also Juan José—and by Carlos Garcia, my great-uncle Chale, youngest brother to my grandmother. Two homicide detectives were reportedly present along with Coroner and Judge Raymond Gerhardt, and two greatcoated firemen, identified as A. L. Rathke and A. G. Pompa, who tried for a half hour to revive the forty-nine-year-old man before giving up. According to the *San Antonio Express*:

> *At first, the police had believed it to be a death by accident, but after Judge Gerhardt investigated the case thoroughly, he concluded that it was a suicide. According to Gerhardt, "Death overcame Santos in the waters of the San Antonio River into which he had imprudently flung himself." It is the fourth suicide of the year.*

The city's official death certificate also makes their conclusions clear:

Manner of Injury: *Deceased jumped in river.*
Nature of Injury: *Drowned.*
External Cause of Death: *Suicide.*

The detectives, Fred Littlepage and Ed Amacker, told the *San Antonio Light* that Juan José left his house at 116 Parsons Street at six that morning, and the family had reported him missing at seven.

> *The body was found at 8 A.M. floating in the San Antonio River. Santos was found by a son, Juan Santos, Jr., and a brother-in-law, Carlos Garcia, near Simpson Street. Santos Sr.'s wife had asked her son to follow his father as he left the house shortly after 6 A.M. She said he had suffered a nervous breakdown several months ago and had spoken Sunday night of "going away."*

The newspaper's account of the events leading up to Abuelo's death ended abruptly by noting that,

> *The pair followed Santos to the vicinity of the river but lost him in the fog.*

Had Uela accompanied my father on the morning of his death? The brief report then says his body was found by my father and great-uncle just an hour later. *La Prensa* reported that Abuelo was employed as a foreman at the Petroleum Machine and Foundry Company, and referred ominously to how he had recently been the victim of *"una penosa y grave enfermedad,"* "a tormenting, dangerous infirmity."

My aunt Connie still remembers with undimmed consternation how *La Prensa* reported her father's death as a suicide.

"It was not. I just know it!" she insists.

In their version, the *San Antonio Light* carried a picture with the headline: "ALL IN VAIN." The photograph shows the earnest young Mexicano fireman, A. G. Pompa, in a cap and heavy canvas peacoat crouched over my grandfather's body, which is wrapped in a thick shroud of woolen blankets. A pair of respirator tubes run from a pump in the background, down into the long thick folds of the blanket, where the fireman's right hand seems to lie gently on Abuelo Juan José's forehead. The tousled salt-and-pepper hair at the very pate of his head is barely visible in the blanket's inky shadow.

8

Aztec
Theater

El Teatro Aztec

*I braid the chain of beads on the old wooden rosary around the white-gloved fingers of one hand. As Padrino to my First Communion, my uncle Richard had just given me the rosary, which he said had been in his family a long time. Standing outside the chapel at Mount Sacred Heart Catholic School, my first grade classmates and I look like initiates in a religious training program for Mexican lounge singers, all of us dressed in immaculate white suits, white clip-on ties, and black shoes, our hair oiled and combed with a tiny wave.*

The aged nuns, who have names like Sister Alfred Euthanasius and Sister Cornelius Dolorosa, hover over us, primping ties and collars, and clasping our hands for prayer in front of us. As we prepare to march down the center aisle, the small chapel is already hazy with new incense.

"Love, love me do! You know I love you!" sings my friend Dennis Perez nervously to himself, standing next to me in the double file we have

formed after the offertory. We are all about to eat from the body of Christ for the first time in our lives, and most of us are dumb with fear.

We had been preparing for weeks, using unconsecrated hosts, but we had been told that in this Mass, the bread would be magically transformed into the actual flesh of Christ, from the body he'd had nearly two thousand years ago. This, we were told, was the greatest mystery. The day before, we had all said our First Confession, reciting the precise phrasing of the opening petition from memory, and then delivering a litany of our misdeeds reaching back to when we were born. After receiving and fulfilling the penance of prescribed Hail Marys and Our Fathers, our souls were again as clean as the day we were born, except, that is, for the indelible blotch of original sin. We were prepared to receive the feast of the body of Christ.

I approach the priest, standing before the altar. After the Communion wafer is laid on my tongue, I remember how we had been instructed not to chew it. That is blasphemy. Instead, I let it dissolve like a piece of lace made of ice as I kneel down in the very front pew. I wonder whether Jesus will return and the world will end in my lifetime. It's a possibility, isn't it? I figure that living through the Day of Judgment is probably better than dying, anyway.

But as I close my eyes to pray the Our Father, as I had been taught, I see something I have never seen before. It is a place, but it has no color or shape. I open and close my eyes again, and it is still there. A place of nothing, as old as creation. To the extent that there is light there in the emptiness, it is present only in the faintest filaments and webs, and utterly still, silent and remote feeling, as if it were millions and millions of miles from everything and everyone I know. Tiny particles of dust seem to be suspended, motionless in front of me. It feels like a place beyond time and the world. It feels like the vacuum of outer space we're launching the Gemini astronauts into, only now there is no planet to come back to. When everyone and everything of this world has passed away and all the light and heat of the universe has been extinguished, there would be only this. A cold, motionless Nada. An ocean without a shore. An infinitude of nothing.

I feel a cold sweat run up my back and open my eyes to see the priest at the altar meticulously wiping the golden chalice clean. I look around me and everything I see is a consolation. My fellow novices are still at their prayers. Behind me, I see my parents and Uncle Richard looking on proudly. Even the polished wood of the pew seems intimate to me.

The world had not passed away—but that place I had a glimpse of was still there, inside of me, beckoning like the true home I would someday return to.

There are mysteries held within a family and there are mysteries held within the deeper soul of a nation. We were of a people that had seen the ground beneath our feet renamed several times over the last five hundred years, a Mestizo nation derived partly by intrepid travelers who had left their Spanish homeland far behind—across a formidable span of ocean—and people who believed they had been living in these lands since the time of the world's creation.

But apart from the mute testimony of the mission ruins, and the quiet, slowly ebbing presence of the ruins of old San Antonio, no one, either family or schoolteachers, had told me that the city we lived in was already nearly three hundred years old before I was born. It had been known for nearly two hundred years first as San Antonio de Bejar, named after the Duke of Bejar; then later renamed San Antonio de Valero, after the duke quarreled with his brother, the Viceroy of Mexico and Marquis de Valero. Over the entrance to the Spanish Governor's Palace in downtown San Antonio, you can still see the Hapsburg coat of arms, colors and symbols of the Spanish royal family in the eighteenth century.

And for centuries before the Europeans had arrived, Indians had lived in these same territories, migrating on foot with the cycle of sea-sons, following the circuits of the planets, the serpentine sky dance of the moon and Venus, awed by the majestic, incremental movements of the deeper, distant stars. They fished the same creeks, the ones we called Cibolo, the Salado, and the Coleta. The ones we fished with cane poles for gray catfish and sun perch.

It wasn't just our family that remained quiet to this past. It was as if all the Mexicanos had forgotten it.

The lands around the city seemed so new and raw, so forbidding and untrodden, even when I was a child. Driving out from San Anto-nio, within a half hour, rickety barbed wire fences ran the borders of land that looked wild and untameable. The landscape to the north was riven with rocky gorges and craggy hills that had slowed the inexorable extension of San Antonio's border in that direction. Instead, for a cen-tury, the city had grown very slowly across the flatlands to the south, east, and west, as farms and ranches were replaced gradually with row houses and San Antonio's first suburbs. It seemed impossible to imag-ine how people had lived before there was a settlement to protect them against the heat, the droughts, the floods, and the scarcity of food.

The Spanish conquistador, Cabeza de Vaca, passed through these riverlands on his shipwrecked odyssey from Florida to New Mexico in the 1530s. Searching for emissaries of New Spain, he found the Indi-ans, Coahuiltecas and Xarames, living a meager life in the hardscrabble landscape where they fished, gathered roots and berries, and journeyed north to hunt scarce deer for venison—and still there was hunger.

The city emanated a deeply old feeling. It was partly the land on which the city was situated, the settled river plain, the countless springs, the open northern views to the hills, the terrain sloping south-ward to Mexico. But there was also something old about the people themselves. The earliest Spanish colonizers to arrive were a group of families from the Canary Islands, itself a place of great antiquity in the Old World. The ancient Canarios from the islands off the coast of Africa buried their dead in elaborate circular stone cairns on high ocean cliffs, and they practiced a form of mummification not unlike that developed in the time of Egypt's great dynasties.

There were only a few *San Antonioenses* who could, with authentic documents and proper titles, trace their bloodlines to those original Canario families, although rumors of this noble lineage periodically swirled around successful Mexicans, like lawyers, doctors, and judges. The most well known were Don Demostenio and Doña Herlinda Zuniga, brother and sister. The last of their august line from the islands, which included some of the early governors of the Villa de San Fernando, they already were in their late eighties when I was receiving my First Communion. These two always seemed to be shipwrecked and abandoned in an alien century. The San Antonio they had known as children was gone.

The only sanctuary for their memories was in the limestone vault of the San Fernando Cathedral downtown, in the front pew on the left side of the aisle, near the giant marble baptistery. This was the place in the old church that had been vouchsafed to the Zunigas by the Creator at the beginning of time. From that perch, Doña Herlinda, petite but strong-boned, dressed in heavy black lace gowns with a silver chignon, wielded her cane against the ankles of Communioners who ventured too close to her prayer space.

Don Demostenio was pale, short, and bald, but very erect in posture and always in a white suit, Panama hat, and a white handlebar mustache. He looked like an Hispano Eric von Stroheim, wearing a gold-rimmed monocle, while he reviewed the lunch special menu at the Mexican Manhattan, a Tex-Mex diner on Soledad Street that was Uncle Lico's favorite. Sitting together in a booth at that diner, Don Demostenio and Doña Herlinda looked as if they had walked out of an El Greco painting and were now stranded here, like two old Spanish angels.

In the early 1960s, it felt as if the long story of San Antonio, however old it might prove to be, was beginning to wane. Born as I was into the budding years of rock and roll, with its incipient electronically communicated international mass culture, the fragments of tales and characters, like the Zuniga siblings, were the few remaining remnants of the inconclusive myths of our city's origin. Even as I was learning to speak and write English properly, listening to the Beatles in my father's pickup truck, mourning JFK, watching *The Beverly Hillbillies,* going to Disneyland, and doing most of the things that made up a kid's initiation into the secret sciences of the American way of life, the streets of San Antonio were an umbilical tether to a past that otherwise seemed to be disintegrating, memory by memory.

The world seemed poised at the gateway to an age when the earth itself might be abandoned, along with its millennial legacy of discord, war, and genocide. I was born in the year the sleek taper of a Russian rocket pierced a microthin vapor mist at the furthest edge of the stratosphere for the first time and set the Sputnik satellite in orbit, a whirling echo of our nomadic longing to see farther and farther across the next horizon.

San Antonio, and every city on the planet for that matter, might soon become merely the places from which we set out, into the vast reaches of space. My uncle Charles worked in Houston for the photographic lab at NASA, which developed all of the pictures from the Gemini and Apollo voyages. Over the years we accumulated an exhaustive snapshot album of the missions. We came to San Antonio after centuries of exploration and moving settlements. The image of an Apollo astronaut, dressed in silvery garments, like a seraph, suspended weightless in space against a backdrop of the planet itself, made the path of further exploration clear to me.

And perhaps this new migration would echo that of the past. All across the Americas, from the great Cahokia mound in Illinois to

Chaco Canyon in New Mexico, ancient Teotihuacán, near Mexico City, and Machu Pichu in Peru, great cities had been built, sometimes over hundreds of years, only to be suddenly disinhabited, left intact, abandoned entirely to ghosts. They left their dead ancestors behind, elaborate buildings standing, painted pots unbroken, setting out for who knows where.

Walking once with a National Park Service archaeologist on a searing, chrome-sky day through the rooms of the crescent-shaped Pueblo Bonito ruins in Chaco Canyon in northwestern New Mexico, I was told that there was no evidence anywhere in the canyon of war, famine, or disaster to explain why the Anasazi left their great city at Chaco behind in the eighth century of the present era. The petroglyphs that dot the length of the canyon's stone walls, of whirling spirals, lightning bolts, handprints, deer, and people, offer no answers that we can read today. Neither do the ceremonial burials of birds, in hundreds of tiny ceramic boxes, the room-size caches of abalone shells, the great bundles of porcupine quills that had all been secreted away and forgotten after they left.

"Maybe that's just how they saw things," the archaeologist said. The place remains sacred today, and Indian people go there for rites and prayers, leaving behind small offerings wrapped in cloth of blue corn, falcon feathers, or red sand in the empty rooms of the ruins.

"Maybe they did what they were supposed to do here, during a certain time, then they just moved on," she said, staring down into the great hollow of one of Chaco's kivas, the sunken circular earth chambers used by the Anasazi for prayer and ceremonies. "They just moved on, to something else."

Maybe it was just as well to be done with San Antonio. In the fifty years since the Santos had made their home there, most of our joys and griefs, private and shared, had been mapped onto the city's streets and barrios, onto its downtown precinct, its hills, and its river. It was a half century of tales told to that place, but the city was a reticent witness.

At the founding of many American cities lurk unsavory tales of invasion and mayhem, usually whitewashed or forgotten. Whether it's the hoary presence of old buildings or a nebula of run-down shacks and other ruins, the evidence of the past—raw, weathered, and scarred—raises accusatory questions. How did this all come about? What price was paid, by whom, and for whose sake? Who was here before the whole story began? Troubled by the wraiths of American history, our cities have been bled by the suburbs and washed in the waters of urban renewal. They have emerged cleansed of the taint of the sin, discord, and, in some cases, the ethnicity of the past.

Yet, the past is recorded, even if imperfectly. On a visit to San Antonio in 1854, Frederick Law Olmsted, architect of New York City's Central Park, felt like an outsider there, writing in his journal of "the dirty, grim, old stuccoed stone cathedral, whose cracked bell is now clunking for vespers, in a tone that bids us no welcome, as more of the intruding race who have caused all this progress, on which its traditions, like its imperturbable dome, frown down."

In the same year, the historian Timothy Matovina tells of a San Antonian who stormed the sanctuary of Mission San Juan and began to demolish the statues and images of Jesus and the saints with a hammer. As he smashed a figurine of St. Martin de Porres, he was stopped by other Tejanos. At the time of the conquest, for many of the Indios and Mestizos alike, the saints of the Catholic sacred pantheon became the focus of the devotions that had once been offered to the Pre-Columbian gods. These Mexican gods were no gods at all, the vandal told those who restrained him. If Mexicans worshipped the true God, he would never have let the Gringos take Texas.

We lived in the ruins of that time, when the faint echoes of the conquest had become mirages and spectacles. On Saturdays, all day long, with brothers, cousins, and friends, we watched Kung-Fu triple features at the Aztec Theater, a cinema palace in downtown San Antonio. The walls of the theater were decorated with colorful panels of Mayan and Aztecan glyphs, interspersed with the faces of various gods, all presided over by the Feathered Serpent God Quetzalcoatl, whose image surrounded the screen as Bruce Lee threw slow-motion aerial drop kicks. Coyolxauqhui, the moon-faced Mexica night goddess, her face pierced and gilded, stared down at us in the red light of the exit signs.

The theater was inaugurated in 1926, after a San Antonio architect sent assistants all over Mexico to collect images and ideas from the ruins of Maya, Zapoteca, Mixteca, Tolteca, and Azteca Indian cities. The curtain painting depicted the first meeting between Cortés and Motecuhzoma, the Aztec emperor. Thousands of people were turned away from that opening, according to one of my great-uncles who remembers being there, having sneaked in early in the afternoon. After the movie, he said, there was a grand Aztecan costume pageant called, "The Court of Montezuma," where the performers enacted the scene on the curtain.

On Houston Street, the Majestic Theater specialized in Godzilla and race car movies. It had its own lavish stone proscenium decked with tableaux mort of stucco turkeys, Indian warriors, and feathered Cherubim. Part Bavaria, part American West, this theater was where we watched double features of *Godzilla vs. the Smog Monster* and *Mothra* beneath a ceiling lit by flickering evening stars, across which wispy desert clouds would slowly pass. Once, when Maria, Grandmother's housemaid, accompanied us, she insisted the sky showed every sign of raining soon and urged us to leave.

The Texas Theater, a block up from the Majestic, belonged to John Wayne and Elvis. We went there on school field trips to see *Red*

River, *The Alamo*, and, finally, *True Grit*, where a one-eyed John Wayne looked broken down and spent. On weekends, they let Grandmother Leandra in for free at the Texas. She had the reputation of being Elvis's oldest fan in San Antonio. Grandmother liked how well behaved he was, even if he made a wrong decision in life, like in *King Creole*. According to Grandmother, he always saw the truth in the end—and he always had a good heart, which was the most important thing.

Further up Houston Street was the art deco Alameda Theater, with its three-story-high neon marquee in the shape of a feather. Here, mariachis on horseback would fill the stage, playing their instruments for a final encore performance of "Guadalajara" at the end of the three-hour-long stage shows, which capped off the day's screening of Cantinflas movies. The audience whooped and sang along as each of the evening's guest stars came out one more time and delivered a verse into the microphone.

We walked amid Moorish beehive towers hewn from red granite, through the shaded courtyard of the Spanish Governor's Palace, past the turquoise and maroon walls of El Tenampa Bar. The wide sidewalks of Houston Street lit up like a Mexican carnival every Saturday night, crowded with strolling old folks, young lovers, cowboys, hippies, and the elegant *pachucos* in their baggy shirts and pants and pointed, black patent leather shoes.

Throughout my childhood, at the end of each day, my parents would pack us into the red Ford station wagon and drive us downtown, first along Houston Street, taking a right at the Alamo, stopping at the plaza in front of the old mission. A street musician named Bongo Joe, whom we heard had come from New Orleans, was usually there, playing two banged-up oil drums with rattle mallets, whistling sultry blues and singing in lower, raspier tones than Louis Armstrong in the hot

Texas night. Sometimes he just let his rolling, melancholy beat go on forever, changing with the shifting warm breezes. The people who gathered to listen threw coins into the giant wheelbarrow Bongo used to carry his drums off at the end of the night.

We would drive up Commerce Street, then pause by the Plaza de las Islas in front of the cathedral to watch the circular colonnade of water of the old fountain that was illuminated in a battery of coruscating colored lights. Sometimes, as a special treat during the summer, we stopped at a watermelon stand out on Fredericksburg Road on the way home, eating great crescent-shaped slices over picnic benches under a corrugated tin roof, spitting our seeds out into the moonlit dirt.

That "San Anto" of memory, already a relic then of a more distant past, was destined, like its precursor, to be abandoned, lost, preserved only in old photographs and in our fragmentary remembrance. Houston Street today is an avenue of ghosts. The Texas Theater was torn down except for its limestone and colored tile facade and box office, left to adorn a telecommunications corporation headquarters. The Aztec Theater is condemned and falling to ruin, the gods' faces marred with graffiti, the stone water fountains green with algae.

After virtually disintegrating by the turn of the century, the mission ruins were restored as national parks. The historic mercado district, all wood and painted plaster, was stripped of its minstrels and chili stands in the 1930s and finally torn down in the 1970s, only to be replaced with a theme-park version made from bricks the color of a Ramada Inn. San Antonio is a palimpsest of erasures, a thoroughly modern and robust Texas tourism and convention mecca, inhabited now by a pueblo of ghosts. It is a hidden-away Mexican city where a lot of old accounts are still being settled, where blood memory runs deep. Not too long ago, an Anglo killed a Mexican American after an evening of drinking at an ice house on the city's western edge. According to the sheriff, "They got into an argument about whether the Anglos had stolen Texas from Mexico, and what happened at the battle of the Alamo."

Downtown bears little testimony to the legacy of conflagration, or for that matter, to the deep history of settlement lying just beneath the apparent face of this place that used to be called San Antonio de Valero. Even the restored Alamo, with its stone walls the color of pristine ivory linen, nestled alongside a sweetly manicured plaza with a gazebo, makes it hard to imagine a bloody battle could have happened there. But just in case you've forgotten the old story of the fight for Texas independence, the IMAX theater a block away runs continuous screenings of *The Battle for Freedom*, which retells the heroic tale and features Davy Crockett wearing a wristwatch.

The newly opened Hard Rock Cafe in San Antonio is a virtual cantina, where conventioneers can sip Lone Star longnecks and hear Tex-Mex accordion virtuosi in secure, suburbanite environs. It sits near an old island in the San Antonio River where the city's gentry once maintained an exclusive club in which no Mexicans were welcome. Across the street and down the Disneyesque riverwalk, a quaintly Spanish-styled Planet Hollywood is the other twin star of the city's new downtown, more patronized by tourists than denizens of San Antonio.

Yet, at Lerma's on Zarzamora Street, you can still do the Aztec two-step to unadulterated live *conjunto* bands. The ancient aqueduct behind Mission Espada will still carry you back in time to the days when these lands were first written into the script of the conquest. Drive the elevated expressways into town and there's a bank office the shape of a Teotihuacán pyramid in your rearview mirror. The Tower of the Americas lies ahead, looking like a UFO hovering over downtown. Floating above the cicada songs and the dense canopy of trees in the barrio are the yellow poblano tile cupolas of Little Flower Church. This place casts a spell that makes the alien its own, that saturates the present and the future in the past, as if it were inescapable, as if the real and imaginary were meant to be swirled in the same timeless south Texas vortex.

My father remained silent, but, over the years, more stories about Abuelo Juan José's death began to emerge, *poco a poco,* in quiet conversations in garages, backyards, and kitchens with aunts and uncles.

They tell me a Mexican circus came to San Antonio in the late fall of 1938. The ornately painted big top was installed in a large field on the eastern outskirts of town. The thick, acrid smell of the unwashed animals hung in the air across the grounds. As most of the crowd made its way into the tent, a surging tangle of spectators in one makeshift wooden arena nearby bet furiously on a pair of already bloodied roosters. Clouds of dust and confetti swirled around everyone's heads.

Juan José was disoriented that night. He hadn't really wanted to go, but several families had planned to go together, so he had felt obliged. The noise seemed to annoy him, the smells of the crowded fairway left him dizzy. When the circus began, my aunt remembers he was nervous and fidgeting. There were bears dressed as Mexican farmers, spider monkeys dressed as nuns. One clown who rushed into the stands with a Chihuahua in his sombrero was made up like Pancho Villa with a big nose and a bigger belly. In the center ring, a phalanx of charros rode the *paso de la muerte* round and round, gaining speed, until an Indio boy made his way from one of the horses onto an unsaddled stallion galloping in the middle of the pack. Juan José seemed disturbed by the number of things going on simultaneously in the three rings. He became quiet. Some in the family say that was where he got the *susto,* the spiritual fright that made him want to take his own life. That was the night he began to grow silent again, distant, and grim.

Soon, he became preoccupied with looking out the front porch window to see if anyone might be lurking on the sidewalk across the street, standing there in the lamplight. It had been a difficult year of mounting debts and worries for Juan José. The foundry missed pay-rolls. They had almost lost the house. The year was coming to an end and he alone knew a moment of decision was coming.

By Christmas, he had been deeply quiet for many weeks. He con-stantly went to the front windows of the house at night, pulling away the curtain to look out and see if anyone was in the street. *"Nada, nada, nada,"* he muttered to himself.

According to one of my aunts, on Christmas Eve my father and my uncle Raul together gave him a black leather aviator's jacket as a present. The family watched him open the professionally wrapped package, nervous about how he would receive it. As he opened the box from Joske's department store and pulled out the shiny leather jacket by the sleeves, he looked at it for a moment, brooding to himself, then threw it with disdain across the sofa and said he had no need for such a luxury. It should be returned.

Uela told her sister Tía Pepa that Abuelo Juan José had spoken of having to go away, though he would never explain why, or to where. He had been sleepless for weeks. On that morning, he got up early, and started looking out the window again, as he dressed himself, as always in suit and tie, for his foreman's job at the Petroleum com-pany. Uela remembered how she had watched him go to the bed of each child before he left the house, bending over to kiss each of the younger ones on the forehead. That felt like a *despedida,* and that terri-fied her.

❦

Toward the end of his life, Colonel Brackenridge had fallen into a melancholy about the fate of San Antonio, and especially the river, which had suffered and dwindled as a result of the rise of the city. In a late letter to a friend, Colonel Brackenridge had written, "I have seen this bold, bubbling laughing river dwindle and fade away. This river is my child and it is dying and I cannot stay here to see its last gasps. . . . I must go."

The colonel had been a believer in life after death, and after his death in 1920, at the age of eighty-eight, his elderly sister Eleanor sought to keep the house and the large estate on Burr Road ready for his expected return. Yet, with her brother and all his loud delight gone, Eleanor lost the spirit for the socials and recitals that were the center of life at Fernridge. Soon, the beige paint began peeling off the endless porch grilles that encircled the main house, and the limestone columns developed dark splotches of mildew and fungus. The glass greenhouse conservatory that my grandfather tended was closed, and the Santos family moved out. Abuelo Juan José took his first job as a die-caster at a foundry—Alamo Iron Works, near downtown San Antonio.

When Juan José visited the estate for the last time, in 1938, he found the once exquisite greenhouse conservatory in shambles. The stalks of elephant ears had collapsed under the weight of their giant leaves and lay dried, willy-nilly across the cobbled walks. Dried chrysanthemum petals were blowing in a warm breeze coming through a broken pane. One of my uncles remembered how his father quietly found one rose bush that was not yet entirely dead. He brought the pot onto the lawn outside, where he watered it with a bucket of spring water drawn fresh from the well.

No photographic record of the house on Burr Road, the first the family lived in together after Mexico, has survived. But in one photo-graph taken in 1920 by an official photographer of the colonel's, my grandparents stand side by side, their expressions solemn, each of them gripping the handle of a baby carriage where Aunt Connie sits wide-eyed. To one side, Uncle Raul sits astride his tricycle, wearing a white blouse with a harlequin collar and shorts, staring suspiciously at the photographer. My father, two years old, stands to the other side, in white smock and shorts, gripping his sister's hand in the carriage, and looking afraid. They are all in the shade of an arbor of giant hanging grape leaves. But in the background, visible only in the shade of the vines, are the great white columns that ran along the house's large wraparound porch. The house was torn down in the late 1930s, leav-ing only the foundation, covered in Johnson grass, to testify today to the place where the Santos and the Garcias had made one household together.

The last house Abuelo Juan José lived in lies beneath the ex-pressway downtown, somewhere underneath a massive embankment between the southeastern corner of Hemisfair Plaza and the new Alamodome. It was from this house, at 116 Parsons Street, that he had made his final journey on that morning in 1939.

Driving toward town on South St. Mary's Street, passing Roo-sevelt Park, where my father found his father's body, always gave me a shiver of emptiness, as if the cold, colorless atmosphere of deep space somehow gathered and eddied there, in the middle of the city. Yet, his last walk from home to that place was etched, invisibly, into the earth, each footprint marked, every breath drawn that day was traced out in the atmosphere to its faintest curl. Accelerating into the curve onto the bridge over the San Antonio River, afraid to look, I caught only glimpses of the water, the old rail bridge, the tall grasses and reeds along the bank.

I had a dream one night that I wrote in my journal back then:

I'm in a San Antonio cemetery, decorated with Mexican
paper flowers. I have the feeling I'm at my grandfather's grave.
The ground feels like a fabric stretched over an armature of taut
twine and hard clay. I reach down and slowly press my hand
through the easily parting ground. Underneath is air, cold air,
as if for miles and miles, and I put my arm in all the way to my
shoulder. I retrieve my hand, and it smells of nothing.

After the family gradually married and moved out of the house
on Parsons Street, Uela continued to live there until the late 1960s,
with Madrina and Uncle Manuel, Madrina's husband. By then it
was a neighborhood of mostly old Mexican dowagers. Their well-
kept houses were large and empty, nestled inside lush front yard gardens, and overhung by expansive, aged oak trees. When the city was
preparing for the 1968 Hemisfair, this pocket settlement of *Viejitas*
was an easy target for the developers' plans to find a corridor to
build an expressway straight into the heart of the city. Uela moved to
one last home, on Cincinnati Street, on the west side of town. The
Parsons Street neighborhood, which she never returned to, was
razed.

The old Mexican precincts downtown weren't the only sanctuaries for ghosts. San Antonio's suburbs were haunted, too. There were
lots of new houses being built in the wooded northern hills of the city,
out Vance Jackson Road, well beyond the onetime reach of the old
missions. With the swarm of developers competing with each other
to build quicker and cheaper, the houses were inexpensive. Bearing
names like Colonial Hills, Colonial Oaks, and Colonies North, the sub-
divisions evoked a polite, generic image of the city's Spanish past that
had been, by then, all but erased in time and forgotten by most of us.
Old barrio streets that were two hundred years old bore names like
Morales, Ruiz, Guadalupe, and Colorado. In the neighborhood we

moved to in the 1960s, the freshly named, newly laid streets were Marlborough, Hopeton, Dudley, Belvoir, and Tiffany.

We were at the city's northern frontier, already in the low, rising steppes of the hill country of central Texas. Deer, weasels, skunks, and rabbits ambled through the neighborhood on cool mornings at dawn. If there had been rain, they would go down to the wide limestone arroyo that cut the neighborhood in half.

Once, while driving my great-uncle Frank home after a party at our house, he suddenly pointed at a lawn we were passing at the corner of Marlborough and Dudley, and said excitedly, *"¡Tlacuaches! ¡Mira no mas!"*

I stopped the car, "What is it, Tío?"

"Un tlacuache," he whispered. "Possum."

Older than Spanish, the word's primordial rasp—*Tlacuache*—came from the name for possum in Nahuatl of the Aztecs. It hung in the air as we watched the startled mother possum leading two babies crawling behind her across the plush carpet of viridian St. Augustine grass in a neighbor's front yard. It was not so late, but there was a complete silence over the neighborhood, except for the crickets. Porchlights glowed through webs of oak tree branches, floating and swaying slowly in the air like amber-colored mandalas. Uncle Frank's gaze stayed fixed on the small family of possums, leaning forward, mouth agape, as if he were awaiting some message, some dispatch from the time of the Tlacuache.

The conquest, as distant in the Mexican past as it is, runs through most of our Mexican American families like an active fault line. Some think of themselves as Mexican, but never Indio. Others think of themselves as Spanish. Among many Hispanos in the United States, this was often regarded as the preferred family origin. After all, Spaniards are European. My suburban upbringing, where Mexicans were still few, only had the effect of magnifying this divide. One cousin even went by the nickname "Sanka," instead of Santos, for a while.

To be a child in San Antonio, dark-skinned, with a Latino sur-name, to be "Spanish," was to be something other than a "Taco Ben-der," a "Wetback," or a "Greaser," something other than poor, downtrodden, backward, and desolate, which is how Mexicans had been made to feel over our long history in Texas. Eventually, we took those feelings into the secret holds of our own hearts.

When I rode in my uncle Manuel's 1954 pearl-colored, wing-finned Chevrolet, rumbling thunderously with its great, roaring *mofle* through the new, white neighborhood we lived in on the city's north side, I ducked under the backseat window, fearful some of my new friends might see me in that hulking behemoth jalopy, which was very definitely an old Mexican's car. I wasn't ashamed of Uncle Manuel, but I knew the Anglo kids from my new public school did not understand the glories of these vehicles, decked with *conjunto* music radio, saints' cards, dashboard religious statuary, and furry dice, and I was too young not to give a damn. For his part, Uncle Manuel was infinitely proud of his car.

At Mount Sacred Heart, the school where I had been before we moved to the new neighborhood, many of the kids were Mexicanos like me. When we took our First Communion, we had looked like campesinos in our pressed white suits and caramel brown skin. It hadn't seemed odd that we were all Mexican since, although it was hardly ever hostile, segregation between whites and Mexicans was still common in San An-tonio then.

Every year, during San Antonio's annual Fiesta Week, the city celebrated the victory of the Texans over Mexico in the Battle of San Jacinto, known as the Battle of Flowers, the last battle in the war for Texas independence in 1836. We would be visited on the school grounds by the newly crowned King Antonio. He served as the regent for the two weeks of festivities and was elected from an exclusively white, century-old social organization in the city called The Cavaliers. We would all be assembled on both sides of a marching promenade as he was driven onto the campus in a polished powder blue Cadillac convertible.

With each year's new king, I was always astounded at how white he looked, as if the skin of his face had been powdered with talcum. He was seated atop the backseat of the gleaming car, truly as a king would be, dressed in a military cap with a shiny patent leather visor, a turquoise and magenta military uniform, festooned with massive golden epaulets and braided roping, and a jaunty half cape slung over one shoulder. You could see that he was wearing shiny black equestrian boots that came all the way up to his knees. His driver held a microphone to his mouth, announcing, "Ladies and gentlemen, King Antonio, of the 1963 Battle of Flowers Fiesta!" From the slow-moving car, smiling distractedly, he would wave at us with one hand, tossing us gilded wooden nickels with his picture on them with the other.

One year, my friend Dennis Perez and I hatched a seditious plot to throw "speargrass" at King Antonio, to see if we could stick him as his car went slowly by, but we were caught after just a few attempts by the fearsome Sister Alfred Euthanasius and had to perform penance by staying after school, writing multiplication tables for weeks thereafter. But the struggle against the conquest was still alive.

I can remember feeling, since long ago, that my generation was destined to be the end of our ancient family lines. Maybe not in terms of offspring, but the end, once and for all, of that old life of rivers and ranchería, the life that began to ebb when we first left Mexico. Of knowing which stars were where and what that meant to rustling fields of corn. Of the Garcia knowledge of the strength of esoteric metal alloys by their timbre and weight. Of the smell of wild dove soup, con limón. Of freshly cooked *menudo* in the winter. Of all the properly starched collars and serious brown faces, dressed like Europeans for a wedding. Of the society of pecans and *cabrito*. Of river-cooled watermelon, eaten in a large circle of relations. Of the last of Mexico left inside of Texas.

We were born to begin the last chapter of a very old story.

It seemed conceivable when I was a kid that the whole world would end soon, as if the apocalypse we were taught about in catechism classes was going to erupt out of our south Texas dirt. The face of Jesus, with his crown of thorns, was reported to have appeared on a tortilla in Harlingen. At school, one of my friends showed me a picture of a woman in India who had been pregnant for fourteen months, and now the child inside her womb was reciting from the Koran daily and delivering strange prophecies of doom for the world.

My first-grade teacher at Mount Sacred Heart, Sister Alfred, a nun of the order of *El Sagrado Corazón,* showed our class a slide-show presentation about the visions of Mary at Fatima, Portugal, accompanied by a narration on a phonograph record. The faces of the three children who had seen the Virgin speaking to them out of a cloud looked as familiar as my cousins, their expressions warm but melancholic, with deep-set eyes. The eldest of the visionaries, Lucia, even had the surname dos Santos. But we all took notice when we learned that before their visions of the Mother of Jesus took place, the three were given Communion by an emissary angel, with hosts that dripped blood. The voice on the phonograph told how, during the six visions of Mary, which took place in 1917, she spoke to them of the World Wars of this century and warned humanity of the evil rise of a *Great Bear of the East,* which, we were told, was most assuredly the Holy Mother's way of describing the godless communist Soviet Union. On the day of the last of the visions, in a wide valley near Fatima, thousands of onlookers were said to have seen the sun dance in the sky, and then it seemed to fall upon them.

I was frightened when Sister Alfred later spoke to us about the mysterious "third secret" of Fatima, a vision so horrible that Pope John XXIII was said to have collapsed after reading it, and it has remained hidden away in a Vatican vault since.

"They say it's about the end of the world," Sister Alfred added in a solemn whisper, as if she were sharing a company secret with us. "And, I will tell you, from my trip to Rome, there are only three more tombs for Popes underneath Saint Peter's."

Surely, I thought, the end of the world would come in our time.

Los Santos never wandered much once they settled in San Antonio. They never much needed or sought to know anything of the world that lay to the north of Elgin, east of Houston, west of Uvalde, in Texas, and south of Monclova, in Mexico.

"This is where I'm from, right here," my father would say, surveying the live oak woods on the family's small ranch just outside of San Antonio, near Pleasanton, Texas.

"This is the greatest place on the whole earth."

I certainly couldn't see any use in learning a language other than Spanish and English, thinking, if I didn't become an astronaut, I, too, would always dwell in these same lands. Perhaps this was the family's final migration. There had been stragglers among the Santos, vaguely remembered circles of the family who had stayed behind, scattered throughout towns along the old pilgrimage route out of Mexico during the migrations of 1914. In Mexico, there were a few cousins in Nava, Cloete, Allende, along the main road, Carretera 57, and other relations had settled in towns along Highway 90, on the way to San Antonio.

One family Uela used to visit had taken refuge in Villita Unión in Coahuila, just south of the border, eventually building an adobe house alongside a small stream, with financial help from my grandmother and her sister, Madrina Tomasa.

Another part of the tribe had remained in Hondo, in the country on the south Texas plains dotted with towns like Dhanis, Knippa, Sabinal, and Uvalde. Hondo is one of those Texas towns suspended in time—run through the middle by the highway. On one side are the railroad tracks and the bank, with a large painted sign reading BANK, a redbrick dry goods store, an old hotel. On the other side, a strip of gas stations, hardware stores, taco stands and barbecue joints, and the townspeople's homes.

Those Santos of Hondo were meant to be ornery, even though many were the offspring of the wandering prankster José León, my abuelo's half-brother, he of the great resounding oversized cowboy boots, who could keep everybody in the old house on Burr Road howling with laughter well into the night. Maybe he didn't spend enough time with his children, always moving between the houses of his brothers and sisters in Texas and Mexico for long visits—and that ended up making them ornery.

With the passing years, the ones who had been left behind along the *peregrinaje* road were mainly rumored about, since even Aunt Connie, the "keeper of contact" within the Santos family, had long ago lost touch with them. But we were all from this place, this long narrow homeland of stragglers scattered along an old pilgrimage road that stretched from San Felipe de las Minas in the south, through Palaú and Múzquiz, Piedras Negras, and Eagle Pass, all the way north to San Antonio. If it wasn't possible to ever fully know my grandfather's story, there was still this road, connecting our present to our past, north to south, a current running in reverse. If San Antonio contained the fading remnant of Mexico, what was Mexico itself?

9

Rain
of Stones

Lluvia de Piedras

 *You always know there is rain coming up in the mountains by the scent of wild oregano, suddenly suffusing the atmosphere with its pungent spice just before a storm.* Lulled nearly to sleep by the long, slow trail climbing to the high ranch of Dr. Mata, the horses were startled by the first dry lightning flash that lit up the twilight sierra landscape around us. From the saddle, for just an instant in that already darkening hour, the large, silent green mountain, corrugated with ravines, was completely visible before us. Thick, stone-colored clouds hung so low they tore inseams along the giant maguey plants decking the peaks with their spear-shaped fronds.

The road into the Mata ranch in north Mexico had been washed out from recent heavy rains. We were going out to do a tally of the nearly four hundred head of cattle, some of which had reportedly been lost in flash floods through distant mountain pastures. We were also carrying sup-

plies for the vaquero, *lashed to a burro laden with food and provisions. We had been riding all day. My cousin Chickee from San Antonio was along on the journey. My friend Abrán Mata, son to Dr. Mata, a dear friend of my father's, was leading the way into his family's remote Coahuila spread. Don Tiburcio, the* vaquero *from the Mata ranch, was tending the burro tied to the horn of his saddle.*

This was the same wilderness that had surrounded my ancestors before their journey north. By then, I was a university student, studying philosophy and literature, but I came back to the Coahuila ranches on spring breaks and during the summer, to help with roundups, to mend waterworks, to clear pastures for grazing, and to write. The Mata ranch was farther out on the Mexican sierra road to Boquillas del Carmen, and higher into the mountains than the Rancho Los Generales, beyond telephone lines and the long reach of the smog from the coal mines in Nueva Rosita and Palaú. The farther out we went along that trail, the further back in time the horses seemed to be taking us.

Rains that heavy were unusual in Coahuila. The night before, the vaqueros *at the ranch we stayed at had spoken about how the rains had come as a result of a spell cast by* la Diosa de Maguey, *"the Goddess of the Maguey," a sinewy blue-green Mexican cactus that grows to the size of a truck and mixes into the sierra in Coahuila alongside stands of ponderosa pines and juniper trees. Meticulously picking mites out of the flour we would use to make our tortillas, the* vaquero, *Tiburcio, insisted that the rains were the work of a goddess, "La Colorada," as he called her, who had a reputation for appearing as a beautiful woman to* vaqueros *in the mountains, then seducing them, never to be seen again by their families.*

"All the magueys were drying up after this winter, and she brought the water to save them. She didn't care about the rest of us up here, though. She probably wishes we'd all go away. We just have to take it, I guess."

Later, after dinner and shots of warm brandy, Tiburcio's bronco-loud snores, carrying the sound of some doleful animal plaint, had made it impossible for any of the rest of us to sleep, and I sat on the patio, covered in a blanket, counting the shimmering satellites arcing periodically overhead, anxious for the first flares of dawn. In the moonlight, the steam of the horses' breath passed like luminous clouds into the pasture. Tied up in a small corral nearby, they shifted nervously from hoof to hoof all night long.

The next day, after eight hours on the trail, the clouds that had been gathering along the mountainside since midafternoon began to unleash their sheets of cold, gusting rains. The winds ripped through the pastures, shaking and bending back the trees, as if they were reeds, rumbling the earth with a booming roar of thunder that came from all directions.

"I told you she didn't want us out here!" Tiburcio shouted back to the rest of us, barely audible over the rising tempest and the din of the raindrops hitting our ponchos. The burro, wide-eyed and braying for mercy, was becoming frantic in the bustle of the flashes, the lashing rain, the flying leaves and branches, nearly pulling off Tiburcio's saddle in an effort to run in any direction for shelter.

Terrified and bucking wildly, the burro had to be tied to a mesquite tree in a clearing and all the supplies, including meat, flour, and sugar, covered in several layers of oily canvas tarpaulins. Except for fruit and potatoes in our packs, we had no other food, but it was more important to reach the shelter of the ranch, and we could return for the provisions the next morning.

As we climbed the final mountain approach to the ranch, the horses stumbled to find their footing in the rocky terrain of the ravine. I could hear the rattling steps of the horses of Chickee, Abrán, and Tiburcio further on, looking for the trail that would take us down the other side. When the lightning flashed again in one great phosphorescent hoop across the sierra, we were already at the summit of the hill. Far below, in an expansive valley the colors of jade and wet sand, I saw the small ranch house that was our destination. Near the house there were corrals. A small river wound through the landscape, glistening in the fulminating light of the storm.

As we began our climb down, the red mare I had been riding all day began to grouse under my weight, whinnying so loudly in the tumult of the downpour she drew bothered retorts from the other horses. Wrapped in darkness, leaning way back in the saddle to compensate for the hillside's angle of descent, I felt every step strike the earth like a chime, finding for a moment some quiet refuge from the driving tormenta.

We had been descending for nearly an hour, heavy rain still falling, though by then the lightning had left off, making the ride a blind crawl. Having lost track of my companions, wondering how close we were by then to the valley floor, I tightened the reins to slow us down on a path of loose rocks. I felt the mare take one long step, then, before I could draw her back, another, into open air. As the hind legs left the earth behind us, I leaned forward, gripping the wet, warm fur of her neck, reins flying like streamers. Too breathless to let out a scream, the two of us plunged even deeper into the inky Coahuila night.

On my mother's side, the Lopez and the Velas were from the small town of Cotulla, in south Texas. On Sundays, before Grandfather Leonides's death, the families would join his brothers José and Blas, and take all the relatives out to a small ranch, a *granjita,* outside of town where a great lunch of barbecued goat was already being prepared. The closeness of the *rancho,* the size of the town, at under a thousand families, nestled Cotulla in a time that felt unchanging, and well away from the locomotion and bustle of the American cities.

After my grandfather Leonides's death there in 1935, Grandmother moved her family to San Antonio for the schools, and to be closer to her sister, Fermina. In San Antonio, by then already a large city, no one knew her. She walked down Houston Street unnoticed by the myriad pedestrians, a widow from one of the oldest Mexican families in Texas, the Velas from Mier—now become invisible. In Cotulla she was widely known and deferred to throughout the town as Doña Leandra, the wife of Don Leonides, the grocer who always wore a suit. She hated being called Señora Lopez.

The *Norteños* of the family, the Santos and Garcias of north Mexico, always claimed to be ready to move back to the countryside, with a little land to farm, maybe a few head of cattle, but always delaying, always longing perhaps, but never really planning to leave San Antonio, ever. Instead, most weekends we retired to the ranches and the creeks, the rivers and the pastures surrounding San Antonio.

Paradise, for many *Norteños,* would be a modest ranch, even a dry, scrubby little piece of sandy land like the Pleasanton *ranchito,* to settle on for eternity. You hear this life sung about and celebrated, sweetly, bitterly, in Tex-Mex *corridos*, and *ranchero* music of north Mexico, and in the glossy, new Day-Glo Mexican colors of popular Tejano music. What is left of the *ranchero* life of south Texas and north Mexico is as old as the New World itself, no matter what its trappings today. Out of its origins in the fierce horsemanship of the Españoles, and the Indians' knowledge of the terrain, a whole civilization emerged, built with mesquite, leather, rope, corrugated tin, and an infinitude of barbed wire.

That world began for me on a *ranchito* in Medina river valley sand, the flat, golden territory southeast of the city, where spindly live oaks grow alongside mesquite and huisache trees, and the whole landscape is dotted with dense clusters of flowering, scarlet-fruited cactus. On iridescent summer days, squeaky tin windmills churned so slowly in the sluggish Tejano breezes that the pumps only managed to pull enough water from the ground to produce a syrupy trickle into the large cement tank. Across cleared pastures, under an unquenchable, bleaching sun, a few cattle would huddle in the shade around a block of salt. And always the song of thousands upon thousands of cicadas, chirping in the hot, still air.

My father, a veteran of World War II, had bought the small ranch, which never really had a proper ranch name, with a loan from the Texas Veteran's Land Board. It was near Pleasanton, Texas, just south of San Antonio's outskirts. Most Friday afternoons, after school, we loaded up the station wagon and made the journey across town and out to the *rancho*. As we passed through the city in what seemed an interminable trek, it was always unfathomable to me that this world of crowded shopping-mall parking lots, busy railroad crossings, and stalling downtown traffic around the bustling mercado existed almost side by side with the silent, remote world of the ranch. From the sandy road that led to the entrance gate, I saw haunted, abandoned clapboard ranch houses dotting the horizon, over sprawling fields of dry grasses. We entered the ranch through a rusting wrought iron gate that creaked with the sound of an eagle's cry, and the older oaks alongside the road formed a tunnel over us, a mosaic of sunlight. We drove the half-mile-long sandy road to where the house was.

My pressing concern was the garden. The sandy riverine loam there nurtured my watermelons, which blossomed and grew in a staggering abundance. In addition to uncles and aunts, *compadres y comadres,* cousins, and a pony called Brown Beauty, the weekend ranch society included white-tailed deer; armadillos; slithering, dreaded poisonous copperheads; hawks; and mockingbirds. My father and uncles would make a big fire as soon as we arrived, preparing for our hecatomb *parillada* of grilled goat, brisket, chicken, wieners, and roasting ears of corn. On special weekends, they dug a hole to bury a cow's head with burning coals, to slow roast the Sunday-morning breakfast delicacy of tender tacos of the stringy head meat called *barbacoa*.

Walking out from the spacious oak grove where we had a small army surplus Quonset hut into the dry brush country, I had the familiar, contradictory feeling that this was a place of great antiquity, and utter newness. It seemed age-old but untouched, with no signs of human presence there ever before. Years later, visiting a farm of a girlfriend's grandmother in New Hampshire, I was taken aback by how handled the forests were—trees bearing crosses, X's, circles, and arrows, moss-covered paths, stone walls half-fallen, mended, crisscrossing far into the woods, far from the nearest road.

One of the main attractions of the ranch was Brown Beauty, a squat, husky Shetland pony my father had bought for twenty-seven dollars at a livestock auction in Pleasanton. At these auctions and rodeos, Mexicans and Anglos met around mesquite corrals, iron pens, and sand-filled rings to haggle over prices. They did business then just as they had for the last two hundred years, trading heifers, mares, bulls—and mad ponies.

She was *"prieta,"* the ranchhand, Isác, had said. That was dark brown, like the color of tobacco resin. And she was ornery enough to acquire a reputation, after stomping toes and tossing children, for being downright mean. For a year, Brown Beauty stubbornly carried cedar posts, bucking and baring teeth, to build the fence around the ranch. Maybe it was that year of hard labor that made her wild.

While riding Brown Beauty, I could feel the whole world rush forward suddenly at a tilt, careening down a two-track sandy road, holding the reins like tethers, voices of family members screaming in the distance, a vague blur of familiar noise. She would take you deep into the woods in an unexpected whoosh and then, just as suddenly, leave you airborne, aiming for a stand of flowering cactus. One cold Sunday morning out on the Pleasanton ranch, so cold there had been ice on the inside panes of the windows in the bungalow, everyone was milling around the fire outside, talking and drinking coffee and hot chocolate. My cousin Robert was riding around the clearing on Brown Beauty when the pony bolted forward in a beautiful, short-legged curvetting leap and carried Robert off into the brush. We all envied him. All he could do was to grasp her neck and duck low, to keep from getting hit by branches. It happened so quickly, we all stood silently watching. It was an hour before we found Robert, bruised and scratched. Brown Beauty stayed missing for another week.

On Sunday evenings, we made our way back into the city, already lit up with Dairy Queen signs and multiplex marquees. Driving sleepily through downtown streets of San Antonio, we saw the strings of lights hanging from towering cypresses along the banks of the river. Bongo Joe was playing in front of the Alamo. On Broadway, we looked at the pedestrians along the sidewalk, snickering and trying to spot my father's cousin Jimena, who had been a prostitute in San Antonio for thirty years. Gradually, we fell back under the spell of San Antonio de Bejar.

We didn't have the ranch near San Antonio for very long. It was sold in the early '60s so my parents could buy the house in the suburbs, where my brothers and I would be able to go to decent public schools. The deal for the ranch had one drawback. It included Brown Beauty.

Once you pass through the sierra town of Múzquiz, heading west on the highway, it's all arroyos, canyons, and stands of pine, juniper, and mesquite mixed in with cactus. For nearly three hundred miles, the landscape surrounding the remote Mexican blacktop is all green pasture, burnt brown mountains, and a big blue sky. This is the road to the Rancho Los Generales, the Guerra family cattle ranch, near their home of Sabinas, Coahuila, which I visited most summers home from college. The Texas border is just one hundred and fifty miles north for most of its length, but the traditions of old Mexico remain strong here.

Even with industrial development encroaching, the road is still a window onto Mexico's past, as it cuts a path through some of the most stunningly beautiful rugged wilderness I have ever seen anywhere. Eagles, hawks, and vultures trace invisible currents across the sky. Lions, deer, and bear are plentiful, as are the menacing javelinas and rattlesnakes. And the many ranches along the road are stocked with large herds of Black Angus, orange-and-cream-colored Hereford, and white Charolais cattle.

This is where my real life with ranches began. Along with Alejo, the chief *vaquero* of the ranch, and various cousins and uncles, we undertook the day-to-day chores and rigors of a working ranch. This could mean an early morning on horseback, out in a far pasture by seven, looking along the ground for the telltale puddles of a leaking pipe that must be dug up and mended with rubber-tire-tubing tourniquets. We gathered for roundups, sweeping through the hills to convene the herd, straggling pasture to pasture in a great looped circuit around the *rancho,* until all eight hundred head of white Charolais were accounted for and brought together, glowing in the moonlight, across a high plain.

The next day, we would descend to the pasture with the corrals in a tumult of dust and fur. Once in the corrals, the cattle were shuttled through baths and vaccinations, steers were castrated, and, if they were calves, branded with red-hot irons with an *A,* the ranch brand, which stands for Alejandro Guerra. The animals seemed so aware, so sentient, if unable to express themselves. Watching them in a pasture as three dozen stood, staring emptily at me, I had to shudder to think of their destiny. Many never made it to market. They were attacked by bears or pumas, or lacerated after getting tangled up in a barbed wire fence.

Once, a prized pregnant cow had been lost for several days, despite Alejo's and my searches up and down the hills of two pastures where she was thought to be. My father was with me on the ranch, and on one ride together we noticed a hillside oak glen where the trees seemed to be covered in a canopy the color of tar. As we got closer, the canopy became a living thing, undulating and heaving as one, but revealed as a horde of expressionless *sopilotes*, "vultures," which had congregated to consume the carcass of the lost cow and her unborn calf. She had been struck by lightning; a great burn mark was still evident on her neck. The *sopilotes* had left the singed flesh, but her ribs were so perfectly white they looked bleached. In that still, carrion air, some of the vultures shook out their old rugs of wings. My father and I sat in our saddles, uneasy with the utter silence of the desolate scene, dust motes hanging in the afternoon sunlight. It was as if we were in a church, the vultures perched in the trees like a choir all around us, a strange sanctuary devoted to the memory of an accidental death.

The time on the ranch also gave me a chance to read and write on my own. I knew these were bad times to be a poet. It was a time when no one listened to the poets anymore, when the words of poets went unheard by all, rich and poor, by politicians and judges, police and factory workers. But that was what I thought I was then, not by choice, but by some personal vocation. Out there on the ranch, it was De la Barca, Spenser, Sidney, Browne, and Traherne. After a long ride out, I read in the mesquite groves in the valley of *los Viejos*, or up on the hill with the great water tank, from where the burnt orange light of sunset made the pages look like they were on fire. On the screened patio, in the shade from the full bake of midafternoon, it was Smart, Blake, Lorca, Kerouac, Burroughs, Borges, and the gnawing idea of an unfortunate destiny. In a journal, I described myself then as "a laughing vaquero poet at the end of twentieth century."

During Holy Week at Easter, and in the week between Christmas and the New Year, we would join the entire Guerra family, up to thirty of us, at Los Generales for several days of cooking and eating, afternoon tequilas, horseback riding, and impromptu rodeos. Meals were served on one long wooden table, set in the shade of a sycamore tree we had planted some years before, next to the patio. Tacos de chorizo, *de machacado,* with beans was breakfast. A breast of dove in a clear lime soup, with rice and peas, might be lunch. Most evenings, Alejo would build a great mesquite fire in a vast cast-iron barbecue pit, and the steaks and *tripas* for dinner were grilled alongside onions, garlic, corn, and chiles for late suppers.

One Easter, after dinner, most of the adults retreated to the sitting room of the ranch house around ten o'clock, the women drinking limeades, the men sipping from snifters of El Presidente brandy. While the subject of discussion at the Guerra table back in Sabinas was usually Mexican politics, out at the *rancho* the talk ran to long Mexican jokes, old family tales, and, as it grew later, ghost stories.

"The old house in Sabinas was haunted, for many years," Tía Bertha said, as I leaned in, listening from the kitchen. "Yes, it was in the closet in our room," she added, pointing to her sister Beatriz sitting nearby. "Late at night, we heard slow footsteps inside the closet. Sometimes we could hear, like a whispering voice, saying *'Dios mio . . .'* It was a very, very sad voice."

"Tía, how terrifying!" my cousin Alejandra said, holding her hands to her face. "How could you even sleep there?"

"Ticha or I would tell it to shush, so we could sleep! And that's all it took. An old woman who came from the church said it was a ghost of an old banker from town. In our closet! She said she saw his face in the grain of the wood on the door and brought the widow of the poor soul to stare at it and say prayers."

"There was always praying going on in their room," their elder sister Julieta offered, drawing snickers from the room.

"But do you know that Mama had to pay a spiritualista to lure that spirit to come out? The man was dressed in a big cloak, and he was a little, you know, 'Forty-one,' effeminate, and he kept screaming at the closet, 'Now you come out of there right now! Naughty Spirit!' " Tío Alejandro erupted with laughter at his sister's impersonation of the spirit medium.

"And did he get the ghost out?" Alejandra asked.

"That was beautiful." Tía Beatriz, or Tía Ticha as she is known, had been silent as her sister told the story. Her face was serious, and she spoke in slow earnest tones. "It was in the middle of summer. From the closet door, through Julieta's room, into the hallway and out onto the porch, and then across the plaza, this old *brujo* left behind a path of the orange petals of *zempaxuchitl* flowers. He said he guided the spirit through the streets of Sabinas back to its grave in the nearby cemetery. You could see the flower path for days."

"And, *fíjate,* that ghost never bothered us again," Tía Bertha added with great pride.

Tío Alejandro told how once, as a child, on an old *rancho* near Múzquiz called Las Rusias, the family had been visiting friends on an ordinary Sunday afternoon in the summer. "We were playing in a pasture and the skies suddenly darkened. Then there was some rain, but it wasn't water. It was small black stones that stung when they fell on us. We ran to the house, but I turned around and saw the rain of stones falling across the sierra, as far as you could see. *Bien curioso.*" Alejandro's brother Miguel, along with his sisters, nodded in solemn agreement.

It was nearly midnight, and there was already a constellation of sleepers on cots spread out across the patio in the open night air. Tío Alejandro popped an old corroded bottle of Cognac Napoleon that he said had belonged to the emperor himself, and it looked as if it might have. As he chipped away at the tar-colored plaque on the bottle, he remembered with us how his father had come from Oaxaca City, in the south of Mexico, where his grandfather, who was puro Indio, had a livery company. Alejandro Senior had fought in *la Revolución* and had ridden into Mexico City with Pancho Villa's Dorado army.

"And in that famous portrait, you know the one, of Villa and Zapata sitting together in the Presidential Palace, both of them in their grand thrones just after victory—off to the very far left of the picture, peeking into the frame, you can see Papá's nose."

As everyone laughed over my uncle's protestations that it was the truth, he poured out thimble-size *copitas* of the aged cognac and passed them around the room. Seeing me in the doorway, he called me over and asked me to recite something I had performed for him earlier in the day. In high school Spanish class, I had learned a speech from *La Vida es Sueño,* a seventeenth-century Spanish play by Pedro Calderón de la Barca about a prince, Seguismundo, who is condemned to live in a tower after his father, the king, receives prophecies that the youth will bring great calamities to the kingdom. Deciding to give his son one chance, the king has the prince drugged, and, upon awakening, the prince is told he is king. The affairs of the kingdom are soon wrecked, and he is returned to the tower, where he makes a powerful speech.

As I recited in the quiet sitting room, I could hear the sound of crickets outside when I paused to take a breath. My voice sounded alien to me, more insistent than when I had rehearsed the words before, the Spanish more flamboyant and rhythmic. I saw Tía Maye, Alejandro's wife, nodding in approval when I came to the last words which I nervously tried to deliver without stumbling,

> *¿Qué es la vida? Un frenesí.*
> *Qué es la vida? Una ilusión,*
> *una sombra, una ficción,*

y el mayor bien es pequeño:
que toda la vida es sueño,
y los sueños, sueños son.

What is life? A frenzy.
What is life? An illusion,
a shadow, a fiction,
and the greatest good is small:
that life is a dream,
and dreams are dreams.

Amidst the whooping and applause which I acknowledged with a bow, Tío Alejandro offered me a copita of the rare cognac, which I raised in a toast to everyone in the room. When it went down my throat, it felt like an icy smoke that tasted of ancient oranges.

"*Shhhh-shhh-shhh,*" Tía Bertha whispered, quieting the room. "*¡Ahora, Johnny!*"

My father stood up and cleared his voice, lifting his hands for quiet with a nervous smile. He raised his copita up in the air, looking for a moment at me, and said to everyone with a sweep of his arm, "*Les voy a cantar una canción.* I'm going to sing you all a little song."

Aside from an occasional wedding or funeral, he hadn't wanted to sing among friends for a long time. Back in San Antonio, he liked to sing in a room of the house off on his own, when you could barely make out the lyrics of Agustín Lara's song "Noche de Ronda" in the sweet falsetto section of the song where it says,

Lu-na que se quiebra sobre la tiniebla
de mi soledad.
¿Adónde vas?

Oh Moon that shatters over the storm
of my solitude.
Where are you going?

Out at Los Generales that night, in a room lit by lanterns and candles, he told the group with great formality that he had written a song he wanted to sing especially for them, a song in honor of the Rancho Los Generales, which he dedicated, cognac held aloft again, to my Tío Alejandro.

"You know how close our families are," my father said, beginning to choke up.

"Somos familia," Tío Alejandro responded. "We are family."

My father rushed out his words as his cheeks quivered with emotion, "And this is for everybody." He sat down and brought the guitar onto his lap. He closed his eyes as he strummed the instrument gently, humming through a cascade of chord progressions and flowery pickings. Finally, he was ready to begin. My father was in his early sixties, and "El Corrido del Rancho Los Generales" was the first song he had written.

My father was *ranchero,* even though he had grown up as a city boy. The ranch off Pleasanton Road was a refuge where we could leave behind the San Antonio of expressways and shopping malls and return to the old time of Texas earth—something Abuelo Juan José had always aspired to.

But the real *rancheros* had been the old Santos, the Santos before they came to Coahuila. My great-grandfather Juan Nepumencio Santos had worked around ranches of the region and was known as a keen-eyed roper. *Visabuelo* Nepumencio, as he was called, lost his first wife in the 1870s during a difficult childbirth before she was twenty-two, leaving him with four sons—Pedro, José León, Guadalupe, and Jesús María—to raise alone. As the sons grew up, they worked the cattle with him at the *ranchos,* and José León, in particular, is said to have become an adept cowboy.

A distant cousin in Austin turned out to have been told some of these tatters of Abuelo Nepumencio's story by her father. In those days, she said, the family lived in the remote dusty village of Espinazo, in the flat, dry countryside between Monclova and Monterrey, which was also the birthplace and home of José Fidencio Sintora Constantino, the famous and widely sought after Indian healer known as El Niño Fidencio, whose disciples still gather every year in the tiny town, reachable only by dirt roads and railway.

It was there that Juan Nepumencio Santos apparently met my great-grandmother Paula Sandoval, a young midwife, who had come to visit the healer Fidencio along with her mother and other *parteras,* or "midwives," who were interested in the wondrous works of the Indian miracle healer. She was about eighteen then, and Nepumencio already nearly forty. After marrying, he moved his four children and their few belongings by buggy to San Felipe, Coahuila, where Paula came from, and where he was able to find work on ranches near Sabinas, hoping someday to be able to afford to buy a small *granja* on which the family could live, keep a few goats and chickens, and grow its food, and still have enough to sell at the markets.

In the diocesan baptismal registry of San Felipe, kept in Sabinas, just as Uncle Sid had reported, beginning in 1882, the names of my grandfather and his brothers and sisters are entered, in flowing ornamental script, one by one, over the next twelve years. There was Mariano, the deaf-mute, who became a barber in Texas and could fix watches, even though he had never received any formal training; and

Tío Uvaldino. Then Juan José, my abuelo, followed by four sisters, Andrea; Francisca, known as "Panchita"; Jesusa, whom everyone would
know as "Chita," the prankster; and Manuela, known simply as "Nela."

It's impossible to say where the haunting in that family began, the
hidden-away distraction, the fearful despair, threading through my
grandfather, uncles, and aunts. Impossible to say how far back in time it
began, like a fossil of some tragic lost knowledge. Once ancient Mexicans had been gripped in a perpetual cycle of obligation to sacrifice to
fend off the destruction of the world and the constant encroaching of
the void. The French anthropologist Jacques Soustelle called this the
"cosmic mission" of the Aztecs, "fighting off the incursions of nothingness day after day." The shadows of that *compromiso,* that solemn duty,
that fearful memory of nothingness, may have lasted long in the hearts
of Mexicanos, for generations after the conquest, to the present day.

Or it may just have been that my grandfather's generation was
deeply shaken by having to flee their home during the revolution, like
so many others leaving behind the only way of life they had known in
Mexico. No one today remembers any talk of Nepumencio or Paula being prone to *complejos de nervios*—nervous disorders, depression, or
madness. But there were rumors about Nepumencio's four sons by his
first wife.

As the elder half-siblings of Nepumencio's first family, they always
seemed like outsiders, *renegados,* often disappearing from the family
home for intervals. Jesús María, the youngest, was a notorious *llorón,* a
crybaby, prone to fits of weeping, often in public, at funerals, as well
as weddings, baptisms, and later, strolling through the streets of San
Felipe. These bouts of crying carried on well into his elder years, after
he had come to Texas. The Santos have remained strangely quick to
weep, and not just in moments of great sadness or joy. In the middle of
singing a song, my father can suddenly be engulfed by tears, trying to
persevere, but often having to stop in midverse to collect himself. The

urge to weep can sweep into me like a wind, during a phone conversation, watching a close horse race, reading a newspaper article about a cataclysm abroad.

Another half-brother was José León—remembered for his great resounding cowboy boots, a handlebar mustache, and telling hilarious yarns—whose nomadic ways kept him out of the family's close embrace. He worked ranches throughout south Texas and later back in Mexico. José León was so restless he never stayed at home. His own family in Eagle Pass grew accustomed to living without him. Moving alone with his own haunting, he crossed the border between Texas and Mexico at Piedras Negras so often he said there was a rut in the bridge there from all of his walking.

The last two half-brothers, Tíos Pedro and Guadalupe, are remembered least. When the family moved north across the border in the days of *la Revolución,* they stayed behind in Hondo, Texas, an hour south of San Antonio, on the road to Piedras Negras. They lost touch with the rest of the family, never answering letters, never visiting San Antonio or receiving visitors, and finally there were rumors, never confirmed, of a suicide.

With Abuelo Juan José, the family's long history in *la vida ranchera* became in him a desire to farm, even after the Santos had arrived in San Antonio. Amidst the new city, he still dreamed of the life the family had lived before. The work Abuelo had done in the greenhouse conservatory of Colonel Brackenridge, tending the ivory lilies, the crimson amaryllises, and the trellises draping with ivy, only deepened those desires, even if planting and minding flowers and ornamental plants was a caprice compared to the age-old cycle of planting and harvesting that drew at him like an ineluctable tide.

In 1934, five years before his death, twenty-one years after coming to Texas, Abuelo was finally able to save enough money to buy a lease on some sharecropping land outside of San Antonio, in a large piece of acreage known as the Belgian Gardens. Great-grandfather Jacobo, Uela's father, joined his son-in-law in the venture, contributing eight hundred dollars he had saved over the years to match Juan José's investment.

Abuelo quit the job he had held for nearly ten years at the Alamo Iron Works after the old colonel's death. Great-uncle Gilbert remembers there were several good years for crops then, with plentiful rain to nourish big harvests of watermelons, cantaloupes, sweet potatoes, tomatoes, and green and yellow squash. The whole family, including uncles, aunts, and cousins in the Santos and Garcia clan, from the *chavalillos* to the *ancianos,* contributed to the work required to farm the fifty rich acres of leased land. During harvest, Great-grandfather Jacobo and his twin, Abrán, would sit on chairs set out in the middle of the fields, surrounded by the youngest of their progeny, brushing the dirt off the vegetables one by one, wrapping them in newspaper and arranging them neatly into boxes to take to the bustling produce truck bazaar in Haymarket Plaza, in downtown San Antonio.

Uncle Frank had two trucks at his disposal from his machine shop in town, and after the harvest was complete, the men loaded them up at dawn for the drive to the market. But the produce cartels were strong, and it was difficult for smaller farmers to win an advantageous position in the wide plaza from which to sell their fruits and vegetables. Juan José and great-grandfather were consigned to a parking place well off from the busy precinct of the downtown market, selling their goods from the back of the trucks.

"And people still didn't have any money. That was the other thing," recalled my great-uncle Gilbert, who had accompanied them. "In San Antonio, especially with the Mexicans, it was still the Depression and everybody was broke. We sold a few watermelons, maybe *unos melones,* but every day we came back with the truck full. It made my father, Jacobo, sad, and Juan José even sadder. They lost everything then. Everything."

Boxes of squash began to stack up in the backyard of the house on Parsons Street, slowly starting to rot inside their newspaper wrapping. Eventually much of the harvest that wasn't eaten by the family or given to friends had to be dumped. And when the same thing happened the second year, the family's financial resources were finally depleted. Abuelo Juan José was left deeply in debt. They came close to losing the house, but Abuelo was able to get a loan from the officers of Colonel Brackenridge's bank, who still remembered him from his time working at Fernridge and the way the old colonel had cared for him. But Abuelo was disconsolate about losing his father-in-law's money in the venture at the Belgian Gardens. Despite finding another foundry job, the feeling of mounting calamity and chaos must have become insurmountable. It was then that he entered the first long spell of haunted silence that most who knew him thought he would never emerge from.

There are two historic paths to the sanctuary of the Mexican soul—the one from the north and the one from the east. The road from the east is the route that Cortés and his army took from Veracruz on their march to Tenochtitlán in the conquest of the Azteca empire. The one from the north is the oldest one, the ancient road, the one said to have been traversed by the ancestors of the Aztecas, in search of their long-prophesied home.

My family's first journey south of Coahuila to the heart of Mexico was in 1976, along that road from the north, past Nueva Rosita and Sabinas, Monclova, Saltillo, San Luis Potosí and Querétaro, to la Capital, Mexico City. The road from Aztlán, the fabled homeland of the Aztecas, has been paved over and turned into a four-lane Mexican highway. Highway 57 is the way of the journey from Aztlán, "the place of whiteness," as the Aztecas called it. This mysterious place of origin was also known as the place of the seven caves, also known as Chico-moztóc, also known as Zuyua. It was a preordained path, divined from the prophecies of a living god. For it was said that the god Huitzilo-pochtli lived among the people whom he had commanded to wander. They were the people who became the Mexica, the Aztecas, the people who built the imperial city of Tenochtitlán, which Cortés would lay waste to.

In the codices, the "hummingbird of the south," as their god was called, is pictured as a crowned head protruding from a tightly bound sacred bundle. He is carried, papoose-style, on the back of one of his elect priest-bearers. According to the codices, they lived in caves first, then in houses made of braided plant stalks and broad leaves, deco-rated with improbably brilliant plumes and feathers. At the place known as Culhuacán, or "curved mountain," they walk along in a sin-gle file, heads bowed, their bodies wrapped in tunics. The god is talk-ing, with the telltale curling glyphs for speech coming from his mouth.

They had set out after years of famine and icy winters, and their wanderings through Mexico lasted hundreds of years. Our family was on a three-week summer-vacation trip. Along the highway in the desert before Querétaro, vendors selling iguanas, monkeys, and parrots held their animals aloft to entice buyers as the cars sped by. If you stopped, they would throw the animals into your car, the monkeys immediately crawling under the front seat, parrots flying back and forth, an iguana settling on the armrest. In the plaza at Potosí, a man would engrave your name on a grain of rice, confirming it with a magnifying glass. In Mexico City, you could have your fortune told by a parakeet, picking prophecies in scrolls out of a small teak box.

I was astounded by how vast Mexico was, how many worlds it contained, from the baroque malachite city of Guanajuato, glowing green in the mountains, to the vertiginous, hazy megalopolis of Mexico City. The day we arrived there, I drove into the city, swept into the swiftly changing currents and eddies of capitalino traffic, circling the *glorieta* roundabouts, accelerating onto the wide, cypress-lined straightaways, passing the VW bug taxis, until, nearing our destination downtown, the movement on the boulevard was abruptly halted as thousands of students marched for hours into the evening, down Avenida de la Reforma, protesting recent hikes in their university fees.

Before it got dark, we had to leave the car parked in the street to look for our lodgings, which were on the other side of the avenida. As we crossed Reforma, walking against the grain through the throng of demonstrators, all kinds of Mestizo faces were there—brown broad-cheeked Indios, paler thin-nosed Criollos of Spanish descent, and every permutation and pigment in between. When they weren't chanting and shouting their slogans, the marchers were arrestingly quiet, and you heard mainly the sound of their breath, and shoes rasping against the pavement, like a parade of people lost in reflection. Inside this quiet there was the inexplicable feeling of some slowly gathering intent among them, as if something were about to erupt from their collective silence.

I had never seen a Mexican metropolis before, only the towns and pueblitos of the north, only the secret, disappearing Mexican city inside of San Antonio. Like San Antonio, Mexico City was built over the ruins of an older settlement, only considerably older, in the case of Tenochtitlán, the seat of the Aztec empire that preceded la Capital of the modern era. The remains of temples, aqueducts, and the old roads of the Aztecs poke out of the earth, chipped and weathered, all over the city, inviting Mexico City's inhabitants, the *Chilangos,* as they call themselves, to live with the constant reminder of that world that had existed before the arrival of the Europeans.

On the grounds of the Museum of Anthropology, in a clearing in the verdant Chapultepec Park, we saw a group of Indian *Voladores* performing the same mesmerizing aerial ritual I had seen at the Hemisfair in San Antonio in 1968. As the five flyers climbed up the long, rope-braided pole, Helen Anthony, an old friend of my mother's and our Mexico City guide, explained how the ancient dance was in fact a record of exact counts relating to the calendar of the ancient Mexican people. Within its very precise rotations and gestures, based on the numbers four, thirteen, fifty-two, were the counts corresponding to the number of days in a year, and the number of years in the great cycles, between which the world might be destroyed or reprieved.

"It was a good way of tying that knowledge to the world, so *we* wouldn't forget, no?" Helen said, looking overhead, as the four Indios pushed off from their perches and began their slow whirling around the pole, arms folded across their chests, in their upside-down spiraling descent. The fifth man kept beating his drum and blowing his flute, spinning around on the pinnacle.

At the plaza at Tlatelolco, where Mexica ruins mingle with a colonial-era church and modern high-rises, Helen first told me how the old Mexicans had built their pyramids over old pyramids, just as those had been built over older pyramids before them. Every fifty-two years, the world was either to be destroyed or reprieved and continued, and a new pyramid would be built over the old to commemorate this passage.

In our time, it was believed that the Templo Mayor, the Great Temple of the Aztecs, a double pyramid which had been destroyed by the Spaniards, lay underneath the downtown cathedral, which Helen explained on the day we went to visit the shrine to the Virgin of Guadalupe, in the area of Mexico City known as Tepeyac. It was a hill where the Aztecas had long venerated the Goddess Tonantzín, and it was in the same place, ten years after the conquest, that the Indio Juan Diego reported seeing the apparition of the brown-skinned female who told him she had come to be mother to all of the people of those lands.

Today, the hill at Tepeyac where the visions took place is littered with the smog-blackened shells of four abandoned church shrines, built by the faithful since 1535—the year of the apparition of La Virgen.

These old churches were in the traditional Mexican style, with two spires, a nave, elaborately carved stone windows, and lintels. And, over the centuries since the vision, each one has been slowly reclaimed by the vast, ageless lake still lurking beneath Mexico City. As the stone chapels sank, crooked into the earth, their marble floors cracked and the granite walls pressed together like chalk, until they were inevitably condemned. The artworks and elaborate statuary of saints that could be salvaged from the old sanctuaries were carried out and stored, to be placed in the next shrine to be built nearby.

The last of these historic shrines was ruined not by ground water, but by an anarchist's bomb in 1926, left in a satchel behind a spray of white alcatraz lilies, near the altar and tabernacle, over which the mystical image of La Virgen was hung. The sacred *tilma,* the Indian cloak on which the image of the woman in a starry shawl appears, survived, but only because a massive, solid iron crucifix in front of the altar absorbed most of the fiery blast. The crucifix was found in the rubble, the Christ molten, entirely bent over backward on itself. Now, the misshapen debris is revered as a miraculous object in its own right and kept in a glass case where the *peregrinos* to La Virgen stop to pay homage and leave offerings of coins or flowers.

The day we visited, there were campesinos praying and crawling on their hands and knees across the smooth stones of the plaza toward the new basilica, some of them with spiny cactus stems lashed to their backs with twine in a gesture of secret atonement. The new, ultramodern, arena-style shrine, inaugurated in the 1960s, with its tentlike, unevenly fluted roof, looks like a golden space station set down in the middle of the paving stone plaza. There are Masses offered and prayers and confession said there around the clock. Among the pilgrims, even

those who dislike the new building compared to the cherished old ruined churches of Tepeyac, admit that it is a wonder: it is possible from
wherever you stand in the great domed circle to see the dun-colored sacred artifact, the image of the Virgin of Guadalupe on Juan Diego's old
Indian cloak, which, seen from afar, almost seems to glow and flicker
through the clouds of incense as it hangs suspended high on a wall set
back from the altar.

Devotees seek to get as close as they can to the mysterious image,
hoping that simply being in the physical presence of a divinely anointed
object in this world will bring a powerful blessing. In the new shrine,
this means going downstairs into the crypt, where you find the corridor
that leads to three moving sidewalks, the kind you see between airline
terminals, which carry the faithful, at a steady, if somewhat too rushed,
pace for them, passing beneath an aperture in the ceiling with the clos-
est view possible—twenty feet above—of the haunting, wistful image of
the Virgin.

From there you can see the round features of her face, a remote,
contemplative, even melancholic expression on her face. She is wearing
a turquoise blue rebozo, draped over her head and decked with golden
stars. Her peach-colored smock is adorned with golden filigree in the
shape of flowers, leaves, and interwoven stalks. Her hands are clasped
and, under her garment, her left knee seems to be moving forward. All
around her body there is a corona of fading ochre light, shot through
with spear-shaped rays of brownish red. She stands on a crescent
moon, and a winged cherub holds the hems of her garments.

Some of the more frequent *peregrinos* have discovered a way to
jam the gears that drive the moving sidewalk, using wooden doorstop
wedges they bring to the shrine expressly for that purpose. That day, I
watched as one pilgrim inserted a wedge into the rubber handrest belt
track, and the sidewalk ground to a halt. At that moment, all of the pilgrims fell to their knees praying directly to the Virgen's image, exalting

in their fleeting intimacy with her until a security guard arrived to dislodge the wedge from the works and the sidewalk resumed its inexorable circuit.

In a sooty, candlelit subterranean chapel further beneath the basilica, I kneeled before a simple statue of the Virgen. I watched an old Indian woman finish her devout prayers and then reach around her back to grab her long, rope-thick gray braid. In one swift stroke, her lips moving again in prayer, she cut it off with a large knife. Very slowly, she then laid it at the feet of the statue, crossing herself, thereby accomplishing some secret promise she had made for some intercession of powers in her life from "La Morenita," as the Mexicans sometimes refer to the Virgin.

I knew from Uela that she had once come here with her sister Tía Pepa in the late 1940s, to fulfill a promise they had made to La Virgen when their sons went off to World War II, and then came back safely. They spent several days praying the rosary together at the shrine before returning to San Antonio. Thirty years later, I had come to Tepeyac as a tourist, not as a believer in the cult of Guadalupe. She was the most powerful national symbol of the Mexican people, drawing Indio, Español, and Mestizo together in one embrace, but I saw the story of her apparitions as a story only—not a supernatural mystery. Mexicans believed in her because Mexicans, deep down, believed in their own, still unnameable, prophetic destiny. Hadn't they always believed the gods were talking with them and living among them, guiding their steps?

But watching the old woman in her quiet ritual that day in Tepeyac, I realized that I had already been initiated into the Guadalupana cult numberless times before, among all the *Viejitas* of San Antonio, in their sitting rooms, their kitchens and backyards. I had felt the power of their faith when they were at their prayers, lighting a votive candle and reading in their Bibles. I was a student of analytic philosophy, trying to discern how language, politics, and culture created the world around us, and how everything was of this world, everything was of history—nothing was supernatural. Tepeyac may have been a part of the ancestors' world, I believed, and now we lived in a plainer, more pragmatic era. Yet, there in the dark underground with hundreds of candles burning, it felt as if I had already been implicated in the stories of the old gods through the prayers my ancestors offered at Tepeyac. Whatever else I might become, our story had always been connected to this place, and I, too, might someday have to return there, to fulfill a secret promesa.

After our journey to Mexico City, my family returned to San Antonio, and I spent a few weeks back at Rancho Los Generales in Coahuila. It was late summer, the time of the year when the monarch butterflies are flying, filling the air with gamboling orange clouds, moving to the south. Alejo, the *vaquero,* and his family were in town preparing their children to begin school. For several long, quiet days, I was alone there, writing down my recollections of our trip to Tenochtitlán.

I began to watch my dreams. There were dreams of voluptuous women, enticing and elusive. Somewhere in an old red granite castle, maybe in Guanajuato, I think, a radiant, dark-haired woman I felt I recognized as someone once very dear to me kept appearing in the hallways, the courtyards, and the common room. But I could never reach her before she vanished.

I saw the end of the world, over and over, in numerous versions and sequelae. It is dark at midday. Doves and pigeons, their wings on fire, fell from the sky into the great, empty downtown plaza of the Zócalo in Mexico City. Hordes of shimmering lambs, in perfect tiers, descended slowly from the sky, passing like ghosts into the desert floor. An enormous crowd of people were gathered in a long, wide mountain valley. High above us, in a sky as black as obsidian, a sickly, snaking ribbon of crimson light, like a burning nebula, became an enormous angel, hovering over some unknown city. Finally, I rowed out in a flat boat onto a pitch-dark lake on a quiet summer night, knowing the angel had deemed our world unworthy of revelation.

Uncle Roger, my father's brother, had always said these were the "end times." He kept clippings of floods, sightings of flying saucers, apparitions of ghosts and saints, just to prove his point. I wondered whether all of the Santos weren't obsessed with the end of the world, whether by the intecession of la Virgen, UFO's, or the Beast of the 666. Out there on the ranch, up in la Serranía I was in the familiar light of the ancestors, at the latitude and longitude markings inscribed on our DNA. Maybe dreams come more easily in such a place. After the time in Mexico City, more than ever, the past and the present seemed permeable.

In another dream, I was on a beach. It was getting dark, but the pale sand was still glowing, and the rocks along the shoreline were silhouetted against the horizon. Out in the water there was a large, brilliantly painted galleon with great sails, braziers lit on deck, floating alone over the purple darkness of the sea. It was green and yellow and red, with elaborate curving wood designs all over it. There was no sign of life aboard, no other lights, no movement. In my sleep I asked myself: Is this what the Indios first saw when the Españoles arrived? Was this the dream memory of a shipwrecked Spaniard soul? A glimpse of the nighttime arrival of the ancestors? These questions could only be answered in Mexico, and I was convinced when I awoke that I should devote myself to finding out how far back our family memory could reach into the great Mexican story. There were many pilgrimages to make, many stories to exhume and recover, and time was short.

I awoke, and walked out onto the patio of the ranch house to do my morning exercises, just after dawn when the bright morning was still very quiet. Alejo and his family were returning from Múzquiz, their truck just coming into the pasture at the bottom of the hill, throwing up billowing clouds of dust. He waved from the driver's seat, his hand tapping the top of the cab, his kids yelling at me from the back of the truck. Near the house, a whole field of wild red mano de león plants, the color of blood, had bloomed overnight. Standing on a carpet for my morning exercises, hands clasped above my head, I leaned slowly backward, arching my spine toward the ground, taking in one deep, clear breath of sierra air.

At that moment, I felt as if I never wanted to leave Mexico. It would be ten years before I would return.

Volador

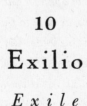

10
Exilio
Exile

As everyone disembarked from the ship across the steep, elevated gangway, I could see the crowded industrial horizon circling the port of Southampton, England, on a gray October day. Numberless chimneys trailed dark smoke across the chalky sky. The British air was thick and damp, and time seemed to pass slower there as a result.

The early afternoon light against the wet red-brick buildings was the color of the desert earth between Santa Fe and Taos. I felt like a naufragio, a shipwreck victim, landing in a place where I did not belong. I was a child of the Mundo Nuevo. I had never imagined even visiting Europe, much less preparing to live two years in the middle of England. I was eager to begin my studies at Oxford, but I felt that I would be an indelible outsider in the ancient university city.

Most of my classmates on board the ship were from European

families. For them, I thought, this was a kind of homecoming. If they weren't British, they still found themselves at the gateway to their home-land continent. As a Chicano of Spanish and indigenous heritage, I was aware that part of my blood was new to these lands. I was entering a New World, just as the Spaniards under Cortés thought they were, when they made their conquest campaign from Veracruz, on the gulf coast, to the Azteca capital of Tenochtitlán in the valley of Mexico.

For days, out in the middle of the Atlantic, the ocean had looked like windblown sand as far as I could see in every direction, sometimes seem-ing utterly still, sometimes like an endless hilly landscape that had sud-denly come alive. Late at night, Russian and Japanese tankers would pass solemnly in the distance, festooned from stem to stern with hanging strands of glowing yellow, burgundy, and lime green lights.

I regretted the passage would take only six days. I could imag-ine spending weeks surrounded by the dull roar of the waves and all their shimmering, apparent desolation. Crossing the ocean, even on the Queen Elizabeth 2, *you know in your bones, with every mile gained, that you have left your familiar world behind. You feel the full measure of the earth and the heavens. On the still nights, the sky glistened with icy blue light, reflecting out along the mirror surface of the seas so that the ship seemed suspended in a limitless expanse of space, heading in no dis-cernible direction. But every day, on a vast nautical map posted on the deck, the thin black line of the ship's track traced across the ocean a little farther.*

From England, Texas and Mexico seemed infinitely remote. That day, on our way to Oxford by bus, passing through villages where people stood, talking at bus stops and factory gates, where laundry hung out on taut lines over well-trimmed gardens, I was thinking of the conquest. I remembered Bernal Díaz de Castillo's description of the approach of Cortés's army to Tenochtitlán:

> *We saw so many cities and villages built in the water and
> other great towns on dry land . . . we were amazed and said
> that it was like the enchantments they tell of in the legend of
> Amadis, on account of the great towers and cues and buildings
> rising from the water, and all built of masonry. And some of
> our soldiers even asked whether the things that we saw were not
> a dream.*

As the bus came down Finchley Hill into the center of town, Oxford
looked like a city made of primordial coral, left behind by a receding
ocean. The Cherwell River was still and muddy. The stone towers bris-
tled against a mesh of telephone and electrical cables. Jack-booted punks
with orange mohawks and black leather jackets smoked cigarettes and
sniffed glue outside a pub.

At dusk, in the center of a pristine circular lawn, the cupola of the
Radcliffe Camera in the Bodleian Library looked like the sun-bleached
caracol dome of an ancient Mayan temple. I was entering one of the capi-
tals of the immaterial empire of Western knowledge, where the natives
would soon open their storehouses to me, as if the old conquest story were
repeating, or rewinding, at some vertiginous tilt.

This was not one of the destinations my family had in mind when
they left Coahuila in 1914. I wasn't sure whether, like a shipwreck, my
real mission wasn't to find the way back home, or, as an emissary of my
tribe, I should seek to travel farther inland, in search of the seat of this
civilization. I might reclaim the plunder of the conquest that was stashed
away in the collections of museums and individuals across Europe:
Motecuhzoma's feathered cape in Vienna, the massive stone sculpture of
a coiled plumed serpent in Frankfurt, painted calendars and codices in
Rome, Paris, and Oxford.

That night, there was a giant harvest moon over Oxford, and the *streets were empty, in anticipation of an IRA march that would take place on High Street the next day. Later, in my rooms, alone, feeling fitful and lost, I read newspapers full of the reports of revolutions in Nicaragua and Iran, uprisings in Poland, Rhodesia, and El Salvador. It was like 1789 all over again, tyrannies were falling, and I wanted my time in the old city, my studies there, to be connected to that, even if it did seem an unlikely prospect as chapel bells chimed at midnight and two swans glided silently down the river outside my rooms. Still, I went to bed that night, thirsty for dreams, thinking that, nearly five hundred years on, maybe the conquest could be reversed. . . .*

"*Todo se acaba. Todo se extermina.*" That's what my uncle Beto had said a week before, cooking a great steaming vat of fresh *menudo,* Mexican tripe stew, his specialty, in the garage workshop behind his house in San Antonio, while leisurely quoting el filósofo Socratés in the middle of an autumn afternoon. "Everything finishes. Everything is extinguished."

I was preparing to leave for England, feeling apprehensive about being away from San Antonio and the family for so long, and Uncle Beto was attempting to explain a broader perspective on the matter. He had come to San Antonio decades before from Nueva Rosita, in Coahuila, and married my aunt Margie, leaving Mexico behind forever, except for occasional visits. People move on. People die. Then, people move on even further. Eventually they die, too; eventually they are extinguished. You can be sad about this, but it wouldn't change anything. The whole process will continue, just as it always has. The old Greek philosopher had gotten that right.

In the years before, we had witnessed the great *despedida,* the deaths, all at once, of the grandmothers in our family. The elder Garcias, Uncle Frank, Pepa, Madrina, and the others, nearing their nineties now, were beginning to slow down. Even my uncles and aunts, and my parents, were beginning to show their age. On a recent morning, my father had opened one garage door and then promptly backed out the other.

The world we had known growing up in San Antonio, the family that had been so accustomed to living together, would eventually be dispersed, swallowed up, along with San Antonio itself, in the always deeper well of time. Along with all of my cousins, my generation was moving out farther into the worlds beyond Texas, further off from the source of the old Mexican time.

Uncle Beto's *dicho* seemed right about how everything in this universe ends and is extinguished—except for the universe itself. An old Aztec song expresses the same sentiment,

> *Can it be true that one lives on earth?*
> *Not forever on earth; only a little while here.*
> *Be it jade, it shatters.*
> *Be it gold, it breaks.*
> *Be it a quetzal feather, it tears apart.*
> *Not forever on earth; only a little while here.*

But this wasn't just an earthly predicament. Astrophysicists had just discovered the existence of black holes—infinite tears in the fabric of the cosmos that sucked matter through churning maws of death to we know not where. Things appeared and perished in the heavens, just as they appeared and perished on earth. Our vast galaxy is itself in perpetual motion, spiraling further outward into the chill vacuum that creation first exploded into. We have left our past—the journeys, marriages, and deaths along the way, all the bowls of *menudo*—scattered randomly across those vast arcs and loops, traced through millions of years, spun out across the void. This was our invisible momentum, always carrying us further from the sources of our stirring.

Uncle Lico died earlier that summer, but his story of our Mexican-ness had remained where he left it, gazing back into the abyss beyond 1770. Near the end of his life, he grew restless and urgent, as if he wanted to rage out of this world with all of his unanswered questions and unfinished family trees.

He had grown thinner, more serious. After thirty years of mar-riage, he left my aunt Mary and moved in with his wartime sweetheart, Amalia, from sixty years before. He drove his Mercury at two miles an hour over the lawns of his neighborhood on West Magnolia Street. On one evening, in front of his house, he brandished a pistol in one hand and a cigar in the other, before falling into a deep, diabetic sleep at his own front door.

After a couple of months of such raving, he returned home and my aunt took him back in. All he'd say about that time is that his damn dia-betes prescriptions were all out of whack, and that his new doctor had things under control.

When he died, suddenly one afternoon, from heart failure, his children, all from an earlier marriage, took over the funeral plans and refused to allow a Catholic ceremony. Those cousins had all become born-again Christians, and they regarded the traditions of the Mexican *velorio* wake, with the long droning prayer chains of the rosary and the blessings and censing of the body, as little better than voodoo and pa-gan superstition.

They removed the San Judás Tadeo cards that people had brought from packages or letters Uncle Lico had sent them over the years. As each friend paid final respects, they laid the cards on his body in an act of homage. Only the card of his brother, Uncle Lauro, escaped detec-tion, when one of my brothers placed it discreetly in an inside breast pocket of el Tío's jacket.

As Uncle Lico lay in state in the funeral home chapel, a slick-haired Chicano minister from Laredo, dressed in a shiny black suit and a wide paisley tie, told us all that my uncle had secretly accepted Jesus as his personal savior. It had happened some weeks before in a private session with the minister.

"He found his peace then. He found his salvation and his ticket to everlasting life with our Lord.

"How many of you would now be prepared to do the same?"

All the old Mexicans shifted uncomfortably in their seats while my mother stared the ancient Mexican *mal ojo* at the ebullient minister from Laredo. Uncle Lico had told me that those born-agains were a bunch of crazy fanatics, and he said it used to drive him nuts how they ended every sentence with "Praise the Lord!" Maybe he changed his mind. Maybe, feeling his death coming very near, he too embraced a new god.

As we had carried his coffin to the waiting hearse, there was a crescendo of Nashville gospel music from the minister's suitcase-sized boom box, as my cousins and their born-again confreres began singing "How Great Is His Name!" At the graveside, after the funeral, Anastasio, a friend of Uncle Lico's who wore a brown straw porkpie hat like Uncle Lico's, just shook his head and turned to make his way back to his car.

"Just ain't the way he would've wanted to say goodbye."

Uncle Beto looked up from the big pot of *menudo* he was stirring, and asked about news of Sabinas. The day before, there had been bad news from Mexico. I had meant to spend that last weekend there, but had missed my ride south after returning late from another trip. Alejo, the ranch foreman, and his wife, Felipa, had a new daughter. They already had six children, but only one son, and Alejo was worried he would grow up effeminate with only sisters for siblings. So they kept having more children—four more—and every time a daughter. A big baptism party is a mainstay of *Norteño* tradition. And the party that night at their small house in town was already well under way, with a mariachi trio singing on the patio, when a group of local toughs, several brothers among them, crashed the fiesta and began menacing some of the guests. Alejo and others ejected them with little resistance, but an hour later they returned, with machetes. In the argument and altercation that followed, Alejo shot three of them, all brothers, killing one, and then went into hiding. After turning himself in several days later, it would take more than a year before Alejo was released on a local judge's finding of self-defense, but he and his family had to leave Coahuila for fear of a vendetta by the surviving brothers of the dead man.

Earlier that same summer, during the long ride out from the stay at the remote ranch of Dr. Mata, far up in the mountains, there had been an eerie scene that had seemed like an augur of these times to come. The horse I had ridden in on had gone lame after our fall on the night of the stormy ride in, so my cousin Chickee and I, with some discomfort, were sharing a horse on the way out. By that time in the journey we all were irritating each other with every word and eccentricity, and Chickee and I let the others ride well out ahead, keeping our own silence, riding quietly through high mountain pastures and low swooping valley trails. Just past midday, as we came into a tree-circled clearing surrounding an earthen water tank, I pulled the horse's reins to halt as we saw a medium-sized speckled doe stepping out of the bush just ahead of us, staring impassively in our direction. For a moment, we stared back, speechless.

The old *vaquero* from the Mata ranch, Don Tiburcio, had complained ceaselessly during our entire stay about the fact that we had lost the meat we had brought in on the night of the storm. After leaving it covered with tarpaulins, we had returned to the piney vale the next day to find the burro safe, but the provisions already looted by vultures or mountain cats. According to Don Tiburcio, he hadn't had any fresh meat in two months, just damn beans, potatoes, some scraps of dried *machacado* beef—and mite-infested tortillas. For all of his cantankerousness about this, the night before we left he still managed to make a delicious fresh milk pudding for us, with sweet cream and aromatic wild mint from the mountains.

But game animals had been scarce all that summer, even the usually abundant rabbits, which were common Coahuila ranch fare. Tiburcio said the recent floods had carried them all away, leaving him hungry, desperate, and crotchety. During those weeks, on a couple of occasions, we had spotted deer, ambling distractedly, far off across a bare valley or standing on a small brushy plateau along a distant bluff. Both times, Tiburcio had taken a long bead and then fired his ancient rifle, only to have the animals jump off into cover, before the bullet was halfway to its target.

The doe was standing motionless, less than twenty yards in front of us. It wouldn't affect Chickee or me if we let the deer go. We would be heading for San Antonio in the next days. Abrán, Dr. Mata's son, would soon go back to university in Monterrey. But Tiburcio would be well stocked with meat for weeks. I wasn't much of a hunter. Out on Rancho Los Generales, we shot rabbits now and then, to cook in very spicy stews with potatoes and fresh chile piquín. In east Texas, under the tutelage of one of our cousins' husbands, my brothers and I had hunted bullfrogs with shotguns and raccoons with .22s. But I had never hunted for deer, and I had never had such an animal in a rifle sight. The only weapon I had with me now was a low-power, collapsible backpacking rifle that was so light it felt as if it was made out of aluminum foil. It had to be screwed together, like a billiards cue stick. And it was buried deep in my backpack.

"Get it!" Chickee whispered from the rump of the horse where he was riding. "We should get it now, while we can! For Tiburcio!"

"It'll run," I replied, reaching behind me, down into the backpack, feeling for the parts of the rifle.

"It's standing still. Get it while it's standing still!"

I pulled out the detached butt and barrel of the rifle from my bag and carefully assembled it. With each turn, the threads let out a slow, high-pitch squeak that sounded like fingernails scratching on a blackboard, amplified by the silence of the wilderness around us. But the doe did not move, did not seem to even blink. Sitting in the saddle with Chickee holding the reins, I loaded a single .22 caliber bullet into the chamber and cocked the firing pin back to fire. At the edge of the tree shade ahead, the doe stood, staring at us, and the cool air was scented with sweetgrass, oregano, and pine.

I took aim for the animal's heart, nestled just beneath the tuft of white fur on its breast, and when the shot pierced the air with a fiery crack, the echoes bounded off in all directions, scattering birds and sending snakes into their holes. We watched the bullet hit its mark, leaving a small red smear on the breast. But the deer did not fall, only taking a few steps forward to continue staring forward at us. The sharp metallic scent of the scorched gunpowder hung in the air around us.

Chickee and I were both taken aback, disappointed that the doe hadn't run, but now the small wound my shot had made would no doubt eventually be fatal. I reloaded and took aim again. The deer looked back at us as if utterly resigned to its own sacrifice, as if there were some inexorable outcome to our meeting. The second shot hit again, this time in the shoulder and the animal flinched and steadied its step, but still did not fall or run. It began to feel as if we had been unknowingly enlisted into a strange ritual execution, with everyone involved following through on some unspoken *compromiso*. As I loaded the next bullet, it looked like a shiny, opalescent pearl before falling into the firing chamber.

It took three more shots before the doe finally weakened at its knees, and then leaned over and fell into a thicket of brush to one side. Abrán and Tiburcio, who had heard the shots, were standing nearby, waiting for the hunt to finish. Tiburcio let out a giddy whoop and rode out from a copse, preparing to field dress the quarry to take back to the ranch.

"¡Bien hecho, compañeritos, bien hecho!" he shouted, trotting forward in a cloud of dust while the two of us were still quieted by the slow relay of shots I had just fired. We watched as Tiburcio quickly lashed the hind legs of the deer up onto the low branch of a tree and began to clean and skin it. He shouted praise for my feat of hunting and held back the neck to show the wounds, spaced like a perfect necklace.

I felt as if I had intruded into someone else's sacrifice, knowing how close the *vaqueros* live to this land that I only visited during vacations. There was no remorse or guilt about taking a deer, especially when it meant Tiburcio eating meat after a long time without. I'd seen Alejo once torture a captured hawk that had been stealing eggs from the ranch henhouse for months, so deep had his personal enmity become for the predator bird. But even if my ancestors had once been of that world in north Mexico, I knew a part of that ranch life had ended for me. At the Rancho Los Generales, the cattle herd was gradually sold off and dwindled down to less than a hundred head. In the ten years that followed, a pageant of lackadaisical *vaqueros* let many of the fences and waterworks fall into disrepair, and the family from Sabinas and Texas didn't visit much. With the news from Sabinas of the shootings at the baptism party, it seemed the life of the *ranchos* was ending everywhere.

Todo se acaba. Todo se extermina.

Uncle Beto dropped handfuls of diced onions and chopped oregano into the boiling stew that had the rusty magenta color of dried chiles de arbol. Stepping away from the hot plate where he cooks his *menudo,* he began one of the flowery oratorical expositions he frequently delivers, based in part on the American citizenship exam he was forced to memorize over forty years ago.

"If, in order to please the people, for the party of the first part, and to guarantee again the principles on which this nation was at one time forefounded, then how can we not, now, being of sound mind, *alejamos de San Antonio,* and the nation on which it stands, saying goodbye to—tamales, *menudo, ranchitos*—so that we may then, perhaps, in the party of the second part, choose henceforth to go to *Inglaterra,* or England, as we sometimes call it, just as our forefathers recommended?"

Stirring the pot of bubbling *menudo* with a long wooden spoon, Uncle Beto ended with his traditional faux CB sign-off: "Obi-Wan Kenobi. Ten-four. Smokey at the front door, over and out!"

London was unnaturally quiet. You could hear birdsong in the trees along the mall by the Thames, as well as the big boats cutting the river water as they went by. All Saturday, downtown traffic was closed off while a giant campaign for nuclear disarmament demonstration snaked its way across the Southbank Bridge, coursing through Piccadilly, up to Oxford Circus, then down past Covent Garden Market, some of us stopping for eclairs and coffee, and then everyone spilling, for hours it seemed, into the great plaza at Trafalgar Square. It was a gray day under turbulent, roiling clouds and the myriad shifting flights of thousands of pigeons inhabiting the square.

This march was the culmination of months of other marches across the country in protest against the Americans placing nuclear-tipped cruise missiles on planes stationed at bases in Great Britain and Europe. As the throng of protesters listened to speeches, milled along the streets with their flasks, sitting on the steps of museums, or hanging from the arms of statues, a circle of orange-robed Buddhist monks drummed and chanted in a changeless solemn cadence. A constant, flat droning hum of far-off bagpipes was in the air as the punk band Killing Joke took the main stage at the demonstration with a paralyzing electric screech, beneath a massive banner with an image of the head of a screaming baby in a seething red mushroom cloud. The drum battery exploded and the crowd was already heaving forward as the caterwauling guitars began to shake the paving stones. I thought to myself: This is what the end of the world will feel like.

In that rumbling din, you could feel the tug of the universe expanding, aging by vast degrees, here, in a fragile world we were ourselves prepared to obliterate, all of it making the end of the world feel palpable and immanent. Some days earlier I had received the news from Texas that my great-uncle Frank had died in his sleep at ninety-five. Francisco was the eldest brother of my grandmother, the family scout in the 1914 migration out of Mexico, Texas homesteader, inventor, father, gentleman, who had once whispered to me, "The way is very simple. Do the good to other people and it shall be returned to you."

His long, delicate hands were rough from caressing metal lathes, pulling apart motors and industrial latches, and hammering planks of white-hot alloyed steel. I had his hands, without the calluses and torn nails. I walked in the same body he had, long in the torso, bony knees, big ears. While he had invented that early version of the dump truck, and a widely used pecan shelling machine, he never became wealthy by any of his inventions. I complained to him that I had received none of the Garcia talent for inventing, engineering, and metalworking. But Uncle Frank disagreed and shook his finger at me, "Your stories and your poems—those are inventions, too!" and he laughed.

From England, he seemed as distant as starlight, as lost as wind. He was the first of the old ones to go after the great *despedida* of *las Viejitas* six years before. Before leaving, I had explained to him that I was going to study for two years in England, and I promised him a full account, as I always gave him after my journeys in Mexico. He nodded, grinning, and his long face lit up.

"*¡Shahk-ess-peah-rrrreh! ¡Qué bravo!*" he shouted, and he showed me his old and yellowed paper copy, missing its cover, of a Spanish translation of the *Tragedies*, which he kept on his night table, next to his bed. Of all that was possible out of our past together, it seemed prophetic or ironic that those were the last words between us in this world. The fearless *abrazo* he gave me as a farewell that day remained a warm presence in a bitter time, far away from the gathered family in San Antonio, giving Uncle Frank his last *despedida*.

The day I learned of Frank's death I had already been scheduled to view the collection of Mexican pictorial manuscripts in the collection of the Bodleian at Oxford. I didn't feel like spending that afternoon inside a library, but it had been difficult getting permission to see the old codices, and the two-hour session had been planned a month in advance. If I were to cancel now, it was unlikely I would have a chance to see them again soon.

All the denizens at their desks in the high-ceilinged reading room of the ancient Codrington Library of the Bodleian stirred as I entered. One of my Tony Lama pigskin suede cowboy boots, once as supple as chamois leather, now nearly rotten from the damp British climate, had developed a squeak in its sole. As I walked across the long chamber to the librarian's desk, the boot let out a series of slow, high-pitched squeals that irritated the scholars and drew a volley of *shushes* and *tsks* from both sides of the aisle.

This was my favorite of all of Oxford's libraries, where I spent a considerable amount of time in those years. There were small study cells with leaded glass windows that had the feeling of ancient cloistered monks' quarters. From the reading room, stuffy from all the alkaline perspiration of scholarship, you could hear the rush of great torrents of water every half hour, sluicing the urinals of the men's room downstairs, but sounding like a running mountain stream, charging the air throughout the old building. And since the library was part of a Fellows college at Oxford, made up of scholars and no students, the clientele at the Codrington tended to be old eccentric dons, a few in their academic gowns, surrounded by piles of yellowing notes, climbing ladders to high shelves, making notes from books while standing on the very top step.

The porter led me to the manuscript room, which was lit through high clerestory windows by the afternoon sun. The four codices, ancient painted books of the Mixteca Indians of Mexico, had already been laid out on a long, cantilevered viewing table, fanned out in narrow accordion swaths of the amatl paper and stiff deerskin on which the colored pictures, from the doorway, seemed to be glowing and spinning. These were among the few surviving documents that predate the conquest, and they had appeared in the Bodleian's collection in 1659, as part of a bequest. How they first came out of Mexico, or where they came from exactly, was unknown.

In long chains of elaborately decorated panels, the manuscripts, painted in rusty ochre, cerulean blue, and cochineal red, depicted genealogies and migrations, battles and concordats, sacrifices and rituals. In some panels, figures in tunics were seated in profile, facing each other on a woven mat, curls of speech issuing and rising from their mouths. Most of the glyphs had been approximated into English.

"The marriage of Eight Flint and Thirteen Lizard, in a place named the Hill of Flowers."

"There once was a lake with an island in the middle, surrounded by seven caves." Then a journey was traced in trails of miniature footprints, from "Cloud Belching Hill to the River of the Lady Six Deer." Beneath a glyph depicting a smoking mirror appeared the place name for the hill of the Intertwined Serpents.

In that room, full of scores of other old books and manuscripts, the velvety brown parchments looked like artifacts from another planet, still radiating the dust of someone else's atmosphere. They were poignant, among the few survivors of the great bonfires that consumed a whole cosmos of known things painted in books just like these. There was a futile, ironic feeling because the books dealt repeatedly with the memory of a place of origin, and all the setting out and wandering in the world, guaranteeing that everything would be remembered, that the knowledge of the past would not be lost. Yet their testimonies were preserved but untranslatable, memories without a rememberer. They looked hijacked, stolen from their vanquished source, each one a broken oracle of a disappeared world.

The old librarian who tended the ancient texts sat at the far end of the table, dozing with his chin resting on his chest, his academic gown tattered and torn along the bottom hem. I thought I might just be able to quietly fold and carry out at least two of the books, the Selden roll and the Codex Bodley, without waking the deeply asleep minder of the manuscripts. I had imagined the plot for weeks. With luck, I would have enough time to mail them from the High Street postal station off to my cousins in Sabinas before the Bodleian Library detectives could catch me. The ancient books could be repatriated in Coahuila, in the *frontera* of Mexico. I had read how a Mexican graduate student in Paris had recently managed to smuggle several codices out of the Bibliothèque Nationale and back to Mexico, by hiding them in the seat of his underwear.

But as I mulled over the risks and rationale for my plot, I was distracted by an image off at the edge of one of the panels of one codex. I hadn't noticed it before because it appeared upside down there, and the later afternoon light was casting long shadows in the stone room. Stepping nearer to it, craning my neck, in one corner of the manuscript, next to a panel of the goddess of maguey seated on a turtle, there was a small, simple painting of the *Voladores,* in the midst of their ritual. The four dancers, faces expressionless, were wearing eagle headdresses and feathers, perched on top of their decorated pole, preparing for the spiraling descent to the earth. Standing on the pinnacle, the *caporal* was speaking, telltale curls streaming from his mouth, chanting out loud the old count of the days, praying that the world would be saved from destruction again.

The longer I lived away from San Antonio, the more it seemed that, as a family, we had passed much of this century setting out. First from Mexico, where the rest of the past was left behind, hidden, then from San Antonio, where the lives and fortunes of the family took myriad paths. Abuelo Juan José set out still further, gradually losing contact with the world around him, carried off in a current of worries, suspicion, and melancholy impossible to resist. Arising on the foggy morning of his death, he must've known he was setting forth again into unknown lands.

After Abuelo Juan José's death, Uela went off deeper into her Rosicrucian studies, using the Bible as a divination tool to seek counsel for her great sadness. Her Bible, which survives, is stuffed with poplar leaves, strips of pink and yellow taffeta, and newspaper clippings about Pope John XXIII. In Genesis, she drew a thick line in pencil around the verses, "While the earth remains, seedtime and harvest, cold and heat, summer and winter, shall not cease."

My father left behind his ambition to become a professional singer after his father's death, taking jobs to help support the family, and eventually joining the army after the Japanese attack on Pearl Harbor. In those days, he had been professionally known as The Broadway

Gondolier, appearing with Richard Cortez and his Gran Orquesta, always in his trademark tapered white suit and gold tie, singing the songs of Agustín Lara and Frank Sinatra in mainly Mexican clubs around San Antonio.

While Uela's family, the Garcias, remained close in San Antonio, they gradually lost contact with the far-flung Santos of Elgin and Hondo, and only seldom visited my grandfather's sister Tía Chita in Nueva Rosita. No one could really bring themselves to speak about Juan José's death, and it was easier if they just didn't see one another, so, over the years, they drifted apart, and the days of several families living together in one large house passed. My aunts and uncles married and moved out into their own homes, and Uela continued to live on Parsons Street with Madrina and Uncle Manuel.

San Antonio was so full of memory for Uela, she mainly stayed inside, visiting or reading, or she tended her garden in the backyard for hours. It was possible to endure, to leave everything painful behind. It was possible to imagine a shell made of quiet that would contain the entirety of the past.

Eventually, for the Santos, there were no more places of origin, just the setting out, just the going forth into new territory, new time. Being in England those years only carried on that tale, even if it seemed a strange destination for a grandson of poor people from Coahuila, Mexico. Uela remembered that one of my Abuelo Juan José's cousins was a professor or a traveling scholar of some kind, and once, a box of books he had sent to San Antonio for safekeeping was said to have arrived at the house on Parsons Street from Cairo, Egypt.

After I read her my first poem, Uela announced that I would be the family's poet, even though I told her the last thing I wanted to write about was the family. There had been inventors and dancers in the family. Uela had been forced by her father to forgo her aspiration to become an actress. And my father had been the singer in the family. But there had never before been a poet. She said she could tell it was my *compromiso,* an obligation that couldn't be denied.

I was already seeking out writers, sending them adoring letters of appreciation after reading their work, and they would almost always write back. I wrote to William Saroyan, Gabriel García Márquez, William Burroughs, Jorge Luis Borges, Ken Kesey, and Octavio Paz, and to poets, like Denise Levertov, Allen Ginsberg, and Gary Snyder. One elder poet I wrote to, Laura (Riding) Jackson, whose strange abstract poems had made a strong impression on me, sent back a ten-page, single-spaced, manually typed letter angrily explaining to me that she had renounced poetry in 1939 for its failure to communicate what she called "basic human truth," and she cautioned me sternly, lest I fall into the same error in which she had misspent her youth, of believing in the "truth of poetry." Inevitably, she said, poetry was more concerned with artifice and elegance of language than with truth. She hadn't failed poetry, she insisted to me in a later letter. Poetry itself had failed.

I had a chance to meet Borges while I was at college in England, after seeing a poster at Blackwell's Bookstore in Oxford announcing "Borges Tonight!" Though he was Argentine, through his fantastic earthly tales of space, time, and infinity, he had been a literary and spiritual mentor to me in San Antonio. In his story "El Aleph," which I had once read aloud in Spanish to Uela, he had described a closet in a house in Buenos Aires where the entire cosmos was manifest in a cipher. He had described infinite archives of the planet's past, enchanted maps that conversed with their cartographers.

That night, he was to be talking about Walt Whitman, another literary idol. The old Sheldonian Theater in Oxford was full, the balcony creaking under capacity weight, and everyone was anxious to see the great Latin American master who rarely traveled. A total hush fell when he came out unannounced, his skin so white against his black wool suit he seemed an apparition at first, led by the arm by an amanuensis, walking cautiously across the wide stage to where a chair and table with his thick manuscript and a glass and carafe of water were awaiting him.

After he sat down, it felt as if he suspended time itself, keeping his silence as water was slowly poured for him and carefully placed in his hand. The transparent skin of his face, tinged slightly with pink, seemed so delicate and tender. His ethereal expression, his eyes milky and palsied, were inexplicably fixed in what looked like the gentlest stare of commiseration I had ever seen, as if he had spent much of his life consoling others.

In his talk, delivered in a brisk, poetic, sing-song diction that sounded like a Latin Mass being intoned, Borges argued that Whitman's imagination had been gradually absorbed into American English. To speak the language itself was to echo Whitman's radical ideas of democracy, humanity, and universality. In a tape I made that night, virtually indecipherable now with age, Borges's voice booms and trembles in a muffled roar, the audience by turns rapt and laughing along with him, as he dazzled the crowd.

After his talk, I stood to ask a question that seemed to cause him to gasp, and eventually to leave the stage. The question, in Spanish, had been innocent, asking only if by saying that Whitman had been absorbed into American English he meant to say there was no reason to still read great poems like "Song of Myself." Wasn't there something in the poetry itself, the long lines, the epic lists, the litanies and epiphanies, that could never be touched or understood by any other means?

First, he asked me to repeat the question, already looking perturbed as one eye twitched warily. But before I could finish, he was already calling on his assistant to escort him from the stage. As I was only the second person called on to ask a question, the audience was stunned. Many turned to look at me with utter scorn. I was quickly set upon by the organizers of the event who angrily recounted how hard they had worked to bring Borges to England, only to have his journey end in this debacle. They insisted that I apologize to the great writer. He would be at a party later that evening, organized by the university. I was put into a car, to be taken there, like a prisoner on the way to the gallows.

By the time I arrived at the fiesta, Borges was already surrounded by other undergraduates, sitting patiently as they read him poems and stories that had been inspired by his work. He looked pained and bored. When I finally found a moment when I could sit next to him, I told him that it was I who had asked the offending question at his talk, and I was sorry if it had insulted him in any way.

Borges broke out laughing, *"¡Es que tuve que mear!"* he said, "I had to take a piss!"

He had told his assistant in a rushed whisper at the very moment I was asking my question, but the assistant had misunderstood and he helped Borges leave the stage. He failed to tell the audience that Borges would return. Then it was too late as the audience quickly began to leave the hall.

After he asked me to fetch potato chips and beer for him, we sat together and he explained that he could see only dim light and colors around him. When he asked my name, it lit up his vast, archival memory. He replied unequivocally that I was Portuguese. Borges spoke in encyclopedic detail of a log from a certain ship from Lisbon in the late sixteenth century that, he claimed, recorded the first time a Santos set foot in the New World.

"Also a Santander. But that Santos must've been your great-great-great-great-grandfather," he declared, laughing more, as content with himself as if he had solved some esoteric ancient mystery. I didn't tell him that, according to family stories, the name had originally been de los Santos, and that in all likelihood it was a pious name some Mexican Indians took for themselves or had placed upon them by zealous Spanish *curas*. Names like Cruz, Angel, Santamaria, Jesus, and Santos.

But maybe he was right. There weren't *any* records or documents of the family past of the Santos and Garcias—my father's tribes—as there were for my mother's family of Velas and Lopez, which Uncle Lico had traced back to the eighteenth century. Maybe their migrations had begun further south than any of us had thought possible.

The pulsing, velvety waves were rounding the smooth concrete abutments at Southbank, then turning swiftly east toward the Isle of Dogs. After the great antinuclear march of that day ended, the sounds returned of all the revving cabs, the lumbering lorries, all the rattling tracks of passing red trains from the Underground, carried off in one surging current. From the bridge, the Thames was matte gunmetal gray in London's sulfurous twilight.

Looking down on the river, debris seemed to hover at its surface, held just above the waters by some eerie reverse magnetism; bags from Wimpy burgers spinning like Chinese fireworks, a sneaker moving like a torpedo, webs of tree branches in a whorl with a piece of a chair, Styrofoam, a dead dog. The lilting falsetto sounds of a Christmas children's choir periodically rose above the din of the old river, and it felt as if I were standing in the middle of the bridge of exile.

With Uncle Frank's death, our family had lost the steady beacon that had guided us out of Mexico and helped create the life we had known in San Antonio. The family was different now, bigger, more spread out. Mexico, and San Antonio, too, had undergone enormous changes. But it was a time when poor people all over the world continued to leave their homes and countries because of joblessness, famine, and wars. Our family's story in this century, of a migration of only two hundred and fifty miles from the mountains of Coahuila to the river plain surrounding San Antonio, was part of a much larger story, encompassing untold millions of lives, all of us setting out once and for all from our homelands—all of us *exilios*—perhaps never to return.

In a journal from that time in England, I recorded a dream of Mexico:

> *This one is the apocalypse at the well. I am in an old Mexican village, ancient looking, with long, hilly streets paved with cobblestones. With a plaza and a church in the middle. Hills in the distance. The village sits above the surrounding landscape, it is itself on a hill. I find myself at a small communal well in the center of the village, and around me are several older dark-skinned men. They are uneasy about something. They are telling me that the world is ending—that the Sun is dissolving. I notice the sky is dark, though it is afternoon.*
>
> *I look up at the sky and can see the Sun's outline, but it is a black Sun, radiating little light and little heat. There is another source of light, but it is coming from an unidentifiable source, somewhere on the horizon.*
>
> *For awhile, I argue with the old men about what is happening. I have some scientific explanations. I am genuinely confused because I feel they have already jumped to rash conclusions. I say, "Maybe it's an eclipse."*
>
> *"Look, the Sun is dissolving!" they tell me, and one of them points into the well. I look down into the water, meeting the stone wall just below the rim.*
>
> *There, reflected on the surface of the water, is what looks like a night sky full of the bright stars. The whole density and*

ovoid shape of the cosmos seems to be mirrored there. But in one place, there is a star—a large star—our Sun, and it is dissolving, the way bread dissolves in water, only faster. And it is not matter that is disintegrating, it is light. I watch as this one brilliant disc diffuses, there in the water, into an ever-widening net of sparks. I remember walking away alone, leaving the others quietly weeping by the well, wondering blankly down one of the meandering streets, in the eerie 3 o'clock darkness of the afternoon . . .

These dreams were not prophecies in the sense of prognostications or predictions. I received them instead as if they were dispatches from a story being told to time by all human lives. In a century so interrupted by conflagrations, deceit, destruction, and dislocation, our dreams would continue to echo these reports. As Uela and Tía Pepa had told me, by watching our dreams, especially if they were haunted, we could strengthen our spirits and prepare ourselves for whatever was to come. They were not to be feared or denied. Just watched, reflected on, and told to others as stories that we had lived.

Larger objects were floating downstream in the Thames now. As I stood on that bridge late in the day, gazing down at the water, it suddenly looked as if a whole village had been flooded out upriver, carrying doors from houses, window frames, broken gables, a galaxy of wooden roof tiles. I remembered how such floods had once been common in San Antonio, periodically flushing out whatever buildings or shacks lacked a strong foundation in the downtown precinct. My broken suede Tony Lama boots had been stuffed with dried flowers and stones I had brought back from a trip to Spain, along with the notes, letters, drafts of poems, and essays from the year that I wanted to discard. The boots, whose squeal had only gotten worse, vexing several Oxford cobblers, were bound together by wire and twine, tightly bundled, and hanging from a rope handle. Then, at a moment when the passing traffic subsided and there were no other pedestrians nearby, I hurled them from the edge of the railing into the heavy air of the British evening, watching the long arc they traced downward, past all the lights of London, slipping finally into the rushing, murky Thames with barely a ripple.

11

La Ruta

The Route

 *As I drove south on the highway from Cholula to Cuernavaca, the clouds floated like a luminous crown over the volcano called Popocatépetl. This was the road Cortés's army took, through fields of wild agave, marching weary, bloodied, and sullen toward Tenochtitlán after their massacre of hundreds of Nahua priests in Cholula the day before. They followed the old Mexica road, now the Paso de Cortés, which went up and over one of Popo's desolate stony ridges. I would circle around the southern edge of the volcano.*

Accelerating to eighty-five miles per hour with the windows down in long, warm open stretches through red-dirt brush country, I slowly rounded the ancient volcano on the new autopista and saw its snow-covered peak bellowing to the south in a massive plume of silvery ash that seemed utterly motionless against the sky. The day before, mapless, I asked for directions to the highway to Cholula. An old, uniformed park-

ing attendant in the oak-shaded plaza in Coatepec pointed in the direction of the volcano and warned me that Cholula wasn't a safe place to be, and he said the gathering eruption had been foretold.

"*This volcano waking up now is a sign.*"

Yes, he said, there was a hole in the sky that was making the whole world heat up like a burning coal. He reported that the French were exploding atomic bombs deep below the Pacific Ocean, which he explained would unleash earthquakes across the globe. But Popocatépetl's awakening was something else. This was not of man's making. He said that was a part of Mexico's story. Popo had erupted in the years before the arrival of the Spaniards. In this century, it had erupted during the revolution. The old parking officer said it meant now that we were in the time of the Azteca prophecy of this age's end, the end of the Fifth World, the Fifth Sun.

"La muerte del quinto sol," *he repeated, wearily.*

The night before, after another long day of driving, I had dreamed of the Voladores. *I could barely hear the flute and* tambor *of the* caporal, *floating eerily in the dark. It was nighttime, and the wind was gusting from every direction, shaking the treetops and stirring up the dust in violent swirls. It was only in the instant of a lightning flash that I saw their profiles, high atop their braided pole. As the heavy sheets of rain began to fall and the lightning bolts began to thunder across the sky, the four flyers set off from their perch and began revolving upside down around the pole. I could hear the sound of the ropes stretching over the din of the downpour. The* caporal, *still atop the pole, spinning around, continued to beat the* tambor *and play the flute. As I watched the flyers descending toward the earth in wide scooping arcs, their arms outstretched, I hear a voice from behind me say calmly, as if to reassure me, "They are dancing to keep this world from falling apart. . . ."*

The old parking attendant said this was the time when the earth under Mexico would tremble to its core again, as it did in the beginning, shaking down all things man has made. That had been the Aztec prophecy for the end of this Sun called "Four Movement." The ancient Mayans simply ended their great calendar in August of the year 2012, concluding a long count of days that reached back into the fourth millennium B.C.

"That's why nobody gives a goddamn about la política," the viejito *said. "The sign from the volcano, that's what we still wait for. We act like everything has changed, like things could just go on like this forever. But it could happen any day, like a change in the weather. And then what?" Battered from the millennia of volcanoes, hurricanes, conquest, discordia, and revolución, at last, the fulfillment of our prophetic legacy: the end of Mexico.*

New York City became my home in exile, less a homestead than a place to set out from into the world. I saw the Santos and Garcias of San Antonio less, and years passed between visits to Mexico. On visits home, my abuelo Juan José's name was never mentioned, and for many years, I asked no questions. The long silence around his memory felt like an inviolable equilibrium.

There were other stories, other tales, other enigmas. All of the revolutions had failed, been infiltrated, assassinated, corrupted, or simply became vengeful and vindictive. In the Soviet Union, China, Iran, Nicaragua, Zimbabwe, many others—and Mexico. In those times when all the ideals and fragile aspirations for Utopia were dying, I traveled to places all over the world, telling stories for television of poor people who, despite the states and empires crumbling around them, struggled to survive and gain control over their destinies. I'm not sure how or why that became the story I pursued as a journalist—a story no one was interested in hearing. It wasn't intentional. It was more like sleepwalking through a house on fire.

I awoke suddenly in Khartoum when the window of my hotel

room shattered in a clamor that left behind a deep, tranquil quiet. In that lacuna moment, the brick that had been thrown through the window rolled to a stop, and the curtains bellowed up with an almost cloyingly sweet breeze from the Nile. I got up from the bed to see there was a long demonstration passing by on the boulevard outside with thousands of Sudanese people marching across the bridge from dusty Omdurman, across the Nile, into downtown Khartoum. There had been a coup d'etat in the early hours of that morning and the hordes of people, jubilant and angry, were celebrating the ouster of the unpopular dictator Jafaar Nimeiry, who had made the tactical mistake of making a diplomatic journey to the United States, only to have a military council seize control of the government while he was away, prohibiting his return.

Some of the marchers were throwing more bricks and breaking windows in the hotel. Others ran into the elaborate marble lobby and took clubs to a large framed photograph of a smiling Nimeiry in sunglasses and blue military dress uniform, pulling it from the wall and shattering it on the ground while onlookers leapt up in approval, shaking their fists and cheering with jubilation. Then, all at once, a perfect quiet fell on the marchers, a caesura in time, in which the whole crowd seemed to think as one, running out from the hotel, rejoining the legions, turning and surging up a main avenue into Khartoum.

At the university, the professors lectured to one another in the shaded faculty garden about what to make of their bloodless revolution. The markets carried on as usual, with vendors meticulously stacking their fruits into perfect pyramids. The generals who had carried out the coup promised a transitional government of only one year, with elections for a civilian government to follow. That evening, a stadium full of people in Khartoum cheered, *"Islamiya-miya-miya! Islamiya-miya-miya!"* as they listened to an incantatory speech on Sudan's future as a Muslim state by Imam Hassan Turabi, a previously imprisoned

Muslim leader who had just been released from jail and would eventually become the prime mover in the Sudan. For days afterward, while huge Egyptian buzzards circled overhead, the streets of Khartoum were mostly abandoned, littered with burned-out cars, always feeling as if some conflagration were about to erupt again.

At the same time, all over the country, unrelated to the political upheaval in Khartoum, there were sprawling desert famine camps where thousands of Sudanese and Ethiopian people were starving and slowly dying. Life in the camps was a blend of the everyday and the apocalyptic. Children in tattered clothes played with toys made from baling wire and discarded tops from the large tin cans that contained the powdered infant formula that relief groups distributed to the families. The feeding stations opened three times a day to a frenzy of dust and clattering empty bowls. The Bedouins, abandoning a life thousands of years old, sold their camels, their swords, their silver bangles and bracelets made of colored Venetian glass to buy scraps of food from vendors set up at the edge of the camps. Ansar holy men, Muslim clerics dressed in pristine white djellabas with green sashes and scarlet turbans, roamed the camps, standing on little hills in the relentless sunlight and reciting Quranic scriptures into the wind—while the sound of voices, moaning, shrieking, and arguing, could be heard from tents in every direction.

After weeks among the camp dwellers crisscrossing the country, shooting video, doing interviews, I returned to my room in a hotel in Port Sudan, and along with my companions on that journey, drank bootleg bitter palm wine and wept. Steve, the cameraman, as a boy in Greece during World War II had been in hunger camps like those we had seen. He said he thought such things could never happen again. George, who was reporting the story with me, believed the debacle could be resolved with aid and assistance from Western governments, if only the political will could be mobilized. Many of the people we met in camps near Tokar, El Obeid, and in Mwelih, near Khartoum, were already beyond struggling against the tide of death engulfing them—keeping tallies of the names of the dead on scraps of paper that were guarded like precious ancient scrolls. The latest revolution in faraway Khartoum would mean little to them. One of the camps was within walking distance from a well-stocked market, but the refugees remained huddled in their tents, many too weak to move, others simply too weak to conspire to steal.

In Nicaragua, the people I saw could easily have been from south Texas or Mexico. On the tropical highway from Managua to the Honduran border, passing farmers with their donkey carts loaded with corn and women walking with small veils on their heads, I also saw teenage soldiers lazily thumbing for rides, hitchhiking back to the war with the Contras on the northern border with Honduras. Their stoic faces, the makeshift accommodations of the poor, the ubiquity of things oddly repaired, were as familiar as the denizens of my homelands to the north, and I wondered: How big is this homeland, the empire of the ill-starred progeny of la conquista, how far to the north and south can it stretch, and how many nations are encompassed by its ancient, unspoken accords?

In the dirt-street village of Somotillo, just south of the border with Honduras, there was a Mass commemorating the six-week anniversary of the deaths of a group of campesina women who had been killed along with a Swiss volunteer, in a Contra attack. In addition to the families of the campesinos, the mother of the volunteer was there from Switzerland, joined by the dead man's wife. The two addressed the assembled throng in an open-air church, decorated with palms and white chrysanthemums, telling them how grateful their loved one had been to be received warmly into their community and how deeply they shared their loss with the families of the others killed in the ambush. Then, a host of campesinos stepped forward and offered elegies about the various victims of the deadly assault, while a trio played a dirge outside.

One old lady named Doña Rosa, whose daughter was among the casualties, was helped onto the dais, leaning back for support against the altar, from where she chastised those Nicaraguans who were waging the civil war against their own country. Wiping her hands on her burlap apron, she stood erect and pulled her hair back sternly, imitating the people she called traitors.

"They say: Things were better under Somoza! We should go back to the way things were under Somoza!" wagging her finger, her voice cracking. "Just like the people who complained to Moses when they were in the desert. We're lost! We should go back! But we are in an exodus, just like them! We are on a pilgrimage! I have hope. I have hope because I have faith that we will triumph!" The villagers cheered the diminutive Doña Rosa, who pulled her shawl over her head and looked back at them solemnly over her eyeglasses, repeating *"¡Vamos a triunfar!"* raising her open palm overhead.

Watching their lives through video monitors in New York City made my life feel like a reverse refraction, remote, set loose in time, disconnected from the masses of people pursuing a daily struggle against hunger and chaos. Here, all their faces were traced out in shimmering scanlines in the stacks of monitors, in jumbled green loops on the waveform video corrector. Despite the squalor of the places I had visited, despite the desperation of the people, the video camera could make everything seem beautiful, or even fastidious—the cobbled streets of Somotillo, the pristine porcelain sand of the Sudanese desert in Tokar. But in one sequence, our jeep pulled up into the famine camp in Tokar, camera rolling, as we were surrounded by hundreds of the camp dwellers, young and old, many of whom were putting their hands to their mouth, then extending an empty palm to us for food. They crowded the jeep, leaning against the windows, pleading, "Give us food! We need food!"

I explained through a translator, shouting, that we had no food to give. We were there to tell a story only, to tell *their* story to Americans through television, so that they perhaps would then be compelled to act, to send relief to the beleaguered people of the Sudan. It felt like a pathetic answer to their request, and many dismissed us with a curse and walked away. Others continued to insist on food.

My family had extracted themselves from that world, extracted themselves from the world of the Mexican poor who are a part of the same struggle of the poor that has no origins or boundaries in place or time. Tía Pepa had said it took one hundred years to run our family out of Mexico. "First Santa Anna lost Texas, a piece of the Republic! Then with Guadalupe Hidalgo, another piece of Mexico was lost. Nuevo Mexico, Arizona, California. Then, we couldn't get rid of the old dictator Porfirio Díaz for twenty years! Papa said he would fight if anyone invaded Mexico, but he wouldn't stay while Mexico destroyed herself. So we came here to *El Norte.*" That move changed our family's place in the old story of the poor, forever.

Now, as I watched the story unfolding, in sequences of playback and record, I realized that when asked for relief, all I could do was to offer to tell a story.

The first of the ghosts was the ghost of a city. After years of exile, already a decade of walking up and down the world in many lands far from home, it was the unexpected sign. An augur. A portent. It was on a summer night, tepid, dank, and hazy in the crowded thieves' market along the sidewalk of Second Avenue in the East Village of New York City. It was an apparition, the ghost of one city suddenly taking shape, like someone long forgotten becoming incarnate again. Amid the clamor and panic of the avenue, at a Chinese bookseller's stand, crouching over a carpet spread with yellow incense cones, old LP's, and a pile of antique photographs, I looked through handfuls of tiny, brittle pictures of lost worlds in time. Many of the prints still had the old black card-paper borders that had once fixed them to the pages of an album. There was one small faded print, showing the obelisk and shadow of the Washington Monument, another showed the ruins of some Greek columns, a side view of Niagara Falls, a spaniel in snow, and a series of nondescript houses and buildings in unidentified American towns. On the back of one picture of a two-story house with a wrap-around porch was written in pencil, "Sept 10, 1919, 216 E. Highland, St. Joseph, Mo."

Then there was an image that seemed strangely familiar, but at first unnameable. At the edges, the print had faded to an indistinct silvery glow, but it showed a mysterious, shady pavilion with long, rough cobblestone pillars and a great overhanging thatched palm *palapa*-style roof. Another showed a tangle of narrow, winding walkways through a patchwork of ponds and barren dirt. On the back of one of these snap-shots, a stamp in royal blue ink read: "Wagner's Drug Store, East Houston & Ave. C., San Antonio Texas."

I remembered then this place I had known as a child long ago in San Antonio—the cool, dark Japanese Sunken Gardens of Bracken-ridge Park, which had been built by prison labor on lands that once be-longed to Colonel Brackenridge, near the Fernridge estate where my grandfather had worked. The lush, green lagoon garden had been planted in the abandoned pit of an old stone quarry. In these photo-graphs, the gardens were still bare, the stones newly laid and untrod-den, the fresh thatching thick and low hanging.

By the time I knew the place as a child, much later, these same stone paths had become well worn, traversing the overgrown lily ponds, leading up along the dripping cliffsides where purple orchids hung in long strands from the stone wall. It seemed to me then not like a man-made thing, but a hidden place that had been left behind since the be-ginning of the world, like the one true Garden of Eden.

How had these pictures come to this place? By whose hands? What was their story? How far along in the story were we now? And how far along in the oldest story? How deep into the tally of whirling novae, the annals of the world's implicit tale, the one told over and over in glyphs, stelae, and alphabets? How far into *la crónica?* And where had San Antonio emerged, in the most secret chronicle of old Mexican time? Who knew the number of the suns? Who had kept a count of the days since the first light of this age?

There are few now, if any, who keep that oldest count of the days. Maybe they are hidden away, keeping lonely watches on the heavens in the Yucatán, in the remote hills of Chiapas and the mountains of Puebla. For the rest of us, by comparison, it seems the past has disappeared from view. So many of the old Mexicans are dying—the old Tejanos—the ancestors who left Mexico for Texas at the start of this century of grief. Their names had become beads on a rosary: Francisco, Margarita, Leandra, Lico, Isidro, and on, and on. For years now, as the memorial prayer cards have arrived, it reminds me: How long for me, in exile?

As I riffled through the old photographs, I found more images of San Antonio from the time my family first arrived, but there were many places my family would never have known. The distinctive stone houses of the wealthy on elegant tree-shaded streets of Olmos Heights. The tranquil poolside arbor of the San Antonio Country Club, where the city's Anglo gentry gathered for iced drinks on hot afternoons. It was only in one picture, of the Alamo captured in bright sunlight, that you could make out the small figure of a mustachioed, dark-skinned Mexican, holding a hoe before him, with his face shadowed under a floppy cowboy hat.

Then, at the bottom of the pile, there were several more photographs that were familiar. They showed the wide water swath of the San Antonio River outside the old city, with the characteristic cypresses along its banks, in scrubby south Texas terrain. In one, where there is a big, still bend I thought I remembered fishing, a man in a suit and derby stared distractedly, hands in pocket, from the river's edge into the standing water. Several others captured the river, already encompassed by the city, snapped on the same spot at different hours of the day from a bridge on Commerce Street, near the old entrance to the downtown mercado. It was as if the photographer had returned to the same place time and again to discern some unknown meaning from the many faces of the river in that place. One showed the river glistening with crystalline morning light. Another, taken at midday, had shadows as narrow as reeds, while still another captured the same scene in the darkening tones of an early evening.

As I stood there in the noise and tumult of Second Avenue, the distant, gurgling sound of that slow-running river seemed louder than the city around me. And as if possessing a voice, across the years and miles, this ghost whispered out a simple message:

It is not for your sake that the story continues.

I went back to San Antonio, having received a letter from the city's fire department helping me locate Mr. A. G. Pompa, one of the two now long-retired firemen who had tried to revive my abuelo Juan José on that January morning in 1939. Their names, Rathke and Pompa, had appeared in all of the press accounts of his death, and Mr. Pompa was one of the figures in the photograph in the *San Antonio Light*, crouching alongside my grandfather's body by the bank of the San Antonio River. Along with my father and Uncle Chale, Pompa was the last living witness of the circumstances of that day. The other fireman, a Mr. A. L. Rathke, had died in the early '70s.

When I arrived in San Antonio, the front pages of the newspapers were announcing in banner headlines the report of a visitation of the Virgin Mary in the city, where she had appeared to a young witness in the illumination of a porchlight, reflected off the polished chrome fender of a 1975 Chevrolet Impala. It happened in an old barrio sub-development on the far south side of the city, off the Pleasanton Road, which had once been a stagecoach route but was now a long, faceless asphalt trail of strip malls, feed stores, and massage parlors. The houses there are flat and weathered from the tea-colored sandstorms that blow through that part of the San Antonio River plain in the summers.

The "Chevrolet Madonna" was first seen by a Chicano boy on his sixteenth birthday, after taking out the trash around ten that night. For some weeks, he had been having nightmares that he would be shot in a drive-by killing on his birthday. In his dream, he would be taking out the trash, walking across the dry, straw-colored carpet grass of the front yard, when he would notice a gray Ford Pinto coming around the corner toward his house. As he saw someone leaning out of the back window with a pistol in hand, he would try to run for his front door, but found he was suddenly paralyzed by a mysterious force. He turned toward the house, but the air was as dense as deep water. And each night, the dream would end just after he heard the explosion of the gun firing from behind him.

When he went out to empty the garbage the night of the vision, he said he saw a bright white light descend swiftly onto a neighbor's lawn across the street. He watched as it moved down the street, zig-zagging between ash trees and pickup trucks like a spinning top, veering sharply in the middle of the street in front of his house and coming directly for him. Before he could move away, he screamed, as he felt what he called "the icy light" pass directly through him and float farther on the night air, finally coming to rest against the clapboard wall of the neighbor's house.

When his mother and sister found him kneeling in the yard just minutes later, his hands were clasped in prayer and his gaze was fixed on the house next door. As he looked at the large, jagged splash of light before him, he recognized in it a clearly defined shape where the light was brighter.

"It's our Holy Lady, kneeling, reading the Bible," he told them.

They looked at the wall and saw the same shape there, and they were awestruck. There was a pool of light that might be a bowed head, one edge that could be a large book held open, a wavy glimmer toward the ground that could seem to some to be a kneeling torso. But you had to look deep into the light, deliberately unfocusing your eyes, to see any of this. After holding hands and saying prayers together, the family went inside and built an altar to receive the blessings the Divine Mother was bestowing on them.

Along with the cataclysms, natural and man-made, this has been a century of miracles and visions. The epic of magic remains incomplete. *Promesas* are still being fulfilled. Before an apocalyptic vortex of killing and recrimination descended on Bosnia-Herzegovina, there were daily visions of Mary taking place in the mountain village of Medjugorje. Three youths, two girls and a boy, carried on a years-long conversation with their vision, whom they described as the Virgin Mary, Mother of God. After the attending crowd for the punctual afternoon apparitions grew too large, the venue was moved by begrudging church authorities to the local church rectory, where only a few witnesses were allowed. Appearing so routinely, the Virgin was able to address herself to such otherwise quotidian matters as the inefficiency of public waterworks in the village and the penurious local property tax rates. An uncle went on a pilgrimage there and claimed, along with other followers, to have looked straight at the sun at midday without harming his eyes. Instead, he saw a rapid dance of many-colored light, as if filtered through a prism in the sky. The visions at Medjugorje ended without fanfare when one of the visionaries went off to join the Bosnian army. Another developed brain cancer. Then the war arrived, and it became too dangerous to even gather at the rectory for daily prayers.

The San Antonio papers reported that after the Chevrolet apparition, the family began a marathon of Rosaries devoted to the Virgin Mary. The son fainted and began speaking in a high-pitched voice, while his family held a minicorder to his mouth, recording his every utterance. When he declared the tapwater in the house was blessed, they placed roses in a vase filled with the water, and the entire house was filled with an intoxicating scent of the flowers.

As word spread through the neighborhood and the news media started to report the story, hundreds of people arrived every evening to see the light for themselves. It didn't take the skeptics long to discern that the light of this apparition was nothing more than the reflection of the family's porch light off the front bumper of a maroon Impala, parked in the driveway. On the second night of the apparition, a couple of *pachuco* homeboys who had been sniffing glue all afternoon, started rocking the car and howling with laughter as the apparition bobbed up and down against the beige house siding, startling the devoted onlookers.

Nonetheless, on crutches, in wheelchairs, and in large groups, the hopeful, the devout, the sick, and the curious kept coming. A man with acute colitis was rumored to have rid himself of crippling abdominal pain by touching the wall. Many swooned while just standing along the chain-link fence of the neighbor's backyard.

Then, another neighbor caught a pilgrim urinating on his lawn. Another found a couple, in flagrante delicto, in their own parked car as they had come to attempt to conceive a child in the apparition's glow, unable to do so before without divine intervention.

A local Bishop said the church was "cautiously skeptical" about the matter. "I see the Blessed Mother every day," he told the newspaper. "But I don't necessarily invite the whole community. If it isn't from God, it will die a natural death."

After uncovering his name in the microfilm archives of the newspapers, I had tried to find Mr. Pompa. It seemed he had left the city. For years the fire department had been unable to locate him, until they received a notification of a change of address through his insurance company. After several days' more of inquiries with the San Antonio Fireman's Benevolent Association, I learned he was living in Kerrville, Texas, about an hour and a half north of San Antonio, in the Texas hill country. Mr. Pompa was a patient at the State Hospital in Kerrville, the end-of-the-line facility in the Texas State mental health system. Identifying myself on the phone only as a friend of the family, the nurse I spoke to there would not discuss his condition with me, but said I was welcome to visit, with an appointment.

"You can come on up," she said. "He has good days and bad days, but he don't talk much with nobody."

I dreaded that hospital from one summer during college, when I had a job there doing art therapy with the patients, many of whom are elderly, long-term internees of the state mental health system. The hospital grounds are nestled in the hills outside of Kerrville, and the campus is laid out like a little village unto itself, with its own streets, named after heroes of Texas Independence, and imitation shops meant to give the patients the reassuring feeling of being at home in a real place. After only two weeks of work there, I was haunted by the sounds and scenes from the hospital. While watching a movie, I'd hear the jagged laughter of one of the patients I had been with during the day. I recoiled when I saw the downy translucent flesh hanging from the underarms of patients who had taken prescriptions for decades that had that eerie side effect. I had quit shortly thereafter, and the doctor overseeing the arts program scolded me for leaving, telling me, "It's not so easy to escape these things. You can't quit *them.*"

When I was shown to the patio in the ward where Mr. Pompa was waiting, I remembered walking through that solarium years before, encountering a group of patients there who were watching the film *The Alamo,* with John Wayne and Richard Widmark, in reverse, after some lazy orderly had improperly spooled the projector. But none of the members of the audience seemed to mind, staring silently at the sheet that had been hung as a screen as John Wayne walked backward along the parapets of the fort under siege.

That afternoon, the cicadas were singing at an eardrum-piercing volume as a nurse led me to Mr. Pompa at one end of a covered patio, dressed only in a cotton robe and sitting in a La-Z-Boy recliner, with his bare feet up on the raised footrest. The nurse pulled his seat back upright, and his old, unshaven face was round and freckled, his soft, dark eyes both blank and querulous. His hands were large and rough-scaled, quivering on his bare knees, protruding from his robe. He looked like Diego Rivera as an old man, his white hair standing up like plumes on the back of his head. At first, he took no notice as the nurse introduced me, taking pains to pronounce every syllable with a shout.

"He understands everything. He just mainly don't want to talk. That's all it is, right, Mr. Pompa?"

Mr. Pompa had two Q-Tips hanging from his nostrils, and two sticking out of his ears. The nurse gathered them quickly with a *tsk* and set off back for the ward. Alone on the patio, I pulled up a chair and introduced myself to Mr. Pompa again, which he responded to with only a blink in his wide open stare. I explained to him how I had gotten his whereabouts, and why I had looked for him in the first place. I told him he was one of the last living witnesses of that morning in 1939, when, as a young man of twenty-five, he had tried to revive my grandfather. I showed him the photograph from the January 1939 *San Antonio Light*, where he was pictured.

"Juan—José—Santos. You are that A. G. Pompa, aren't you?"

The Fireman's Association said that, already twenty years retired, he had had a decorated career as a *bombero*. He had put out a lot of San Antonio fires. He had run into hundreds of burning houses to bring out the living. Maybe he had been able to revive untold others of the would-be drowned. But all of that was lost to him now, including the morning of January 9, 1939. Whatever faint echo of that day remained deep inside of him and was beyond his grasp. If he was aware of anything, he was unable or unwilling to let anyone else know. We sat staring at each other silently for another few moments. In his eyes, he seemed present, but abandoned, as if a fire had left only the shell of the building standing. Then he took a long, deep breath and began singing with a still-noticeable Spanish accent, *"The eyes of Texas are upon you . . . all the livelong day . . ."*

On my way back, I thought I might drive past San Antonio, past Uvalde, Hondo, and La Pryor, past Piedras Negras and Nava, and on into the center of Mexico to where all the roads began.

The news from the radio was that it hadn't mattered much to the faithful that the "Chevrolet Madonna" had a perfectly explicable source. Hundreds of believers were still coming to the simple neighborhood every night. Was it not a miracle that the lamplight from the porch had even caught the dented fender of the Impala in the first place? What was the probability of those few shafts of light reflecting off that long, curved chrome surface in precisely the way necessary to project the Madonna's silhouette? Out of the million chance encounters in the ordinary running on of the everyday, this beam was a light breaking suddenly through a curtain, creating an aperture between worlds, showing just how incomplete our own world really was.

But the neighbor on whose wall the apparition reflected was growing desperate as hordes of devotees trampled greater swaths of his lawn and carried on singing and chanting all night long. He decided to illuminate the apparition with two gigantic mercury floodlights, thereby bathing the amber-toned reflection in a fluorescent silver glare that erased any hint of the Virgin Mary's outline and drew gasps and angry shouts from the crowd.

One reporter heard a woman scream at the neighbor, "If you have any love in your heart you will let us see the Virgin!"

"If you believe in Mary, the mother of God, you will turn out the light," yelled another.

The mother of the family of the young visionary collapsed.

In the days that followed, the family repositioned their Impala in the driveway and used camping flashlights to try, without success, to cast the Virgin's reflection against their own garage door. All they managed were jittery Rorschach blots of a shapeless milky light. Once the car was moved, the image of the Blessed Virgin Mary reading the Bible was to disappear forever. For several days, the devout and the nosy continued to come after sunset. For months after they stopped coming, the neighbor kept his modest house saturated in as much light as the Lincoln Memorial.

She had not been a Virgin who had come with much to say. As always, she had chosen an obscure place under humble circumstances to manifest herself. This time there were no clouds, no cherubim, no starry mantle. As apparitions go, she was more of a chimera or a cipher rather than an interlocutor between worlds. For those who believed in her light, she brought the message that the interaction between the mortal and the divine in those lands has not ended.

From her debut in the Americas on a sacred hill in Mexico City more than four hundred years ago, here at end of the twentieth century, she came to a parched, rundown Texas suburb. The faithful had congregated to see in the apparition's low-wattage glow that the enchantment of the homelands is not over.

On the night the miracle-busting floodlights were turned on, when the mother of the young seer of Pleasanton Road passed out, some of the devotees had gathered around her, holding hands, and improvised a song they sang over her as she lay unconscious, *"Stay with me, Lord, stay with me, the spirit of the Lord is moving through my heart, stay with me, Lord, stay with me."*

The air over Tenochtitlán was a brownish gray chemical mist. The chalky haze of fuel exhaust and smog made it hard to see anything but a blur of wet streets, low buildings, factories, and roadways. We spiraled down, drifting in a hush, into the ancient precints of the Valley of Mexico. I remembered one nineteenth-century painting by José Maria Velasco in which Mexico City is seen from the village of Amecameca, circa 1870. The sharply outlined white city is on the far horizon, across an expansive prairie dotted with cactus and maguey. Beyond are the volcanoes, Popocatépetl and Ixtahuitil. The air over the valley was so clear then you could see for a hundred miles.

Now, we float in on the dirty clouds of our century, the nectar of Tlazolteotl, the Aztec deity who brings forth new creation out of the filth she consumes. The spattering rain on the airplane windows looks rusty, corrosive. This is zeitgeist weather for Mexico City in the time of la crisis.

"It's been like this since 'la crisis,' " a cab driver says on the way into town. "Things are really screwed up. Nobody has any money."

He's right. Later, in the Plaza Santo Domingo, no one has change for a fifty peso note, roughly the equivalent of ten dollars.

"La crisis" is Mexico's amazing, perpetually imploding economy. It is the peso, falling in a bottomless fiduciary abyss like a Siqueiros wraith on fire. But it's also the unbreathable air, tracked daily in newspaper logs of the levels of toxic chemicals present in the air. The rot of political corruption, like an abscessed tooth, shakes the nation, from the heady *personajes* of state to shoe-shiner unions. *Militares* are shooting *campesinos* in Guerrero while politicians hurl recriminations of "Bad Spelling!" at one another.

There are village uprisings of Indígenas in Tabasco, in Michoacán. The influence and power of *los narcos,* in tandem with the Colombian drug cartels, is fluorescing. Then, the twenty-seventh anniversary of the 1968 Tlatelolco massacre sparks a riot. Ex-president Carlos Gortari de Salinas is alleged in the press to be the "intellectual author" of the assassination of his successor, presidential candidate Colosio, and the present president, Ernesto Zedillo, may yet emerge as a central witness, probably never to be called. Meanwhile, the "postmodern" Zapatistas, the Mayan rebel army in Chiapas, are staging an ongoing natonal dialogue on political reform as an ersatz graduate seminar media event.

"The wars of the conquest continue." That was the bulletin that the Zapatistas had littered by the thousands around the village of San Cristobal de las Casas, in the first days of their New Year's War,

> *To the Mexican People: We are the product of 500 years of struggle! First against slavery; then in the War of Independence against Spain headed by our first revolutionaries; later for withstanding North American expansionism . . . again when the Porfirio dictatorship denied us the letter of the Laws of Reform and we selected Zapata and Villa as our own leaders. . . .*

We say enough! We are the descendants of the original con-
ceivers of our common identity; we are the dispossessed mass
and we call to each of you to join in this single cause....

By their own account, they were an army of indigenous peoples of southern Mexico, declaring war against the illegitimate government and army of Mexico.

Then, more earthquakes, in Colima, in Chiapas. Hurricane Rachel strikes the gulf coast, then returns to sea, regathers storm force, and lashes the Mexican coast again. And Popocatépetl, the volcano outside Mexico City, which last erupted in the '30s, is fuming. One of my aunts in Coahuila says, "It's like the time of the plagues in Egypt."

"La crisis" is social apocalypse in extreme slow motion. And there is an erotic élan in how the Mexicanos manage to savor the inexpressible melancholy of it all. In a dark serendipity, the center of Mexico City is decked with elegant, somber banners advertising an exhibition of the torture machines of the Inquisition. Another *taxista,* part Greek chorus, part human barometers of la crisis, is quoted in the press saying, *"Esto no se arregla."*

"This cannot be fixed."

The year before, as I drove south along the coastal highway through western Oaxaca, the road had curved through burnished hills for miles without any evidence of civilization or settlement. On the right, the cliffs along Mexico's spine dropped off to flat, chalky beaches. Crawling ocean waves glimmered under a heavy Pacific mist. On the left, countless tiers of large gray granite boulders stood craggy against the hillsides, the gnarled cedars glowing deep green against the scorched golden grasses, the entire landscape suspended in a rare effect of limpid afternoon light. *I know this light.* A tea-colored sunlight suffused the hills, as if the afternoon would dissolve slowly, infinitely, into every shadow, every creek bed, every gorge. *I know this light on this land, in exactly this way.*

I had never been to Oaxaca before. I had never even seen pictures of Oaxaca, except for photographs and drawings from Monte Alban, the ancient acropolis ruins of the Zapotecs, inland near Oaxaca City. It was Bedouin déjà vu—to be startled by sudden familiarity with a constituent quality of light in an unknown place. *My blood has moved through here before,* I thought.

These were the journeys to the center of Mexico that I made:

South from Aztlán, through a phalanx of crowded border checkpoints, bypassing Nueva Rosita on *Cincuenta Siete,* into the heart of Mexico via the two-lane highway of Huitzilopochtli, the first God of the Mexica.

Following the western coast south along the spine, down the Pacific highway past the shrines of Resortlandia—Puertos Vallarta, Azul, Escondido—then Tehuantepéc and Tuxtla Gutierrez and on to Chiapas, where Mexico's next revolution was erupting.

The umbilical journey was that which the Mexicans called *La Ruta,* the erased journey. It is the route that Cortés, our secret, shameful grandfather, and his army took on their military campaign against the Aztec empire, from the sultry nights and sleazy cantinas of ancient Veracruz to the traffic-glutted streets around the ghost of the Great Temple of the Aztecas, next to the Zócalo plaza at the center of Mexico City.

There wasn't a single monument to Cortés left standing in la Capital after the 1910 *Revolución.* The record of the journey had been largely obliterated, excised from maps and commemorative plaques at roadside landmarks. But I had pieced together the route with my mother's friend Helen Anthony, using a recent book by a French historical geographer that correlated the accounts of Cortés in his letters to the Spanish king Charles V and the narrative of the Spanish soldier Bernal Díaz de Castillo with the geography of contemporary Mexico. Sitting together in a booth, at a seafood café in the Mercado de la Ciudadela, Helen and I unfolded a large map based on satellite images of the Mexican landscape.

La Ruta was traced in a Day-Glo turquoise line against verdant green, emerging from Veracruz on the gulf, winding its way up into the coffee bush mountains of Jalapa, descending then in a reticulated pattern, all plains and valleys, crisscrossing the new highway toward Cholula, then over the volcano Popocatépetl, through Coyoacán, arriving, finally, in the mesh of pavement and buildings at the center of Mexico City.

The rented Volkswagen Bug clattered with the throttle all the way open, revving in a high-pitched whine down the empty Orizaba superhighway to Veracruz. Mexico's toll highways are ghost tracks, with many Mexicans unable or unwilling to pay the high tolls, leaving the brightly lit three-lane roads devoid of pilgrims, especially at night. It had taken hours to leave Mexico City, the traffic congealed for miles through the poor precinct of the city known as Nezahaualcoyotl, where the fumes of burning garbage heaps leave a permanent acrid haze over the district. Then, from Puebla on, an unimpeded trail, where I was passed only occasionally by swift and thundering eighteen wheelers, bearing painted slogans like, "IN THE HANDS OF LORD JESUS CHRIST," and "VIRGENCITA, DO NOT ABANDON ME!" Where the road ends in Orizaba, a vast industrial plant looms on the horizon, sending pillars of flame up into the bruise-colored night sky, illuminating a city of gangways, storage tanks, plants, and power stations.

From there to Veracruz it was a dark, two-lane blacktop, where I had to grip the wheel of the Bug to keep from being flipped off the road in the gusting wake of a passing truck. On both sides, farmers were burning their fields after harvest, and the waist-high flames from far off silhouetted legions of cows and goats crowded along the road, making the drive at times perilous and slow. After a meal of red snapper at the Gran Café de la Parroquia, I slept in a room over the plaza, the shutters open to a group of musicians, guitars, mandolins, violins, and bass, playing the doleful, tango-esque musica Jarocha of the city, made famous by the great Veracruz composer Agustín Lara. The singer's pleas for mercy from his scornful lover rang across the plazas, the violins striking small notes as faint as meteor light.

The next day, setting out alone on *La Ruta,* the journey began in the village known as La Antigua, where Cortés was said to have moored his ships to a pair of fat-trunked ceiba trees that still stand on the banks of the river inlet that cuts through contemporary Antigua. The commemorative signs marking the two bedraggled, low-hanging trees are rusted over and defaced, their legends barely legible now, except for "FUCK CORTÉS."

Cortés's original garrison in Antigua is a ruin, the fallen walls grown over with thick, densely woven trunks and vines. Inside, a group of campesinos had built an adobe shack, surrounded by banana trees, their pigs and chickens unloosed through the part of the quarters one map showed to have been the private lodgings of Cortés himself. Nearby is the little chapel, barely bigger than a shed, built by Cortés's men as a sanctuary in which the first Mass was offered on the Mexican mainland, and the Spanish *Requierimiento* was read three times aloud, claiming legal domain for King Carlos V over all of those lands forevermore. If the taproot of the Indian world was lost in time, this modest, still meticulously kept chapel was the beginning of what would become Mexico, part Indio, part Español. Cortés had children with Indian women, among them, Malintzín, the Totonaca Indian slave whom the Mayans had presented to Cortés as a gift. She had learned Mayan, and her original language had been Nahuatl, the language of the Azteca empire. Along with a Spaniard who had been shipwrecked and learned Mayan, they formed the translation chain of the conquista: Malintzín interpreting Nahuatl into Mayan, and the Spanish officer translating Mayan into Spanish. From the very beginning, Spanish and Indian languages were threaded through Cortés and his army like invisible filaments, binding Indio and Español inextricably together.

Along *La Ruta,* I went to the village of San Miguel Tzinacapan, high in the mountains of northeastern Puebla, one of the places where the *Volador* tradition has been maintained unbroken since the time before the conquest. Cortés's army passed near here on their way inland first to Cholula, then onward to Tenochtitlán. Today, you turn onto a winding mountain road that takes you through the Spanish-sounding villages of Grijalba, Oriental, and Zaragoza. Tzinacapan is literally at the end of the road. It is a small, close-knit village of Nahua people, descendants of the Aztecs, who still speak Nahuatl, though they prefer to call it "Mexicano." Up in the mountains of Puebla, the conquest was never completed. The statue of San Miguel the Indians worship so vigorously in a torrent of song and dance is a stand-in for the warrior god of their Nahua *antepasados,* Huitzilopochtli, the god who led the Aztecas on their epic exodus into Mexico from Aztlán in the north.

They live mainly by farming, or working in the nearby town of Cuetzalán, which has an active tourist trade. The lands are densely overgrown highland forests, but close enough to the Gulf of Mexico to still see the palms and ferns of coastal jungle flora. Farming is a constant struggle against the fecund, irrepressible force of the wild, and harvests are always meager. I arrived during the annual celebrations of the feast day of the village's patrón, San Miguel. Much of what little these people have they spend during these days of transcendent fiesta. The fiesta is a three-day-long ritual that, the residents say, is a necessary observance to guarantee the cycle of planting and harvest will repeat again.

As the fiesta began, bands of musicians assembled in the stone-cobbled streets, and several corps of *Voladores* prepared to make their mesmerizing flights from a pole planted just meters away from the main church door in the middle of the village plaza. While they spin around the creaking pine trunk, from 120 feet up in the air, a delirium of dance and music explodes on the ground. *Quetzalinos,* with their brightly col-ored, giant crescent-shaped feather headdresses. Toreadores in mirror shades, dressed like charros, performed furious tapatio steps, punctu-ated with yelps. Mysterious *Matachines* in their sequined costumes and veiled sombreros, repeating a grave minuet. Drunken, menacing *Santiagos* with their wooden swords, commemorate Santiago Mata-moros, the killer of Moors. And amidst all the others, the *Miguelinos,* swooping in waltz-time from left to right, dressed like their patron saint, in a golden conquistador's helmet, a helot's skirt and carapace, and a pair of dwarfish golden wings.

Looking upward toward the sun, I listened to the thick hemp ropes stretching and disentwining. The upside-down flyers were play-ing flutes, arms crossed on their chests, striking birdlike poses, throw-ing sharp flitting glints of light from the mirrors that deck their red cone-shaped hats, casting their moving shadows across the dancing hordes. What could any of this have to do with me and my family, *Norteños* from the Coahuila desert?

Later, back in my hotel room, in the nearby town of Cuetzalán, I felt listless and confused. Aimlessly, I switched the television channels past *He-Man, Master of the Universe,* a badly dubbed Humphrey Bogart movie, and ads for Walter Mercado, the Liberace-esque Puerto Rican astrologer's psychic help line, proclaiming "You are present at the birth of a new Mexico!" A news bulletin reported that a twenty-two-year-old policeman in Mexico City had run amok in the city subway station called "La Raza." Another symptom of "la crisis." In a crowded train, he had pulled out his service revolver and fired eleven times, killing two instantly and wounding several others. He ran out into the station but was immediately captured by police. The bulletin included a long interview with the cop, despondent, roughed up, and bruised, and still standing in the spot where his mug shot had been taken.

"I don't know what happened," he said morosely into the video camera. "I don't remember anything at all."

Resolving to leave, I rose the next morning before dawn to visit the nearby ruins of an ancient ceremonial center called Yohualichan, "the house of night" in the Nahuatl tongue. Like Palenque and Monte Alban, these pyramids, small by comparison, are perched on the rim of an expansive valley, offering a broad panorama of the plain below, and, by night, a wide view of the dome of stars.

The modern village of Yohualichan nestles the old ceremonial center like a wreath around the temple ruins. The main pyramid resembles the famous pyramid of the *nichos* at El Tajín, its exterior pockmarked by galleries of small inset niches that are believed to have been used to place idols in a specific arrangement corresponding to the day of the year and the elaborate calendrical cycles that were part of the way of life of the indigenous people who lived here. A great plaza with a meticulously tended lawn lay in the middle of the quadrangle of pyramids. The people who built ancient Yohualichan were probably Totonaca in origin, but they were later overrun and expelled by the Nahua people of the Mexica empire of Tenochtitlán. It is their descendants whom I had watched dance and fly the day before.

It was a glorious clear morning, and the sounds of tinny radios and morning pans clanging in the little village nearby reverberated between the pyramids. I wondered just what the dances were really about. From what beginnings had they evolved? And what memory were they meant to preserve? Those temple ruins, like so many others across Mexico, testify to a people with an extraordinary sense of their own place in the vast panorama of the cosmos. They built their pyramids, their villages, their cities, in precise orientation to the heavens, as if they sought to yoke heaven and earth in one unbroken chain between the world of men and the world of nature. Much of that world was destroyed in the conquest, but ruins such as these were still living repositories of knowledge, markers left in time for all time to come.

A woman and what appeared to be a group of students listening attentively to her milled about in the plaza center. Sitting atop one of the pyramids, I watched when, with a shriek from the woman, the group of students set out running in one corps along the perimeter of the plaza, kicking up their legs wildly behind them as they ran. The woman then walked toward me with a lithe stride and began climbing the pyramid's steep steps with an alacrity that made her seem very young. When she arrived at the pinnacle where I was sitting, I was taken aback to see she was actually an older woman, maybe well into her sixties, her short-cropped hair completely gray. She approached, dressed in a simple paisley smock and wearing Adidas sneakers with ankle socks. Her brown face was soulful yet stern, and I thought she might by angry until she smiled, showing one gold front tooth, reaching out to me with both of her hands as if she were greeting an old friend.

"*¿Estabas mantralizado?*" she asked, almost shouting.

I wasn't sure what she had said to me. "*¿Perdón?*" I answered.

"You were chanting," she said in English, taking my hands in hers as I stood up. I had been chanting some Hindu mantras hours earlier, as the sun was coming up, but there was no one around the pyramids at that hour. "I was," I replied nervously. "Do . . . you chant?"

"I am Rosaura. I teach anthropology at the university in Puebla, and I am a spiritual teacher. Those are my students," she said perfunctorily, pointing to the plaza below. Her students were still making their circuits, still maintaining their exaggerated goofy gaits, which, at that moment, made me laugh. Rosaura nodded, laughing along with me. "Yes, it is funny, but it makes you very strong," she said, holding up her firm biceps to show me, and pointing to her legs as she performed the motion, bouncing both of her knees in the air as in a Shaker dance.

"What do you teach?" I asked.

"I'm an expert on the Teotihuacán culture. That's what I teach in the university. But I teach them the old beliefs, the old Mexican beliefs. I am Mestiza, but I grew up here," she said, motioning toward the village. "There were many here who knew the old beliefs, Totonaca, Nahua, Maya, and they taught me. They would've been happy to hear you singing here today."

I told her I was from Texas and about my fascination with the *Volador* ritual and asked if she knew anything about where it had come from, or how it had originated. As I spoke, she smiled and nodded at every detail, her eyes anticipating each word. "The *Voladores* came from over there," she said, looking off to the east, where the gulf was faintly visible in the far distance, a wire-thin glint on the horizon.

"But you understand, they've been here a very long time. Way before all the others, all the rest of us. They taught all the newcomers to do the dance, which is a *compromiso* between us and the gods and goddesses."

"*Los dioses y diosas antiguos,*" she repeated in Spanish. "But you must know much more about it than me. It's good you come here to see the *Voladores!* All of Mexico's children will come back, you'll see." Rosaura took one long breath as if to end the conversation and said, "Let me give you a blessing, an old blessing."

She held my arms at my side, and pulled my shoulders up to make me stand straight. I saw several of her students peering up at us as they ran along the far side of the plaza. Then, Rosaura began rapidly whispering, her eyes closed, placing a droplet of her spittle on her index finger and rubbing it first on my forehead and then my sternum. She pulled at my belt buckle and lightly spat into my pants, and then rubbed more spittle onto my boots. As she stood, she bowed to the four directions, and said finally, in Spanish, "and when you leave, leave some offering here, something that means something to you. *Buen camino, hijito.*"

I watched her descend the pyramid in bounds, rejoining her students and ambling off toward the village. Yohualichan resumed its sentinel silence. It had been hard to take Rosaura's blessing seriously, coming unexpectedly after her hurried discourses on Teotihuacán, ancient aerobics, and the *Voladores*. But as I sat on the pyramid alone, the places where she touched me were tingling, as if I had been touched by something very hot. Before leaving, I found a clearing behind one of the pyramids and buried my old Walkman in a shallow hole.

I decided to stay on in San Miguel Tzinacapan for the last two days of the fiesta. The dances continued. The new sixteen-year-old Queen of the Corn was announced and crowned in a long ceremony. And all day, into late twilight when the deep crimson shadows spread out across the Puebla mountains, you could hear the long, whirling descent of the *Voladores*—the plaintive sound of their hemp ropes, pulled taut and spinning even tighter with the weight of the tethered dancers as they gradually approach the earth. As the moon rose, onlookers set off fireworks that illuminated the sky around them.

I was invited to lunch at the simple house of Señor Rosales, the village *mayordomo,* or host, for that year of the fiesta. In exchange for the honor, he would foot the expense of several public feasts and generous supplies of *pulque* and beer. And there was a continuous feast taking place at his house. All of the dancers came to pay their respects to him, doing a small dance in the meeting room of his home, then placing an offering of honey, turkey, or liquor at the main altar. The group of the *Voladores* that I had watched that afternoon marched into the house and performed a circle dance with flurries of intricate steps, accompanying themselves with flutes and drums. Their pointed caps were tipped with a circular fan of colored foils. They wore white shirts with red sashes that had been elaborately beaded with floral designs. Their red velvet tights were beaded along the sides, and they ended in bell bottoms revealing the group's matching Beatles boots. Finishing the little dance, the *caporal* of the group then placed a bottle of Yolixpa Fuerte, an herbal liqueur of the region, on the altar.

Afterward, we sat together in the backyard at a long table set with two dozen places, all of us eating fresh tortillas and a spicy black turkey mole, made by Señora Rosales. I asked the *caporal,* named Florián, "What do you think about when you're at the top of the pole, dancing and playing the flute and drum?"

That afternoon, I had watched as Florián had made his dangerous dance on the pole's top, leaning backward, his arms outstretched and waving from one side to the next. From the ground, he seemed to be speaking to a low-hanging cloud that was poised just above the pole.

"I think about nothing," Florián said, sipping on a Fanta orange soda.

"Nothing?"

"I just play and dance. And then it all happens at once, like a wind that comes and goes."

Cortés's march across Mexico in 1519 left a trail of devastation, death, and debris that the Mexican earth has absorbed by now. Setting out for the west from San Miguel, in Tlaxcala, you can see only sporadic rubble of the great wall that once protected the Indios from all intruders and would-be conquerors, including the great Mexica of Tenochtitlán. In Cholula, the last city the Spaniards encountered before entering the seat of the Mexica empire in the Valley of Mexico, stands a grand pyramid, perhaps the largest ever built by man, buried under soil by the Spaniards for centuries now. Looking like an ordinary tree-spotted hill nestled in a modern Mexican town, the hidden pyramid is crowned with a chapel at its summit that Cortés personally commissioned to symbolize the triumph of Christianity over the pagan worship he had found being practiced in Mexico.

But what was buried once may not stay buried for all times. At the end of *La Ruta* de Cortés was the Azteca capital of Tenochtitlán, today's Mexico City. At the center of Tenochtitlán stood the Templo Mayor, the main temple of the Mexica religion, with a shrine devoted to the worship and ritual obligations of the two gods, Huitzilopochtli and Tlalóc. From the peaks of this steep pyramid, the Mexica made their obligatory sacrifices, thereby perpetuating the cycle of the days that sustained all mankind, throwing the bodies of the sacrificial victims down the gore-stained steps after their hearts had been torn from the living victims.

Once the Aztec empire had succumbed to the Spanish army, Cortés ordered that the Templo Mayor be sacked and destroyed, obliterating forever what he considered to be an abomination against God. It was known that many of the stones from the Templo had been used to construct the great cathedral that now stands in the middle of Mexico City, alongside the Zócalo, adjacent to the National Palace, the seat of government. For hundreds of years, it was believed that the remains of the Templo lay buried forever, beneath the stone foundation of that cathedral.

Then, in the late 1970s, during an excavation of an area in which to extend the Zócalo subway station, about twenty yards away from the perimeter of the cathedral, workers discovered an enormous circular stone which bore the engraved image of the Aztec goddess Coyolxauqhui, her body dismembered, mangled, and misshapen. The stone was known by anthropologists to have been associated with the cult of Huitzilopochtli and the complex of Templo Mayor. According to accounts from the period of the conquest, it was said to have been laid at the base of the pyramid, at the point where the flung-away bodies of the victims fell from the stone steps to the ground.

The remains of the Templo Mayor had survived, and since their discovery have been excavated and exposed to the light of our century, at the very heart of Mexico City. What the Spaniards did not realize was that they had destroyed only the outermost evident pyramid, and left the others, from earlier in time, untouched, deeper in the ground. These, too, have now been returned to the light.

When I arrived at the ruins of the Templo Mayor in Mexico City at the end of my Cortés journey, it was on the day known in Mexico as *el Día de los Muertos,* "the Day of the Dead," the first day of November, when the souls of the ancestors are allowed to return to the realm of the living for one night. Mexico City was decked in the bright, fluorescent orange chrysanthemum flowers known as zempaxuchitl, traditional for that day, and throughout the Zócalo, children were dressed in the makeup and costumes of the *calaveras,* the comical skeleton figures that are the emblem of the holiday.

Walking through the ruins, I passed a succession of slanted walls, each one the shell of another, more ancient pyramid. In the spaces in between, as each old pyramid had been buried, the Aztecas had left behind sacred stones, stacks of conch shells, battalions of stone warrior statues, their arms held stiffly at their sides, medallions of jade or obsidian implanted in their chests, over their sternums. Each wall was a barrier, falling further back in time—until I came to the innermost place of the excavation, where the pinnacle of a hoary pyramid is still visible.

Here, the shrines to Huitzilopochtli and Tlalóc lay plainly before me, painted in bright blues, red, with patterns of black stripes and circles.

According to the archaeologists, there is one more archaic pyramid still sheathed by this one, which perhaps will never be uncovered. At this stage of the excavation, the innermost pyramid is already surrounded by a moat of primeval water, the seepage of the ancient lake that still lies under the pavement and iron of Mexico City.

Some archaeologists say the underlying pyramid awaits more advanced excavation techniques that will allow us to dig below the water table, revealing perhaps the first temple built by the Mexica after their great wandering, at Huitzilopochtli's behest, from their homeland Aztlán, in the north. The Nahua priests who bless the pilgrims at the Templo's perimeter say that water signifies the final threshold of our unknowing, and that the origin of the Mexica, their first sanctuary to their gods, will be withheld from us forever.

The low morning clouds over Rancho Los Generales had burned away by seven. I awoke early again to the gaze of a spotted falcon, perched in the red rafters of the patio roof, staring in through the window at me as I stirred. The corrugated tin roof would offer sturdy shelter against the sometimes fierce sierra winds, but the speckled auburn bird was uncertain whether to build a nest so close to a slumbering human. For days, it had kept a vigil over my sleep, patiently assessing the risk of settling there.

It had been a sleepless night, full of lightning and wind, but no rain: *la tormenta sin agua.* Such nights are the *vaquero*'s bane, wreaking havoc in the pastures—broken fences, missing cows—and the ground remained parched. All night, the winds had keened in slow, haunting arpeggios against the cables that supported the spindly shortwave radio tower over the house. At times, the gusts sounded like cathedral organ chimes rumbling the roof, then gathering to one great hovering tone, before suddenly falling to whispering wails.

After a decade away, I had been back at the ranch for some weeks, returning from my trips in Puebla and Mexico City. A pair of my old boots, cracked, sandy-colored, high-necked Tony Lamas, were still in a cabinet waiting for me. The landscape, rough, unyielding, and sometimes treacherous, was more lush than when I had last seen it. The fences, the corrals, and the house on the hill had all taken on a worn quality. The sycamore tree we had planted twenty years ago now shaded the patio in a broad-leaf canopy, its trunk as wide as a barrel. There had been several years running of good rains, always a momentous blessing in the sierra—and the subject of a great deal of conversation among the *vaqueros,* for whom the lightest mist of a rain is reflected on for its value in keeping the land green. But there hadn't been any rain since the day before I had arrived.

"It was only a little rain, *un aguita,* just enough to hold the dust down," the new *vaquero,* Fidencio, told me the night I arrived at Los Generales, about the previous day's misting. "It didn't even get the leaves wet underneath," he said, helping me to unpack the truck. Fidencio lived on the ranch with his family, a wife and three kids, singlehandedly keeping track of every head of cattle, far-flung through the five pastures, tending the waterworks, mending the fences, setting out the salt blocks and the alfalfa bales across the ranch. He had been the first *vaquero* since Alejo, the first in fifteen years, to master the complicated obligations and esoteric knowledge of the *rancho.*

I had come to the ranch to try to write about the trip I had just made. I barely saw Fidencio or his family. The cold December days were long, quiet, and solitary. Rising at dawn, I would set a fire in the potbelly stove and then jog out on any of the ranch roads to hills where I had endless vistas of the purple sierra, just as the sun was hitting their craggy peaks and ledges with golden beams. Back at the house, after making a plate of *huevos rancheros* and listening to the BBC World Service on the shortwave radio, I would turn everything off and sit down in the screened veranda with my notes, tapes, and readings. A few words might come each day, a piece of a poem, a paragraph. If I'd had a choice, I would have been a singer. I would have sung this story. Not as opera, not rock, not mariachismo, but the kind of singing that takes a thousand years to finish one song, a drum slowly beating, violins so soft they are almost inaudible. It would be sung in a low, worn, raspy voice like Agustín Lara's, in 1948, when he sang those lines in his own rendition of his famous "Veracruz,"

> *Yo nací en la luna de plata,*
> *y nací con alma de pirata.*

> I was born under a moon of silver,
> and I was born with the soul of a pirate.

But I am not the singer in the family. Uela had told me: *I was to be a poet—the teller.* That would be my role in this tale, not inventor, not singer, not the mystic, not the suicide, not the *vaquero,* not the *Volador.* I would be the teller in the family.

What would I tell? What was worth telling? Could you tell a story about centuries of forgetting? I had thought, *Maybe there would be a message, left somewhere in the deepest hold of old Mexican time, that would be revealed.* I could walk anywhere in this world and I would still be numbered in the old counts of the days. At the edge of the dark Gregorian millennium, in the ebbing years of the Mayan calendar, we were all living under the prophecy of the *Nahui Olin,* the fifth sun of the Aztecas, in which the world would end in a great shaking out of the earth. But I couldn't see how my family fit into that great story. And my wanderings around Mexico were a secret pursuit, unrelated to the work

I had been doing back in New York City, making television programs for more than a decade. The story was always postponed, the writing put aside. Now, maybe I had lost the story, if I'd ever had it to begin with.

I awoke the next morning staring into the eyes of the spotted falcon. There was a racket from down the hill near Fidencio's house, where I saw the truck that belonged to Don Armando, my Tío Alejandro's long-time assistant. It was my uncle's birthday, and the day before, Fidencio and I had ridden out into a nearby pasture to fetch a grown lamb that would be slaughtered for the birthday feast. The animal was now tied to the fence around Fidencio's house, furiously bleating and clanging its bell.

By the time I reached Fidencio's house, he had already strung up the lamb, hindparts lifted, from the rafters of the porch. I greeted Don Armando, a portly man in his late sixties, with an *abrazo,* and said good morning to Fidencio, his wife, two daughters, and baby son. While his wife, dressed in a leather apron, gave me coffee with a matter-of-fact manner, Fidencio threw one swift upward stroke with his blade, and the lamb bled out into a basin in a torrent, dying in an instant. He began cleaning it and meticulously removing the skin in scrolls, while giving Don Armando an exhaustive account of the health of every pregnant cow on the ranch. Then Don Armando turned to me.

"*¿Y que hallaste por ese ruta de Cortés, y con los Voladores?*" he said, laughing, and looking at Fidencio out of the corner of his eye, egging him on to join in. "What had I found on the Cortés route, and among the *Voladores?*"

Cracking himself up, he asked, "Did you find Malinche?" referring to Cortés's indigenous consort, Malintzín. Just as I was beginning to tell him about the great ceiba tree where Cortés's ships were said to have been moored, across the pasture I saw a towering *remolino,* "a whirlwind," suddenly appear near the corrals, pulling up dust, hay, and dry brush into its wobbly funnel. We all turned and watched it as it grew wider, taller, and darker, then began cutting a swath through the pasture toward us. The children and their mother ran into the house, but Fidencio continued to dress the lamb. With the roar of a storm, the *remolino* paused a few yards from us, at the fence around the house, drawing a whoop from Don Armando. Just as Fidencio looked up, we were all engulfed by the twister, which seemed to be stationary, as if it had found its magnetic center, and could not move on. In the middle of the whirlwind, Don Armando held his arms up, his belly stretched tight over his belt, eyes closed, with his lips moving, as in a prayer. Fidencio covered his eyes and held a cloth wrapped around the lamb. While the *remolino* churned over our heads, it felt as if the whole world grew incredibly silent. Amidst the wind, as if in slow motion, I saw a black and gray bee the size of my fist carefully land on my mouth. As it came to rest, it seemed entirely natural to offer a refuge in the heavy gust. Its front legs were perched on my top lip, its hind legs on my lower lip. The sound of the *remolino* faded, and in the quiet instant that followed, I heard words being spoken in my head, faintly, but steadily.

> *Scintilla. Barricade. Santa Tierra. Helix inside of helix.*
> *Color of blood. Playa. Covenant. Indelible diaphanous light.*
> *Her words falling like sand. Battalion. Intaglio. Breathless.*

Just as the *remolino* suddenly disappeared, I spat out in one breath to shoo away the bee, amazed it had not stung me. We stood motionless for an instant, Don Armando's arms still outstretched upward.

"This is a very good sign," he said chuckling. "A thousand baths cannot make you as clean as standing in one of those. It can wipe away sins!" That night, after returning to Sabinas, on my way back to San Antonio, I wrote the rest of the words I had heard spoken inside of the *remolino,*

They have brought guns into the garden. The seam is end-less, the weather impossible. Indistinct knowledge, as a Pa-paya. As Frijol. Eyes like mirrors. Heart like wind. Sangria by the gallons. River of souls. Songs pull toward the earth like a magnet. Lost friends. Dead grandfathers, grandmothers, un-cles, and aunts. Holy. Holy. Mystical Revolutions. Five hun-dred years.

12
Una
Canción
A Song

He must have walked out along these tracks, I thought. On a cold, pale gray morning, January 9, 1939, setting out from Parsons Street, Abuelo Juan José must have followed these railroad tracks into the dense fog bank that grew thicker and more opaque as he got closer to the river. In the cleared terrain of the railway corridor that morning, my father, following, would've had to linger far back so his father would not see him. As soon as he entered the fog, he was lost.

Fifty-six years later, just past dawn, on the anniversary day of Abuelo's death, I stood on the same rusted tracks in a desolate rail yard to the east of St. Mary's Street in old San Antonio. Quietly, without anyone noticing, I had arisen and left our house on the northside of town just as the sun was rising on a chill, damp morning. The street lamps lit up the low-hanging clouds in a velvety orange glow. The January San Antonio

*fog was thinner that year, and as I drove the still-empty elevated express-
way into town, a wispy neblina mantle hung on the treetops of the
neighborhoods, pierced by electrical pylons, billboards, and the steeples
and domes of barrio churches.*

*Standing on those tracks, the cast-iron gates of the abandoned Lone
Star brewery were chained shut before me, the portal through which
trains had once carried countless gallons of beer made from San Antonio
River water to the rest of the state. In the opposite direction, I could see
the slow asymptotic curve of the rails moving farther off to the east. Following them back, the wide swath of railway lands abutted the back
fences of family houses, where their inhabitants were just beginning to
stir now—Chihuahuas yapping in the yards, sagging clothing lines
hung with dew-soaked laundry left out overnight. And where the Santos
homestead on Parsons Street used to be, visible from the tracks, now stood
a concrete supporting colonnade of the McAllister Freeway.*

*That morning, Juan José must have walked out from the house on
Parsons, taking a left at Hoefgen Street. After two blocks, when he came
to the railroad tracks, he would only have had to take a single right.*

*From that point I walked alongside the weathered rails for less than
fifteen minutes, and now stood over the San Antonio River where it still
cuts a bright ribbon of viridian light through Roosevelt Park, one of the
oldest parks in town. Little has changed since 1939. The same bridge is
visible in the background of the newspaper photograph of his death. This
is the same knotted earth, flecked with river grasses, under the shoes of
the fireman who attended him.*

*Looking down onto my reflection in the flowing water from the tres-
tles of the train bridge, the river seemed so near, twelve feet away at most.
There was a rumor that someone had seen Abuelo jump into the river.
But it seemed impossible that anyone could manage to kill themselves by
jumping from that height into such shallow waters.*

Down by the bank of this river the Indians had called Yanaguana, I crouched in the winter-dry grasses and listened to the ancient, unbroken, coursing trickle of the water. Except for arrow-point formations of ducks flying low and to the south, the city felt empty, evacuated, under a quieting spell. I thought I might sit there for hours and no one would see me. I remembered old Spanish maps, tracing the veins of this river in brown ink to where they decant into the Gulf of Mexico, and onward then, bleeding into cobalt blue, to where the gulf empties at last into the vast maw of the Atlantic Ocean. What elements of this place, bleached sand, cicada shells, pecan leaves, mimosa and yucca blossoms, were carried out from here to that final, farther home?

We might never absolutely know how Juan José died, whether it was a suicide, a sudden heart attack—un infarto—or perhaps a murder. In this tale, even though it was written into this unchanging place alongside the river, that moment would remain perpetually shrouded. But here was Abuelo's spirit path out of this life, the Rio San Antonio, surging from Roosevelt Park out beyond the city, merging with the crystalline Cibolo, the muddy Salado, all their alluvial clouds invisible under the tranquil surface, winding slowly through the green valley lands to the southeast, pushing out toward infinite waters, Juan José's soul swift and bright as a sun perch, swimming unfettered, disappearing into the deep.

ALL IN VAIN. Those were the words that appeared over the newspaper photograph from the *San Antonio Light* of the scene of my grandfather's death in 1939. With one hand, the young fireman, Mr. Pompa, appears to be gently cradling Abuelo's head beneath the thick woolen blankets. With the other, he holds a respirator over Juan José's face. According to the report, the firemen tried for half an hour to revive him, without success. The caption reads: RESPIRATOR FAILS TO SAVE JUAN SANTOS.

All in Vain.

Since learning of the mystery of Juan José's death during that graveside visit in San Fernando Cemetery—now twenty-five years ago—in journals, letters, poems, and stories, in conversations with family, journeys in Texas and throughout Mexico, I have sought to defy those three words, with little success. I wanted to tell a single story, bound together like an old *amate* codex, to carry the saga of Mexico into the story of Texas, and into the story of our family, walking like a tribe of pilgrims out of a tattered past of conquests, upheavals, revolutions, and migrations.

I wanted to dispel the shame the family has held inside like a hidden wound, to burn off the silence that kept many of us from speaking Juan José's name, except in whispers, for decades. I tell the story over and over again, but the momentum of forgetting is strong. The currents of fear unleashed in the family around his death run deep and long. Now there is another generation, the sons and daughters of cousins among the Santos and Garcias, many of whom like me have left San Antonio, traveling farther still from these mysteries and chimeras, farther from the places and details of our past in Mexico, and farther from the ghosts of Mexico left in Texas. They know even less than we did of the story of Abuelo Juan José and the Santos melancolía that was not extinguished with him.

That old melancolía has returned several times, like an indelible song written into the blood that will be sung, regardless of the singer. In one unrestrainable leap, Uncle Roger had briefly spun down into that netherworld of chaos, panic, and illusions. He was convinced that slow, invisible fires were burning inside everything—trees, walls, sidewalks— gradually rendering the apparent world into ash. During a visit, he stared at me, wide-eyed, gripping the armrests of his chair, darting his eyes out the patio window to see how far along the inexorable process had moved.

"It's a matter of time, *mmm-hmmm,* a matter of time," he kept repeating, while rocking back and forth in his chair. He believed he had become a leper and that the entire neighborhood he lived in had been abandoned and quarantined as a result. His eyes were full of apprehension, as if he were being forced to look at something he would have chosen never to see.

That look was familiar to me, familiar from that inward place I have known since childhood, the infinitesimal tabernacle of the great void left inside of me too, something irreducible, left over after the body, the mind, the world, are all gone. I have always been able to go there, touching the formless cold of the place, the lonely emptiness, but always recoiling in terror, always returning to this world in an instant, when every insignificant detail observed, the smell of tea, the prattle of the radio, a light breeze, becomes a comfort and a beckoning.

We had never spoken of it before, but it felt as if my uncle was there in that place, only he was stranded there, unable to return. All he could see around him was the inevitable ruin of everything. The rest of us learn how to ignore these notions, to forget how all of creation plunges through the frigid void in vast arcs and circuits that will fade, decay, and disappear in the unspeakable plethora of time. Eventually, Uncle Roger found his way back, but he knows now, despite all of the delusions he suffered there, the place he went to is real.

How can we be healed?

Aunt Connie, who fell into her own embrace of the void, was saved by tapioca. Ordinarily very spirited and loquacious, for some months, like a novice in a cloistered order, she had surrendered herself to a virtually complete silence, becoming more and more remote, sitting still, with an expressionless stare, or occupying herself with prayer books, fingering the black beads of an old onyx rosary. Instead of her usual rushing, melodic torrent of jokes and stories, punctuated by flurries of laughs and movements of her hands, she spoke in monotones and murmurs, as if she were resigned to an implacable secret fate that had been revealed to her.

Aunt Connie was living with Madrina and Uncle Manuel, whom she thought of as her second parents, while she sought medical help, "from a real doctor," my father said at the time, "not them quacks and *curanderos.*" Still, after months, the doctors had done little to help her regain her former state of mind. She continued to struggle, barely able to keep the elephant ear plants on the patio watered, and she swept only half of the kitchen at a time.

While I was home visiting from college, Madrina had invited me over for lunch with her, Uncle Manuel, and Aunt Connie. Madrina, in her late seventies then, had never been known for her cooking. Her meals usually consisted of many dishes, somewhat overcooked, in extremely small portions, so that by the time the table was set, it looked like a galaxy of small bowls with salsas, *guizadas,* Doña Maria mole, beans, okra, and rice. On this day, my aunt sat across the table from me, so sullen and withdrawn that she seemed to be absorbing the oxygen out of the air around her, molecule by molecule. We ate in complete silence, and I was grateful for the way the sound of the silverware on the plates, and Uncle Manuel's long, susurrated sips of beer, echoed in the dining room, breaking the pall.

When the time for dessert arrived, Madrina brought in a large porcelain tureen which she proudly opened to reveal a pearly mass of tapioca that she had prepared that morning, still warm and smelling of cinnamon. As Madrina moved to serve everyone, she put the spoon into the tapioca, but it did not give easily. Uncle Manuel mischievously keened his eyes on me, as if he knew a secret about our dessert. Pressing down harder into the bowl, she pulled the spoon up, only to draw out a swatch of the tapioca in one long cord, as rubbery as mucilage.

Aunt Connie's attention, distracted throughout our meal, was suddenly gripped on this perilous maneuver.

Madrina tried to act as if nothing were amiss. She held the thick bolt of tapioca, stretched from bowl to spoon, utterly still, for what seemed minutes. Balancing herself and straining to smile, she laboriously raised another small plate to serve onto, expecting in the meantime some of the pudding would fall away, back into the tureen. Instead, reaching its threshold of tension, the dollop of tapioca quivered first, then slipped off the spoon in a blinding instant, slamming back into the serving bowl with a thwap so loud it sounded like a pistol going off, instinctively causing Madrina to jump back and duck.

As Uncle Manuel and I struggled to stay silent and pretend nothing had happened, Aunt Connie erupted in a burst of laughter, an explosion so strong it helped to dislodge her from that silent, hidden place she had been for months, and from there, she gradually returned to be fully among us.

It had always seemed that over the last one hundred and fifty years—from the time Texas was separated from Mexico in the 1830s, among the Lopez and the Velas of my mother's family, and then again during *la Revolución,* when the Garcias and the Santos crossed the border and left Coahuila behind—the story of Mexico had ceased to be a part of our family, and we had ceased to be a part of it. Separated by eighty years, there had been a double betrayal of Mexico, the negation of a negation, repeated and reversed, across these four families' pasts. Mother's family was abandoned by Mexico—left behind in Texas— while my father's chose to abandon their country, *la tierra madre,* for Texas, during Mexico's hour of greatest need.

We became Americans, and as such, we were no longer a part of the ancient *compromiso,* no longer obligated to keep a solemn vigil over Mexico's destiny, or, if necessary, to sacrifice ourselves for it. By leaving Mexico and being left by her, our forebears had meant to free us from that ceaseless cycle of sacred duties to dance and chant and make sacrifices and pilgrimages, so that the cosmos would continue to exist. The world we lived in now didn't require anything of us to keep the great movements and cycles of the earth and the universe in perpetual order.

This leave-taking from the homelands has been acted out repeatedly since the beginning of the Americas. In Cuzco, Peru, in 1561, the Mestizo historian Garcilaso de la Vega, called "El Inca" (because his mother was Inca royalty, his father a Spanish officer), described how he decided to seek his fortune in Spain. There, he stood to inherit some part of his father's lands and there he could sue for the return of lands in Peru that had been taken from his mother's family.

Before leaving for Spain, he had heard of the recent discovery of a marvelous tomb containing the corpses of five Inca kings. Along with a friend, he went to bid farewell to the mummies of his ancestors. Once inside the chamber, he found the bodies were wrapped tightly in exquisite woolen shrouds, hands crossed over their chests, the skin of their faces pulled tight and smooth by the dry, alkaline mountain air. Over the eyes, the preparers of the bodies had placed small patches of woven gold. De la Vega, never to return to his native Peru again, wrote many years later in Spain of how he reached out to touch the hand of the great Inca Huayma Cápac, as a *despedida,* a farewell. He recoiled at once, feeling it cold and rough, and sinuous, like a vine. Already then, he felt a gulf between him and them that was unbridgeable.

Nearing the end of the millennium, the old Mexicans are dying off in gusts now, some of them dazed and weary, worn out by a century of labor and strife. With each death of another of the old ones left among us, the echoes of Mexico grow ever fainter. Abuelo Juan José's death had the opposite effect. Probably, it was his own decision to move on altogether from this world. He had had enough of the calamities, enough of the humiliations, the indignities visited on Mexicans in those times in Texas. Perhaps he *had* been disconsolate and confused that morning. But maybe he was *not* suicidal. Maybe, in a deep distress, wandering disoriented, he had been overtaken by a heart attack, and he threw himself into the shallow tepid waters of the San Antonio in the hope that the water would wash away his affliction. Or maybe he fell.

And maybe it was murder. Maybe, heavy with trepidation, he had been off that morning to secretly meet with the notorious red-haired Irish foreman who had been abusing him for months at the foundry where he worked, and resented that the company had promoted Juan José, a Mexican, before him. Maybe it had been a treacherous rendezvous, arranged by this nemesis under some false pretense, intending to lure Abuelo Juan José to a secluded place where he could be taken care of, once and for all.

Left in the past as an abandoned tale, Abuelo Juan José's unresolved end hid away all these questions that would awaken in me, two generations and nearly forty years later. I had the *compromiso* to try to complete his story, not because his life was important in history, but because his life was imparted to the lives he engendered, because his life was a missing arc between us and our incalculable origins.

Even though it happened on a morning long ago in San Antonio, my grandfather's walk along the tracks to the river, alone, confounded, into the thick San Antonio fog, left the question of our destiny in Mexico and Texas unresolved in all of us who were to follow.

The anniversary of Abuelo's death several years ago fell on the day before I was to return home to New York City. After making the drive back from my attempt to imagine his final moments in the river at Roosevelt Park, over a breakfast of chorizo tacos and refried beans, I reminded my father it was the anniversary of his father's death, and I asked him if he would like to visit his grave together later that day.

"I'm very busy today," he answered, in a plaintive voice. "I don't know if I'll be able to do it. You should maybe go without me." I didn't tell him where I had just come from. Dressed in a sweater, jeans, and workboots, he cleared his throat, got up slowly, leaving me at the table, and went off to the garage to begin his chores.

I didn't want to push him to revisit the painful recollections of that morning fifty-six years before. Some members of the family had cautioned me about bringing it up with him at all. "He found his peace with it," they said. "You'd best let him be." For my father, in his late seventies, the memories of that day must have been a distant blur of fog and panic and searching, and then a glimpse of his father's shape, seen from the street, fading in the unforgettable fog of that morning. All of that ensconced in a corona of silence for nearly six decades, which was his privilege. When he wasn't sure about visiting the grave that morning, I thought to myself, *They were right, I will push no further with him.*

Days before, at the wedding of a Garcia cousin, I had seen my uncle Chale, youngest brother to my father's mother, who was reportedly with my father that morning in 1939 when they found Abuelo's body. Since the death of his wife, Chale, now in his late eighties, had been in the care of one of his sons, shuttling between towns where the son had undefined "business" in Texas, California, and Oregon.

Uncle Chale had aged dramatically since the last time I had seen him. In old family photographs, he appeared in meticulous studio portraits, his hair perfectly slicked, his mustache precisely trimmed, smiling like Clark Gable. Having traveled the world in the navy, he had always been dashing, quick, and gifted with a natural ease around people that had made him the family's cosmopolitan and bon vivant. Now, his eyes were bloodshot and drooping, his hair standing straight up, dressed in unkempt clothes, the waistline of his pants drawn together at the back with a great safety pin after recently losing a lot of weight. He was missing teeth and had been shy and uncertain of his words at first as we embraced and talked, standing outside of the church together while the ceremony was under way inside. But when I asked him about my grandfather, he suddenly became animated.

"Yes, he was like my second father! El Juan José. I loved him. Very, very much. I lived with them when I was young, and he treated me like a son. For that, I will always love him."

I told him I was trying to learn more about the circumstances of Juan José's death, and I had heard he was with my father when they first found his body in the Rio San Antonio. Did he still remember anything of that morning?

Uncle Chale paused, his hand shaking uncontrollably as he rubbed his unshaven cheeks, long-faded images of that distant day were returning to him in slow motion. His eyes began to well up with tears, but as he began to try to speak, his son intervened and said it would not be good for Uncle Chale to remember that. His health was fragile, his heart still broken over his wife's death. My uncle looked at me, vexed and wordless.

"Maybe some other time, primo," my cousin said, "maybe when he's feeling a little better." He put an arm around Chale, now seemingly as helpless as a dotard, and ushered him silently back into the sanctuary of the church. Uncle Chale looked back at me once, as if he still wanted to speak, but my cousin held his arm tightly and directed his shuffling steps into one of the back pews where they sat down.

In the days shortly after that, the two of them were off again, living in a Winnebago, headed west, and no one in the family has seen or spoken to Uncle Chale since. His story would remain untold.

The rest of the anniversary day was slow and gray. I gathered notes, video and audio tapes, letters, and photographs from the trips in Mexico. I had not been away from New York City for so long in eleven years, and I was traveling with an elaborate mobile headquarters. Late in the afternoon, while I was packing a suitcase, the Tex-Mex music of KEDA, Jalapeño Radio, coming through the walls from my father's workshed outside, suddenly stopped. He stepped through the back door, wiping his hands on his jeans.

"If you want to go, let's go," he said quickly. I wasn't sure of what he had said at first. "It's getting late if you want to go to San Fernando," he added.

"You want to go?" I asked.

"Let's go, it's getting late," he replied.

We stayed off the expressways, taking Vance Jackson to Fredericksburg Road, past the old taco-doughnut shop, down Babcock to Wilson, turning on Culebra to Twenty-fourth, and on to the south, toward the Mexican cemetery of San Antonio, where the streets are lined with headstone engraving shops and vendors' stands selling balloons and memorial blue chrysanthemum arrangements. There was a lot of traffic, since it was already rush hour in the neighborhoods of the far west side. We seemed to stop at every light, idling in an awkward silence.

"What happened that morning?" I finally asked him. "What happened the morning your father died?"

"John Phillip. It was too long ago! I don't remember."

"Do you want to remember? If we don't tell these stories, we'll forget them."

"That's okay," he said, looking out the window. "That's okay with me."

We were nearing the cemetery, stopped at an intersection where the old Agudas Achim synagogue used to be on St. Cloud Street, and I continued, "Did you follow your father that morning?"

Taking a deep breath, he said, "Mama came and woke me up and asked me to follow him. My older brother was there. I don't know why she asked me to go after him—instead of Raul." At that moment, his voice sounded like a child's, complaining about the privileged treatment of an elder brother. "She told me to go after him and watch him, and not to let him see me."

"Why not?"

"Because it would embarrass him!"

"Why did she want you to follow him in the first place?"

"Because, he was sick. The night before, he kept talking about going away, going away. He had been sick for months already. He never really recovered from failing with the farm at the Belgian Gardens. So, the night before, he had been saying, *'Ya es tiempo. Ya me voy. Ya es tiempo,'* and nobody knew what he was talking about."

"But Uela did," I added.

"She knew something was wrong with him."

"And then what happened?"

"I tried to follow him, but the fog was very thick. I lost him. It was very hard for me with Mama after that, because I felt responsible, but I lost him. One minute he was there, walking by the old Alamo Iron Works, then he was gone. I looked everywhere but he was gone."

"And then how did you find him later?"

"I went to his job, just in case he had been going there, but he was walking in the opposite direction, and no one there had seen him, so I ran home."

"How did you find him in Roosevelt Park? Why there?"

"Uncle Chale and I drove around in the truck, thinking we might still find him walking along the streets. He liked to walk in that park, picking weeds from along the river. We thought we'd check for him there."

"How did you spot him? Did you see him from the street? Was his body *in* the river?" All of the questions I had harbored secretly for so long came rushing out in a messy litany. The tall palms of Las Palmas shopping mall, across from San Fernando Cemetery, were already becoming visible on the far horizon in the pearly light of early Texas twilight.

"I don't remember! In the water, I think," he said. "It was a long time ago, John Phillip. It was a hard thing for me for a long time after that. It took me a long time just to deal with the guilt. It felt like it was all my fault. I had nightmares about it for years, when I was in the army. I couldn't sleep. I just wanted to forget about it."

"But there was nothing you could have done."

"It didn't feel like that then. I thought I could have saved him."

"Do you think it was a suicide?"

"Of course! What else could it have been?"

Finally, we turned the corner at the Las Palmas mall, crowded with shoppers preparing for the feast day of the Three Kings, *el Día de los Magos,* the last celebration of the sacred calendar of Christmas in Mexican tradition. There were long shoals of low clouds, scalloped across the sky and illuminated in dark pinks, yellows, and blue. With darkness soon setting in, the first stars were visible over San Antonio as we turned into the entrance way to the great arches of San Fernando Cemetery. As we drove in, we saw the two Mexican caretakers locking down the bolts of the gates for the night. It was still ten minutes from the posted closing time, but, they said, the cemetery was on "holiday hours" and it was already empty—and they wanted to go home. Abuelo Juan José's grave might as well have been a thousand miles away.

"Come back tomorrow!" one of them shouted from behind the gate. "We'll be open all day long . . ."

My father grew silent, and we left off our talk about Abuelo and that day long ago. An amber waxing moon was now rising over the old city as we drove down Commerce Street, heading downtown. We turned onto Zarzamora Street, where the *tortillerías, panaderías,* Mexican restaurants, Tex-Mex clubs, and ice houses make it a thoroughfare of the Mexican west side of San Antonio. Before heading home, we stopped by Henry's Puffy Tacos to share an order of puffy chicken tacos. I was nearly forty, my father nearly eighty. All that remained unspoken now could just as well be offered up to the sun and burned off once and for all, the way morning clouds disappear by noon in north Mexican sunlight.

And perhaps my father was right. It is okay to let go of the stories. In the end, they don't really tell you anything. It is okay to move on and to forget, to seek the blessing of forgetting. Through the century, the family had kept moving, from the countryside of Mexico and south Texas to San Antonio, from the barrio to the suburbs, and from Texas outward to a myriad of places, around the world. I had already lived for more than ten years far from the bones of the ancestors.

The puffy tacos buoyed my father's mood. After we returned home, he said that he was willing to sing a couple of songs, if I were still interested in taping him.

"If we're gonna do it, let's do it. I'm tired," he said.

For the last several days, I had been asking him to let me videotape him singing a few of his original compositions. He had been reticent at first, complaining that he couldn't sing anymore, that his fingers were stiff, he didn't have a guitar pick—now he suddenly became determined, quickly setting up his kit in his study; first his microphone and stand, then plugging his guitar into a squat Marshall amplifier, plugged in under his desk. His swiveling desk chair squeaked, so he sat instead on a stool, in the formal posture of a *flamenquero,* leaning forward, cradling his guitar tenderly on his leg, one foot propped up on the amp. I set up some lights for better shooting, basting my father in an incandescent glow that made him squint at first.

Then his ritual began. He strummed through several chords to tune the guitar and then adjusted the volume to kill the tinny feedback. He cleared his throat while he picked a few quick arpeggia. With stereo headphones on, attached to the video camera, I could hear the crickets outside in the few moments of quiet.

"Ahora sí," he said, with one last nervous cough and a quick shuffle on the stool.

After a long breath, as he began to sing, his face relaxed so completely that it was as if he had walked into another body, unfettered by everyday cares. He began with what has become his *Norteño* standard— the "Corrido de Los Generales," his song about the ranch in Coahuila that he had debuted there long ago. The song began on a dulcet chord, shimmering as he held the first word, *Que . . . ,* singing it in a quavering tenor note that hung in the air until, at last, he began the song in a lazy polka time, with,

> *Que—bonita es la vida,*
> *Que bonita es la vida en el rancho!*

> How beautiful life is,
> How beautiful is life on the ranch.

As he sang, the skin of his throat quivered, hitting all of the high notes with polish and innocence. His voice was still velvety, welling up from way down in his belly, with the slightest sense in every note that he is not far from weeping. He sang gazing forward, letting his eyes drift off to an imagined horizon when he sang about fences that ran like lines without ends. He sang in praise of beautiful cattle, in praise of bountiful water and trees, in praise of the blessed land, ending with a loud, *"¡Sí Señor!"*

Excited by hearing his own voice again, his fingers moved lightly across the strings plotting out his next song. "Remember this?" Then he sang "Texas Born," a twanging country-western song he wrote in my honor when I went off to study in England.

> *I wear a pair of shiny boots—a big ten-gallon hat,*
> *and every time I go somewhere,*
> *there's always someone who*
> *asks the same old question,*
> *"Mister, where're you from?"*
> *And this is when I tell them*
> *that I was Texas born,*
> *and I come from San Antone . . .*

He followed with two love songs he'd written for my mother, "My Beautiful Wife" and "Si Yo Pudiera (If I Could Only)," with melodies that moved from the coloratura of romantic 1940s Mexican movie music to warbles and trills that sound almost Arabic. "Now, I'm going to do an old, old Mexican one," he said, striking the first chord of "Noche de Ronda." As he sang the old song by Agustín Lara, he seemed at complete peace, able to strike each note as if the song were just being written. He was surrounded by pictures on the walls of his parents, the last portrait of Juan José, taken months before he died, and Uela, wearing her stoic expression, a few years before she died. My father finished his concert with his "Corrido de Múzquiz," a song for the Coahuila town at the edge of the sierra from where his great-grandfather Teofilo Garcia had been kidnapped by the Kikapu Indians. In that song, he sings of the town's local waterfall, the renowned beautiful women of Múzquiz, and how, of all places in the world, he would choose to die there. When the song concluded with a fierce double strum, my father let the guitar echo his final notes. As the last chord faded, the quiet of the night returned and the room was still. He drew the guitar up from his lap and leaned on his stiff knees to get up from the stool.

"That's it!" he said, switching off the amp and the microphone, gathering his cords up into neat loops. And when I ask him why he says in the song he'd like to die in Múzquiz, and not San Antonio, where he has lived his entire life, he replies, "That's just the story, John Phillip. That's just the story in the song."

Epilogue

Back in New York, I feel the city at once alien and familiar to me. The planted malls along Park Avenue could have been lining boulevards in Paris, Rome, or Barcelona. The weathered monument to Columbus on Central Park South became the angel of victory on the monument to La Independencia in Mexico City. Little seemed recognizable from my time before, as if my presence here for ten years had been excised from the city's spiritual census.

In the subways, the faces of the thousands of passengers—Vietnamese, Ethiopian, Mediterranean, East European, Latino, African American, and others—were mixed in now with faces more recognizable from my recent travels—Maya, Mexica, Zapoteca, Chichimeca. Never a significant presence here before, the people of Mexico had arrived in New York City. The city was unmoored in the ocean of humanity. Eventually, the entire world would come here, everyone bearing their old gods and their ancient obligations, silent and inevitable.

I spent my days rearranging the notes, routines, and drafts for this book, moving them around daily in numerous kaleidoscopic arrays. I wondered, for the first time in a long time, if I shouldn't be back living in my homeland, among the rivers, creeks, and hills—in San Antonio— the ruin city of my birth, where the ancestors are buried, and where the family's past has settled over creation in the dust of a hundred years.

There would be no conclusion to Abuelo Juan José's story. Only Juan José knew what pact was being fulfilled there in Roosevelt Park on the last day of his life. The memories of those who remembered any- thing of that day would never be gathered into a single picture, a single tale. The old Mexicans who had secrets would eventually take them along on their own journeys out of this world.

For all my obsession with telling the family story, my brothers and I, still childless, might yet be the end of our family line, the end of the story the ancestors have been telling to time for millennia. Perhaps it makes no difference that we have all left San Antonio, with one brother in Houston, the other in New York City. Like our forebears, we have moved on from our given homes, leaving the ancestors behind, setting out beyond the farther border, remembering and forgetting our origins, and always looking for signs.

A brown eagle hunted for days in the air over Central Park. For nights on end, I watched a comet from my terrace. Lightning struck an old tree in the park, hewing it in two in a single, resounding crack. It was in those days, newly back in Manhattan, when my uncle Raul visited me one more time. While I was away, several guests said they had seen a ghostly presence, like a silvery smoke, in my living room. An Indian friend, Tully Spotted Eagle Boy, said he had seen a man in my apartment, dressed in white work clothes as I had seen

Uncle Raul once before, sitting quietly in the burgundy velvet reading chair.

"Don't worry," Tully wrote in a note, "He's friendly. He says he's happy. He wants to help you. Very big blessing."

I hadn't been dreaming since my return, only deep stony sleeps for weeks. Then, one night, I awoke with a start. When my eyes focused, I found myself suspended in a ball in midair in my living room, my knees pulled up to my chest. It felt as if I were being cradled from behind, when I suddenly was moved in a blur across the room, coming to a stop over a shelf cluttered with old family photographs—Uncle Frank, Uela and her sisters, the whole tribe, gathered one Easter in front of Uela's house on Parsons Street. Then swiftly and silently, I was spun across the room again, stopping just in front of my bookshelves, long enough to glimpse an edition of Cortés's *Letters* and the Velázquez Spanish dictionary. "This is not a dream," a mischievous voice said from behind. I turned around to see Uncle Raul, standing before me, laughing. As when I had seen his spirit before, the skin of his face looked youthful, his body fit and energetic. When he touched me, wordlessly, I remembered many of the times we had shared together, playing with his dog, Stupid, eating a lunch of tacos in his kitchen, arguing politics at a wedding reception in Mexico.

In a flash, we're outside on the streets, and Uncle Raul has a car that is made of air. In it, he is able to drive with me into the nighttime skies high above Manhattan. Accelerating rapidly upward and spinning, the city below looks like a nebula in space, a swirl of moving lights and beacons, glowing far into the atmosphere in every direction. Swooping down, I see the illuminated pinnacle of the Chrysler Building. Heading south, the twin towers of the World Trade Center, blurred with speed, stand like dolmens at the river's edge. Along the way, though he is inaudible over the rushing wind, Uncle Raul is talking continuously, laughing his tommy gun laugh, passing us so close to the stone arches of the Brooklyn Bridge that I can feel the chill of the cold, sooty granite on my cheek. Then we climb into clear sky again, and I can see a long queue of lights to the north from planes waiting to land at La Guardia airport. The streets of the city look empty.

All at once we stop and hover, floating high above one building on the Upper East Side of the city. Looking far down, we see a door open on the rooftop. Uncle Raul points downward with a giggle as an old, tired-looking man dressed in the eagle warrior costume of the ancient *Volador* dance walks wearily out onto the roof. In one hand he has a drum, in the other a flute. Perched on top of a large platform, he begins to play the flute and beat the drum, starting a slow, methodical dance, bowing his shoulders to the north, to the west, to the south, to the east, and rocking from one leg to the next, lifting his knees in high steps.

The old man's mournful singsong melody, like the sound of lost birds, reaches us on the winds. Uncle Raul looks at me with a sad nod of recognition. "This is not a dream," he says once more. Soon, the man below is joined by others, old and young, all of them dressed in tattered feathered suits and eagle headdresses, until the roof is crowded with the costumed dancers, each one facing out toward the city, keeping the same melancholic, mesmerizing cadence on their drums. In perfect synchrony, they all bow and spin, first to one side then to the next. The old man's drumming grows louder, his flute screeching across the whole island. Then the music stopped, and all of the dancers remained perfectly still. In the night air, I can hear Uncle Raul's breath next to me. We watch then as each of the dancers in sequence leaps from the roof's edge and flies out over the city, tracing large arcs and loops over midtown, descending slowly, disappearing finally into the streets in small clusters.

Cool gusts churn in the dark against my face. The Big Dipper flickers in and out of focus, one star at a time. As the faint, airy sound of the old man's flute song wafts over us again, I look out over the brilliantly illuminated nighttime cityscape one last time, marveling silently with my uncle at how here, too, in Babylon-on-the-Hudson, Mexico's invisible enchantment is already under way.

Tent of Grief

An Afterword

 Winter in San Antonio came on with an early frost in 1998, blighting my father's backyard pecan crop. In good years, he gathered several tin washtubs of smallish, juicy pecans from his two forty-year-old trees, the pride of his garden. Invariably, a shoe box full of the nuts would arrive in New York, rattling like a maraca. But not this year.

The blighting of the year's pecan harvest wasn't the only presagio of ill tidings. For months, Madrina, now ninety-nine years old, had been suddenly awaking in the middle of the night, screaming. She now lives with my aunt Bea in San Antonio. She no longer asks if all the Santos have died. Now, she asks Aunt Bea, "When am I going to die?" Then, one night, my aunt heard her scream and ran downstairs. She found Madrina in her pajamas, on all fours on the floor, her face taut with fear, weeping in a slow guttural growl while she clawed the dark air above her with one outstretched hand, in a furry pink glove. After calming down in Aunt Bea's arms, she complained of being haunted by a mysterious *bulto,* which she described as a churning black mass, hovering in the middle of the room, threatening to engulf her.

Five days after I finished this book in early December, my father was killed in a horrific automobile accident near our home in San Antonio, Texas. Mother barely survived, and continues to recover. It was late dusk and they had just gone to Mass, stopping at a grocery store on the way home to pick up a few things. They were making the last left turn to enter their neighborhood, a turn we have all made thousands of times. A nineteen-year-old kid in a Mitsubishi Eclipse was coming from the opposite direction. He hit my parents' car broadside, in mid-turn. Weeks later, I saw the result in a car graveyard, a twisted wedge of torn blue metal. My father, who was sitting on the passenger side, must have been killed instantly.

We had not known we were counting his breaths. He was eighty-one years old, enjoying every day with my mother, writing new songs, and as he liked to say "doing a little real estate on the side," every now and then selling a house or a few acres in the countryside near San Antonio. The day before he died, I had been on the phone with him and he was strangely foggy, confusing me with one of my brothers, losing his train of thought, as his voice seemed to flicker with uncertainty. On the day of his death, we traded calls all day, failing to reach each other. In my last call, I had left them a message saying, "Y'all must be out on the town or something! I'm home."

Then, sitting in my apartment in New York City, a voice in my head said, *"You'll never speak to him again."* I dismissed the doleful thought and ate dinner alone. It was near midnight when my brother George called from Houston. "We've got a big problem," he said, his voice grim and determined. "Mother and Daddy were in an accident tonight, and Daddy was killed."

We gave him a great *despedida* on a bitterly cold December day in

San Antonio, a farewell that resounded with mariachis, Mexican trios, and a performance of one of his last songs, "Si Yo Pudiera." In the months since his death, I have missed him greatly, longing still for the story he was never able to tell me about his father's death. Likewise, he never read this book. I was always waiting until it was really done. He had read parts of it, and he had heard me read from it at the main San Antonio Public Library last May. "Sounds good," he had said afterwards, "sounds real good." In the weeks before his death, he had seen the book's cover, with the photograph of his family in 1920. He had framed it, adoringly, in a gilded wooden frame.

And the story I waited so long for him to tell me—the story of the interrupted life of his father—has become mine.

MARCH 1999
NEW YORK CITY

Acknowledgments

So many have supported me through the years I have spent writing this book, none more than my parents and my brothers, Charles and George, and my sister-in-law, Cindy. Thanks also to Stephanie Brummer, who endured much of my soul wrestling while I tried to imagine the book. *Mil gracias* to *toda la familia,* living and gone, for sharing so many of their stories. I'm particularly indebted to my great-aunt Josefa Garcia Valdes, Tía Pepa, for the hours we spent together in the last years. As the Native Americans say: To all of my relations! And to la familia Guerra of Sabinas, Mexico, for giving me a family, and a home, in the old homelands—the Rancho Los Generales, where I wrote much of the first draft.

Deep gratitude to Carina Courtright for all of her support throughout; she shared many of the outward, and inward, journeys in the book with me and listened to these tales told over and over. Naomi Shihab Nye, my poetic ally since creation time, read early drafts and spirited me on through many peaks and valleys over the years. I would never have tried to be a writer without the encouragement of my poet-mentor, Ernest Sandeen, who died two years ago. He first heard the story that was hidden inside all of the forgetting, and he and his wife,

Eileen, created a home that nurtured a host of young poets. Another great mentor, Father Virgilio Elizondo of San Antonio, helped me to understand the profound implications of our heritage in the *mestizaje* of Mexico. Pamela Cadwallader Illott, my executive producer at CBS, first opened the entire world to me. Later, she gave me shelter on her ranch in Texas, where I wrote part of the book. And all honorifics to my theoretical conspirators for the whole saga: Tom Levin, James DerDerian, Adam Ashforth, Kendall Thomas, and Deborah Esch. My comrade Tom Keenan helped me find the book's title, hidden inside one of its tales. An *abrazo fuerte* to *mi compañera,* Lisa Heller, for her patience and companionship through some of the darkest times along the way. And thanks to Pedro Lujan for his prophetic paintings and our many conversations over the years about the *Inframundo*. He and Leah Gitter opened their home to a rabble of Latino artists and writers, helping us to discover a common vision.

My great colleagues at the Ford Foundation have always urged me on in this writing, especially Alison Bernstein and Bill Duggan. My agent, Janis Vallely, comrade in the dharma, believed in me from our first meeting, which made everything possible. And deepest gratitude to my editor, Jane von Mehren, who gave me the unexpected blessing of enormous energies from her own soul to refine this book and reveal the story I wanted to tell.

A PENGUIN READERS GUIDE TO

PLACES LEFT UNFINISHED AT THE TIME OF CREATION

John Phillip Santos

An Introduction
to *Places Left Unfinished*
at the Time of Creation

"There are mysteries held within a family and there are mysteries held within the deeper soul of a nation," writes John Phillip Santos in this lyrical memoir. *Places Left Unfinished at the Time of Creation* interweaves those mysteries to show us that by preserving and retelling our own families' stories, we keep humanity's deepest legacies alive. In Santos's case, the family mystery concerns the death of his grandfather, Juan José, who vanished one morning on his way to work. Was it an accident? A heart attack? A suicide? A murder? No one in the Santos family seems to know. After fifty years, they don't even want to talk about it. It isn't until John Phillip is an adolescent that he starts to ask questions about what happened to his *abuelo*. These questions lead to, or were always part of, an even greater curiosity about Santos's heritage.

Mexico, Santos tells us, is a country whose history lies buried beneath layers of sand, ash, soil, and water. Even the most extensive excavations cannot uncover its ancient beginnings. The roots of Mexico are in the indigenous world, but it has become a country where many bloods—Indian, European, African, and Asian—blend into *La Raza Cosmica*, a Mestizo people with heritage in many nations. It is also a diasporan country that has seen its inhabitants driven out of their homes time and time again.

Two generations ago, Santos's family fled Mexico in the wake of a revolution that had made life in their small town too dangerous to bear. They settled in the San Antonio area where they prospered, working in factories and tending gardens. Like many Mexican Americans, Santos grew up straddling two cultures. But unlike most teenagers, Santos was obsessed with stories of the past. He surrounded himself with his grandmothers, great aunts, and great uncles, talking to them about their lives in Mexico and in Texas, listening to their tales of family lore of magic and miracles. But Santos realized that as those people grew old and died, so to did the memories they carried with them.

Now that the last of the Santos clan has long since left Mexico, what is the family's destiny? And what, Santos asks, is Mexico's destiny? To answer these questions, Santos sets out from his home in New York City to trace his ancestors' roots in Mexico. He returns to the North Mexican ranch where he spent time while growing up. In the mountains of Puebla, he searches for the origins of the hypnotic *volador* ritual. He follows *la ruta*, Cortés's march of conquest across Mexico, arriving in the present day megalopolis of Mexico City, built on the ruins of the Aztec capital, Tenochtitlán.

Finally, Santos confronts his family's, and his own, voluntary exile. As he reaches toward the past he is overwhelmed by the surviving spirit of Mexico; by its beautiful and desolate landscapes; its quietly soulful people; its struggles to reclaim its ancient heritage and to recover from its violent history. In the end, his grandfather's death is no less a mystery, but John Phillip Santos's search for the truth has left him not only wiser, but also certain that the spirit of Mexico is resilient, and that the legacy of his family's past, with all its mysteries intact, is alive and well inside his own heart.

TELLING THE MESTIZO STORY
(A NOTE FROM THE AUTHOR)

How can you remember and tell the story that one family has told to time over many hundreds of years? How much of the ancestors' knowledge and feelings still live in the hearts of our families today? How far along are we in the story and where is it leading?

Places Left Unfinished at the Time of Creation is a memoir, but only partly autobiographical. It is a *testimonio* from a simple Mexican American family in San Antonio—a family tale told against the backdrop of the great epics of Mexico and Texas.

To tell the story I wanted to tell, eventually I had to return to Mexico, to retrace the journey of Cortés's army on their cataclysmic campaign to conquer the Indian world they had found. The Cuban writer Jose Martí once observed that the conquistadors "stole a page from the universe." The Indian empires were vanquished, but the Indios have survived into present day Mexico, and a memory of their Indian past still lives in the Mestizos, the Mexican race that is part Indio, part Español.

My book embraces the Mestizo traditions that have shaped me, the ranch life on the rugged landscapes of Texas and North Mexico, the poetic styles of Edmund Spenser, of Sir Thomas Browne, Christopher Smart, William Blake, and Walt Whitman—also Herman Melville, Jack Kerouac, Carlos Castañeda, and Jorge Luis Borges. *Places Left Unfinished at the Time of Creation* is a memoir with a poetic intent: a conversation with the dead. In the end, no mysteries are solved, but the act of storytelling renews a bond to the past and dispels the silence and forgetting that has haunted our family throughout this century.

Places Left Unfinished at the Time of Creation is an American story, a story that is one part of our emerging Mestizo republic of stories from all over the world that we must first conjure and remember—and then we must tell them to each other.

John Phillip Santos
New York City, January 2000

ABOUT THE AUTHOR

John Phillip Santos was born and raised in San Antonio, Texas, and spent much of his time growing up going north and south across the Mexican border. The first Mexican-American Rhodes Scholar, he was educated at Notre Dame, Oxford, and Yale. He has won numerous awards for his writing, including the Academy of American Poets' Prize at Notre Dame and the Oxford Prize for Fiction. Since the early 1980s he has written reviews, opinion pieces, and features for newspapers and magazines such as the *Los Angeles Times, The New York Times*, and the *San Antonio Express-News*.

Over the last ten years, he has written and produced more than forty television documentaries for CBS and PBS on culture, religion, spirituality, and politics. He received Emmy nominations for his films *Exiles Who Never Left Home*, about Mexican-American spirituality, and a documentary series on AIDS, *From the AIDS Experience*. He has also served as an advisor to the White House on a Presidential Commission investigating the current crisis in the education of Latino youth. He currently works in the media program of the Ford Foundation.

A CONVERSATION WITH
JOHN PHILLIP SANTOS

One of the book's most delightful aspects is the recollection of your colorful family members, and of your relationships with them. It seems rare these days for young people to share—let alone enjoy—time with their elders. Do you think this is a trait common in most Mexican families, or did your curiosity about your family history compel you to seek out these older relatives? Do you think your relationships with them helped make you a better storyteller? If so, what did they teach you?

My tribe of Texas Mexicanos were extremely close, but this family intimacy, among the elders, uncles, aunts, and cousins is a great Mexican tradition though it is becoming, sadly, less common on both sides of the border. We were all raised to revere the elders. I felt a special curiosity to learn as much as I could from them. Their wisdom and poise stood out for me amidst what I felt were the more superficial values of an emerging American consumerist society. Through their stories, their strength and rootedness, I felt connected to an ancient tradition of story, which has affected my writing and my filmmaking.

One reviewer of your book wonders about your frustration with your family's failure to preserve any evidence surrounding your grandfather's death: "It sometimes seems as if Mexicans are to forgetting what the Jews are remembering," you write. "We have made selective forgetting a sacramental obligation." This reviewer ponders whether this attitude is typical not of Mexicans but of the generation that bore the brunt of the Great Depression. How do you respond to this? Could your parents' vagueness about the facts surrounding that period of their lives be a kind of generational—rather than cultural—defense against painful memories?

The Mexican impulse to forget that I describe has origins in the distant past, long before the specific hardships of the Great Depression, or any of the other challenges Mexican Americans have faced in the United States. This impulse is bound up in the mystery of Mexico's painful birth in the conquest, and the *mestizaje* of the Indian and Spanish worlds that followed. Mexican Americans have an important stake in the history, and future, of this country, but we also have an important place in this older story, a deeper *compromiso* to find ourselves in that story, and to communicate it to the whole world.

Why do you think Mexicans have been more inclined to claim European or Spanish heritage rather than their Indian or pre-Columbian ancestry? Is that attitude changing today?

This is a complicated question that mirrors the shape-shifting identities by which Mexicans have discovered and described themselves since the era of the conquest. In those times, arguments raged in the courts and churches of Europe as to whether the Indians even had souls so the new Mestizo peoples who were being born of both cultures naturally allied themselves with the culture of the victors. With the Mexican revolution of 1910, and particularly through the work of Mexican philosopher Jose Vasconcelos, Mexico began to officially embrace its indigenous roots and Mestizo identity. This is particularly evident in the late-nineteenth century paintings of Hermenegildo Bustos, the first Mexican artist to realistically portray Mestizo faces. His work exerted an enormous influence over later painters such as Diego Rivera and Frida Kahlo, whose imagery of the Mexican world helped to forge the Mestizo image of Mexico we know today. As evidenced by the recent Zapatista uprising of Mayan Indians in the southern Mexican state of Chiapas, the struggles of the conquest are far from over. As in the United States, Mexico's indigenous communities continue to suffer marginalization, poverty, and racism. A true reconciliation with our indigenous forebears still awaits us, on both sides of the border.

What, if anything, distinguishes life on the border between Mexico and Texas? Is there a distinct culture there? Do you think your family's life would be different if your grandparents had settled farther north into Texas?

My best answer here is to go and see for yourself! From San Diego/Tijuana to Brownsville/Matamoros, *la Frontera*, as we call the border, presents a uniquely rich and varied culture of traditional heritages, *conjunto* music, spicy Mexican food combination plates—and countless pathways back into the historic past of the region. It is not a zoo exhibit though, but a place very much in metamorphosis, producing ever more dizzying cultural combinations: from pop stars like Richie Valens and Selena to the Aztec hip-hop of contemporary Mexican bands like Plastilina Mosh. These borderlands first became the subject of study only fifty years ago in the work of Jesuit historian Herbert Eugene Boulton. Today, diverse voices such as Gloria Anzaldua, Virgilio Elizondo, and David Carrasco are helping to reshape border studies, bringing forward for the first time, the *testimonios* of the people who have lived in this contested terrain for centuries. Other Mexican families traveled farther north, to far-flung destinations in Washington state, Missouri, and Michigan. As in Sandra Cisneros's evocation of Chicago in *The House on Mango Street*, there are many writers to come who will speak to these experiences of the Mexican Diaspora throughout the world.

How would you encourage Mexicans—or descendants of any culture for that matter—to preserve their heritage? Why is actively remembering and passing down stories from one generation to the next so important?

My best way of preserving heritage is through storytelling. I believe that as the United States becomes an ever more ethnically and culturally diverse nation, the strength of our democracy will rest on our collective understanding of the innate worth of each other's oldest stories. This is a shift with extraordinary ramifications for institutions such as our schools, libraries, universities, and museums: They must become the places where we meet to share and reflect on this great legacy of the world's stories being gathered in America. This was always our true manifest destiny.

What do you think of the recent influx of Latin culture into American society? Is it possible for Mexicans living in New York City to carry on and preserve native traditions?

Rather than recent influx, I think of it as long-overdue recognition. We've always been here. In the last years, population growth and immigration have increased the American public's awareness of this Latino presence. The legacy of the Mexican story that I carry has always been present throughout my time in New York City, shaping the way I see the world. Today, I have been joined by a legion of new Mexican immigrants from central Mexican states such as Puebla (the home of the *voldadores*) and Oaxaca. Along with them, finally, great Mexican food has arrived in this city. Their vision of New York is likely to be equally marked by their bonds to the Mexican past, reshaping this great American city in the twenty-first century. Stay tuned for the ad campaign of the future: ¡*Orale Nueva York!*

What have your travels to other lands in which ancient cultures once flourished revealed to you about your own link to the past?

I've always had a great fascination with the ancient world and its civilizations of star-gazers, pyramid-builders, and tireless pilgrims in

9

search of we know not what. My travels to places like India, Mesopotamia, and Egypt have been deeply moving, spiritually transforming journeys, demonstrating how other peoples of the world have remained connected to their ancient origins. I believe there are secrets hidden in the past that contain keys to where we should go in the future. Think of it as time-release wisdom. This is not an ethnic question; the significance of these ancient traditions is a universal human truth that we all have a stake in.

As a documentary filmmaker you make your living documenting and preserving people's lives and memories. How did you come into that line of work? To what extent are your efforts to record daily life around the world a reflection of your regret about your own family's lost history?

I began making TV documentaries as a way of telling stories about politics, spirituality and social change that could reach more people. I grew up as a poet, but a poet who watched a lot of television, from the hapless misadventures of Wile E. Coyote to the landing on the Moon, and the great documentaries of the CBS Reports tradition. It was only in retrospect that I saw my programs for CBS as a kind of involuntary pilgrimage through some of the poorest communities in the world, exploring how people use their beliefs and spiritual values to transform society and achieve justice. When I return to filmmaking, my work will be different, more personal, more poetic in its styles. In truth, nothing has been lost. We are in the same struggle, and the story continues.

Why did you write this book? Were you expecting, in your research into your grandfather's death and in your journeys throughout Mexico, to uncover concrete truths about your family's history? What do you mean when you write, "Perhaps my father was right, it is okay to let go of the stories. In the end, they don't really tell you anything. It is okay

to move on and to forget, to seek the blessing of forgetting" (p. 271)?
How has writing this book changed your perspective on remembering
and forgetting?

This book was a part of my own *compromiso* with the ancestors, and the telling of the story is its own song. I came to see my father's way of dealing with the story, his singing and his silence, as a powerful testimony, celebrating the mysteries that our tradition preserves. My early quest for certainties paled in comparison. In the end, I came to recognize how little differentiates forgetting from remembering; like photonegatives of one another, whether as figures or traces, the shapes remain the same. Our appointment with the past is inevitable.

QUESTIONS FOR DISCUSSION

1. What does Santos mean when he says of his family, "We became Americans, and as such, we were no longer a part of the ancient *compromiso*, no longer obligated to keep a solemn vigil over Mexico's destiny or, if necessary, sacrifice ourselves for it . . . The world we lived in now didn't require anything of us to keep the great movements and cycles of the earth and the universe in perpetual order."(p. 264) How is the difference between American and Mexican history reflected in its citizens' understanding of family and cultural heritage?

2. How does Santos parallel his attempts to seek the truth about his grandfather's death with his own journey through Mexico? What is he trying to accomplish in each effort? To what extent does he succeed or fail?

3. Throughout his memoir, Santos mentions the *voladores*—Indian dancers who swing from the tops of wooden poles. What do these figures represent in both Mexican history and in Santos's life? What is the significance of Santos's final vision of the *voladores* swooping down from the rooftop of New York City apartment buildings?

4. Madrina tells a story about "The Valley of Silence," in Coahuila, Mexico, a place devoid of sound, which, she says, is one of many places around the world that "God had, for some unknown reason, left unfinished at the time of creation . . . places where the world had no shape or substance." (p. 55) Why do you

think Santos chose this phrase for the title of his book? What does it mean for a culture to be "unfinished?"

5. What do you think Madrina meant when she declared, soon after moving to San Antonio, that she "had been taken to Purgatory?" (p. 118) What is the significance of the seizure and visions she experienced after seeing the truck carrying a caged wolf?

6. How would you describe the way the book is constructed, with passages of recollections about Santos's past woven into the story of his grandfather's death and the details of his journey following Cortés's path as he conquered Mexico? What is the effect of interspersing personal memory with ancient history, the author's own recollections with the remembrances of his ancestors? Is there any kinship between the book's four sections of three chapters and the ancient calendars Santos writes about?

7. Do you think that Santos would be better off not pursuing the story of his grandfather's death? Where did his research get him? Do you think he reads too much into his family's grief about the past? Why or why not?

8. How does your reading of this book affect how you think about the trend toward multiculturalism in this country? What are the ramifications of integrating cultures from outside the American mainstream into our daily lives? Should we work harder to preserve and carry on the traditions of our native cultures? How is America likely to change as more of these cultural traditions from around the world enter our public imagination?

9. As a group, discuss each member's heritage, the steps you have taken to preserve it, and the connections you feel between

your lives and the lives of your ancestors. Ask each member of the group to share a family story that has been handed down between generations.

10. How has reading this book changed the way you view your own family's history, if at all?

For more information about other Penguin Readers Guides, please call the Penguin Marketing Department at (800) 778-6425, e-mail at reading@penguinputnam.com or write to us at:

Penguin Books Marketing Dept. CC
Readers Guides
375 Hudson Street
New York, NY 10014-3657

To access Penguin Readers Guides on line, visit Club PPI on our Web site at: www.penguinputnam.com